THE
CIGAR
CONNOISSEUR

THE CIGAR CONNOISSEUR

AN ILLUSTRATED HISTORY AND GUIDE TO THE WORLD'S FINEST CIGARS

NATHANIEL LANDE

AND

ANDREW LANDE

with the collection of Dr. Orlando Arteaga,
President, Asociación Cubana Vitolfilia

Special photography by Yancy Hughes
Additional research and text
by David Gibbons with Tony Fins

Clarkson Potter/Publishers

New York

Grateful acknowledgment is made to the following for permission to
reprint illustrations and photographs:

Arents Collection: pages iii, v, vi, viii, xiv, 3, 5, 6, 8, 9, 10, 13, 14, 15, 16,
17, 24, 25, 31, 36, 40, 41, 43, 47, 58, 62, 63, 64 (right), 67, 69, 71, 104,
107, 110, 115, 126, 141, 142, 156, 157

Yancy Hughes: iv, 2, 51, 53, 74, 84, 147

Photograph by Walker Evans, reprinted by permission of
The Metropolitan Museum of Art: xv

C. Meunier, *Ladies of Seville*, Royal Museum of Art, Brussels: 7

Bettmann Archives: 12, 19, 64 (left), 65, 72, 113, 119, 116, 120

Nathaniel Lande: 22, 82, 85, 98

Gianni Constantino, courtesy Habanos S.A.: x, 23

Domingo Batista, courtesy Davidoff: 27, 28, 29, 34, 90, 100

Enrico Barone: 27 (inset), 89

Premium Advertising Havana: 30

Dr. Orlando Arteaga: 44, 66

Courtesy Pentagon papers: 52, 53

Courtesy *Epicure* magazine: 55 (above)

Courtesy Davidoff: 76, 79, 97, 128, 138

Courtesy Dunhill archives: 77, 148 (above), 150

Andrew Lande: 92

St. Petersburg Times: 94

Courtesy J. R. Tobacco: 103

Courtesy *Cigar Aficionado*: 118

Catherine Leuthold: 122, 132, 146

Courtesy Elie Bleu, Paris: 146, 148 (below)

Courtesy Gene Walder: 149

Courtesy Grand Havana Room, Beverly Hills: 124, 151, 154 (above)

Courtesy Club Macanudo: 153

Courtesy City Wine & Cigar Co., New York; photograph by
Steve Freeman: 154 (below)

Courtesy Monte's, London: 155 (left)

Courtesy James Fox, London: 155 (right)

Courtesy American Airlines: 158–159

Copyright © 1997 by Nathaniel Lande and Andrew Lande

Published by Clarkson Potter/Publishers, 201 East 50th Street, New York, New York 10022.
Member of the Crown Publishing Group.

Random House, Inc. New York, Toronto, London, Sydney, Auckland
http://www.randomhouse.com/

CLARKSON N. POTTER, POTTER, and colophon are trademarks of Clarkson N. Potter, Inc.

Printed in Japan

DESIGN BY HOWARD KLEIN

Library of Congress Cataloging-in-Publication Data
is available upon request.

ISBN 0-517-70846-9

10 9 8 7 6 5 4 3 2

ACKNOWLEDGMENTS

*This book was crafted with
the help of our friends and pals,
Laurie Liss, Roger Vergnes of
Copperplate Press, and Pam Krauss.*

*The book could not have been
produced without the help of*

Lew Rothman
Simon Chase
David Ilario
Habanos, S.A.
Premium Publicity, S.A.
William Styron
José Ilario
Epicur magazine
Niki Singer
David Brokaw
Barbara Palenberg
The Office of Foreign Assets Control
Cigar Aficionado magazine
The Pentagram Papers
Mark Goldman
Richard DiMeola
Austin McNamara
Dr. Glenn Westfall
Warren Pfaff
John McLaughlin
Margot Schupf
Alexander Wallace
Ama Lopez
Emilia Tamayo
Tatiana Camacho
Liliana Portuondo
Biblioteca Nacional José Martí
Benjamín Menéndez
Carlos Fuente, Jr.
Ramón Cifuentes

Gay Talese
Edward Sahakian
Tasha Lande
Linde Hope
Nicholas Freeman
Hendrik Kelner
Avo Uvezian
Dr. Ernst Schneider
Davidoff
Dunhill
John Campbell
Christopher Boon
Johnny Oliva
Frank Llaneza
Jorge Concepción Luna
Felipe Ventura Narbara
Domingo Batista
Julio Caesar Molinet
Jennifer Lee
Earl Christian
Jane Lahr
Victoria Bartow
Ted Teodoro
The Arents Collection
The New York Public Library
Sandra Levinson
The Center for Cuban Studies
Bernardo González
Mary Posses
Yancy Hughes
    and
Shaye Areheart

*Their friendship and
contributions are invaluable.
The authors thank them with
deep appreciation.*

CONTENTS

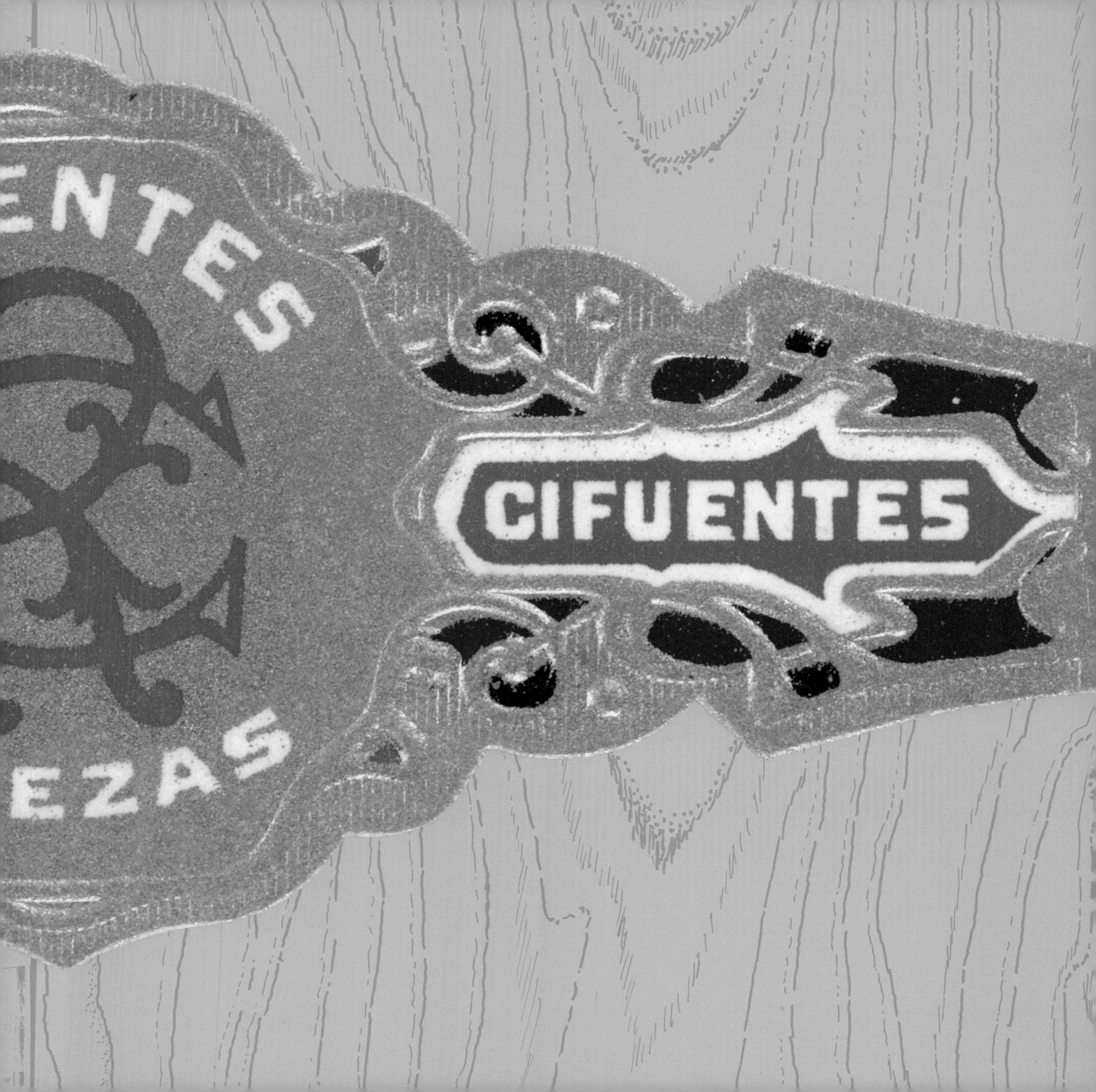
ENTES
EZAS
CIFUENTES

FOREWORD

MAKING PARTAGAS CIGARS has been my passion, as it was my father's, for a lifetime.

And now, just as my father and I once worked side by side, the distinguished journalist, author, and scholar Nathaniel Lande and his gifted young son Andrew have combined their talents in a handsome book dedicated to the past and present of the finest cigars in the world.

With a team of skilled researchers and several notable contributing writers, the Landes have created a rich tapestry of historical facts, vivid illustrations, contemporary interviews, personal reminiscences, amusing anecdotes, and valuable guidelines in a volume unlike any other I have known. As a result, its pages resound with the unique heritage of cigars and the people who have made them the inspiration for composers and poets as well as the pleasures of presidents and kings.

A timeless odyssey of the spirit, the book takes you to far-off places, from Cuba and the Dominican Republic to Spain and Cameroon. All through the journey, you will meet men I have known, from cigar masters such as Benjamín Menéndez to cigar aficionados like Ernest Hemingway. Most of all, you will sense the mystery and romance of a hundred works of art that transcend all of the boundaries that all too often separate countries and cultures from one another.

So let this memorable tribute to cigars and all that they stand for unfold before you, one revelation after another. With or without a cigar in your hand, I know that you will treasure it as I do.

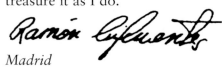

Madrid

PREFACE

HAVANA. The first time I saw this rich romantic colonial city was with my father in the fifties. He was a distinguished doctor, a visiting professor at the University of Havana, and a friend of Ernest Hemingway's. He took me along to be a guest at Finca Vigía, Hemingway's home, sitting above a pastel-painted hilltop town called San Francisco de Paula. I was just a child, loving the adventure of it all, and I remember the images framed with music and words, like a Walker Evans photograph: a dapper man in a white suit by a shoe-shine stand; the grand wedding cake called the Hotel Nacional; Hemingway's cool *mojito* at the Bodeguita del Medio; the spectacular moving nighttime mambo bands outdoors at the Tropicana; the pretty girls strolling past the colonnades in their summer dresses; and music playing on every corner in the old city, always the music. I remember.

Forty years later, I have returned to this magnificent island as a fellow at the Center for Cuban Studies, to find the same colors painting the same timeless landscapes found only in Havana. In the evening, cigars are smoked in this interlude of memory.

The music and themes of this city are notes transcending time. The aroma of a Partagas, like music, takes me back to

that earlier time. The smoke floats through open shutters and Palladian windows, to the sea, following the Malecón. With that memory, I realize that Havana may have lost her passion, but she has not lost her spirit.

Not far from Havana are the lush green rolling hills of the Vuelta Abajo, a landscape that has played a significant role in the history of the cigar. Here in this countryside my interest in cigars as a repository of the Cuban spirit was awakened.

My journey would ultimately take me to the great *casas de tabaco* of Cuba, the plantations in the Dominican Republic, the humidors at Dunhill, the tobacco factories in the Canary Islands, and the original *fábricas* still standing inside old Havana.

Along the way I would meet some of the great cigar

personalities who have shaped this industry and spearheaded the renaissance of smoking. I had the pleasure of meeting with Simon Chase at Hunters & Frankau; the incomparable Lew Rothman; Richard DiMeola of Consolidated; Austin McNamara of General Cigar; Ernst Schneider in Geneva, who carries on the Davidoff tradition; Benjamín Menéndez, once a creator of H. Upmann and Montecristo and now the overseer of Macanudo; Ramón Cifuentes, descendant and director of Partagas; Frank Llaneza of Hoyo de Monterrey and Punch. I spent time in the *Epicur* world of David and José Ilario in Spain, and with Tampa's late Angel Oliva, who pioneered the transplanted Cuban seed in Nicaragua, Hon-

the production of the finest cigars in the world. I'll never forget them.

They are the keepers of a legacy living in a rich soil. Another keeper, if you will, is the premier collector, Orlando Arteaga, whose collection of *vitolas* and *vistas* graces the National Gallery in Cuba and whose private collection from the Litográfica de Habana illustrates the pages of this book. His enriching friendship and contribution are immeasurable.

And it is a great pleasure for me to write this book with my son Andrew Lande, whose knowledge and elegant style are a great source of pride.

The cigar has been identified with power, prestige, and privilege. But in its soul there is more. Along the journey there are moments of companionship and conversation with new friends and old feelings. And these are the times to be remembered.

Nathaniel Lande
New York

WHAT STARTED OUT as a simple curiosity about smoking a cigar has developed into a daily ritual that I truly love.

It all began several years ago, when I used to pass an old tobacco shop near Grafton Street, Dublin, on my way to classes at Trinity College, where I was a student. My interest was initially aroused by the aroma of Havanas coming from that shop. Because Cuban cigars are legendary—and illegal, where I come from— I realized this was perhaps a perfect opportunity to sample a Havana, an opportunity I couldn't miss. I soon found that actually smoking one provided great enjoyment.

My journal documents my visits to the Dublin cigar merchant as they increased from weekly to daily. I look back at my time in Dublin not just as a traditional educational experience but as a chance to familiarize myself with all the available Cuban cigars.

duras, and Ecuador. I was privileged to visit Château de la Fuente, the plantation that produces the Opus X, and to listen to Avo Uvezian compose another great smoke. With Davidoff's poet of the cigar, I visited Hendrik Kelner at Tabacos Dominicanos, S.A., and spent afternoons with the wonderful Emilia Tamayo, the managing director of Cohiba, an extraordinary lady in a Havana men's club who oversees

When I returned home, I worried that I would soon smoke my way through the small supply of Havanas I had brought back to California. I knew no other cigars than Cubans, and under the influence of their mystique and prestige, I felt there *was* no other cigar. The evening came when I finally smoked my last Havana, and the next day I had no choice but to venture into a Los Angeles cigar shop—uncharted territory, to be sure. On the advice of a very knowledgeable and understanding tobacconist, I tried a Honduran Hoyo de Monterrey. Since I was familiar with the Cuban Hoyos and had enjoyed Epicure No. 2s and Double Coronas, I figured this might be a safe choice. As I smoked this cigar, I was surprised. It was different from the Cuban version and a very good smoke, a full, rich cigar like the Hoyos I knew, but with slightly different flavors. I was gratified.

My interest in cigars of different brands and countries grew, with Partagas, Puros Indios, and Avos, and with cigars made in the Dominican Republic, Jamaica, and Honduras all becoming part of my repertoire. After smoking a considered selection, I was thrilled to discover that I liked these cigars as much as my Havanas and that they were available to me in the States. I sometimes noticed that their construction and quality were even better than the famed Cubans, though I always maintained that when a Cuban is good, it's great.

My affection for cigars was compatible with my love for food and wine, restaurants, and cooking, though as a young man in my twenties, I felt odd spending my money collecting wine and cigars, while my friends were buying electronic audio and video equipment. There was something about a fine cigar that I found truly irresistible.

Throughout the day I find myself looking forward to my after-dinner cigar, the time when I enjoy a cigar most. Often during the day I think of what cigar I will smoke after dinner, never making a definite decision because moods change and certain moods favor certain cigars. But the moment comes! Before I light my cigar, I love to look at it, admiring the quality of construction, the beauty of the wrapper leaf. I like the way an after-dinner cigar finishes a meal and allows time to reflect upon the day, giving me a special time to relax and focus on whatever I want—a conversation with a friend, a problem to work out, an idea to develop. Sometimes I enjoy listening to music or watching a film on video while smoking a cigar. Usually my most memorable cigar experiences involve just me and my cigar. I find that it's almost meditative to smoke a cigar alone and allow whatever thoughts or feelings to surface. I often get my best ideas while smoking a cigar; sometimes inspiration comes from an Opus X No. 2 or a Cohiba Robusto. It's as though my cigar becomes my companion for forty-five minutes, or more, depending on whether I'm ready to make a commitment to a double corona. From the moment I light the cigar, it comes alive, changing flavor as it is smoked. The rich smoke fills my mouth, and I experience an intensity that invigorates my senses.

By the time I reach the end of my cigar, I've grown very comfortable with the way it feels in my hand, and it's not easy to let go. Abandoning a cigar in an ashtray becomes a sad moment. Sometimes it's just too difficult to put down. It's like saying good-bye to an understanding friend.

Andrew Lande
Los Angeles

1

A Glorious Tradition

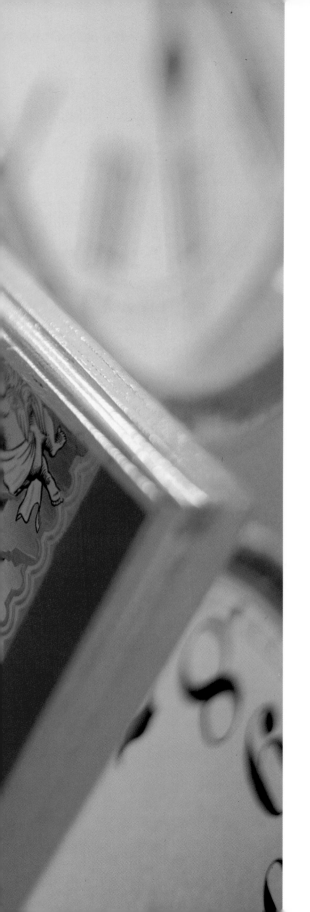

ROMANCE, REVOLUTION, AND RENEWAL

THROUGH THE AGES, political drama has always attended the making of cigars. While cigar smoking is certainly fashionable, it has never been a passing trend. Ever since the pre-Columbian era, cigars have signaled stature and ritual, creating their own art forms and traditions in a world of taste and inspiration.

THE DISCOVERY OF TOBACCO

THE FIRST KNOWN recorded reference to tobacco is in Christopher Columbus's journal. When he landed in Cuba on October 28, 1492, he sent two of his sailors, Luis de Torres and Rodrigo de Jerez, on a fourteen-day trip into the interior. They came back with the astonishing information that the natives were "drinking smoke" from bundles of tobacco wrapped in leaves called *cohibas*. Rodrigo de Jerez is believed to have begun smoking on a daily basis—the first European ever to do so.

The discovery of the New World opened up unlimited commercial markets for tobacco, and from that point on, as documented by the historian Samuel Eliot Morison, "tobacco spread throughout the world faster than any religion." The chief explorers who ventured to the other half of the globe, including Amerigo Vespucci and Ferdinand Magellan, all played a role in popularizing tobacco, not just in Europe but in the Far East.

CUBAN TOBACCO COMPANY INC., SUCCESSOR
SUBSIDIARY OF THE AMERICAN TOBACCO COMPANY

For centuries tobacco had been cherished across Central and South America. Long before Europeans ever set foot in the New World, the Mayan, Incan, and Aztec civilizations had used tobacco, often mixed with grasses, for religious ceremonies and as a medicinal herb. Priests would blow the smoke to the four winds and sometimes in the faces of warriors to bless them before a battle. Mayan images from as early as the fifth century show people smoking sticklike objects. There are examples of cigar holders from Mexico more than two thousand years old.

The natives of the Americas discovered that inhaling smoke reduced their hunger pangs and increased their stamina. Nicotine offered a mild intoxication that enhanced ceremonies marking important events, such as contacting the gods or negotiating peace treaties. It's not clear how the original Americans learned that tobacco must be fermented and cured to achieve its desired effect. One likely theory is that they picked the leaves and let them collect in compost piles, which were later burned, at which point they noticed how pleasant the smoke was.

Folklore and fantasy have always surrounded the discovery of tobacco. One myth is that the Chinese grew and smoked it before the discovery of the Americas. Actually, the Chinese learned about it when explorers of the late sixteenth century brought it to China from the New World. Another myth is that Sir Walter Raleigh was the first Englishman to smoke. In truth, it was Sir John Hawkins and his sailors who brought tobacco to England in 1565, after seeing the French colonists and natives smoking in Florida. Raleigh, only thirteen years old at the time, learned about it from Sir Francis Drake and his men, who in 1586 brought it back to England from the colony on Roanoke Island in what later became Virginia. Raleigh did popularize smoking in the court of Elizabeth I, however, and the queen successfully taxed it for revenue.

By the beginning of the sixteenth century, tobacco had been introduced as a medicinal herb into Europe. Many take credit for the introduction of tobacco into the Old World. The Spanish point to Cortés, who they say brought seeds to Charles V after the conquest of Mexico in 1518.

ABOVE: VISTA CREATED BY LITOGRÁFICA DE HABANA, CIRCA 1882.
OPPOSITE: NINETEENTH-CENTURY CUBAN LABEL DEPICTING COLUMBUS'S DISCOVERY OF THE NEW WORLD. OPPOSITE BELOW: THE KING'S PROCLAMATION.

The Portuguese claim that Hernando de Toledo brought it back from his voyage in 1520, to establish a plantation in Lisbon. Meanwhile Dutch experts hypothesize that it was Damien de Goes who presented the leaves to King Sebastian of Portugal. In France, Jean Nicot was originally credited with "discovering" tobacco, but more recently this achievement has been attributed to André Thevet.

Nicot went to Lisbon in 1559 as French ambassador to Portugal and in 1560 brought tobacco plants back to France, where it was grown for medicinal purposes and was a favorite of Catherine de Médicis, widow of Henri II. Nicot made wide-ranging claims about its properties as a curative; it could alleviate everything from bad humor to gout, he claimed. The plant was named *nicotiana* after him in 1570. But Thevet is believed to have brought tobacco back from Brazil four years earlier than Nicot. He liked the flower and cultivated it in his garden, never promoting any practical use for it.

At first, smoking was limited to the Spanish and Portuguese aristocracy and to the sailors and explorers who had ready access to the leaves. By the end of the sixteenth century, however, the French, Belgians, Germans, and Dutch were regularly using tobacco.

Different methods of smoking became popular in different European countries. The British, for instance, took up pipe smoking because that was

how the natives of their North American colonies smoked. In fact, cigar smoking didn't fully catch on in northern Europe until the nineteenth century, although it had already been a major habit in Iberia for three hundred years. France became the first northern European country to accept cigar smoking, but not until Napoleon's armies brought the practice home after the Peninsular War (1806–1812).

As tobacco gained acceptance in sixteenth-century Europe, it also began to draw critics. Centuries before the current antismoking movement, James I of England issued proclamations against and penalties for smoking what he called the "stinking grass." His action was not unprecedented. When Columbus's Rodrigo de Jerez exhibited how natives smoked grasses after returning

Kositzky's Beft Virginia *LONDON.*

to the Old World, he was sent to prison for affronting high society. Monarchs from Pope Urban VIII to the Shah of Persia penalized smokers in a variety of ways. European smokers, for example, risked having their stashes confiscated, while Middle Eastern puffers risked imprisonment if caught inhaling. The great 1650 fire in Moscow was blamed on a smoker who allegedly fell asleep while smoking.

"True lovers more admire by far Thy naked beauties. . . . Give me a cigar!"
Lord Byron

But governments soon realized that legislating conduct was difficult. The advantages of taxing tobacco rather than penalizing it soon became apparent, and many companies established a trade in tobacco. A French tobacco monopoly was set up during the reign of Louis XIV, and the French West Indies Company enjoyed exclusive rights till 1730. Most European countries followed suit with their own national enterprises.

ABOVE: EARLY EIGHTEENTH-CENTURY DUTCH TOBACCO DOCUMENT. RIGHT: *LADIES OF SEVILLE*, AN OIL PAINTING BY C. MEUNIER, WHO VISITED SPAIN ON MANY OCCASIONS BETWEEN 1860 AND 1890. THE ORIGINAL PAINTING IS HOUSED IN THE ROYAL ART MUSEUM IN BRUSSELS.

THE DEVELOPMENT OF THE CIGAR

FOR SPANISH MONARCHS, the tobacco tax was more than just a source of revenue; while they used the gold mined in the Americas to build armies and wage wars of conquest, they invested tobacco revenues in the building of factories in Seville and eventually throughout the country. Indeed, for the next century, Spain would be the leading manufacturer of cigars using tobacco supplied by its crown colony.

The first cigar factories appeared in Seville in 1676; in 1731 the royal cigar factories were established there. By the beginning of the nineteenth century, Spain's cigar industry had grown to employ five thousand workers, who churned out millions of their trademark *puros*—to this day the popular Spanish word for cigars.

An offshoot of the cigar was the *papelito*. Made from leftover tobacco, it was a poor man's cigar, the precursor of the modern cigarette. From the mid-1700s, the lower

ABOVE: AN EIGHTEENTH-CENTURY ETCHING FROM THE NEW YORK PUBLIC LIBRARY'S ARENTS COLLECTION FROM A SERIES ON THE EARLY PREPARATION OF TOBACCO.
OPPOSITE: EARLY NINETEENTH-CENTURY TOBACCO STAMP FROM VIRGINIA; A LETTER FROM GEORGE WASHINGTON DOCUMENTING HIS SUCCESSFUL TOBACCO CROP.

and middle classes in Spain took factory scrapings and rolled them in paper for a quick smoke. *Papelitos* were widely available by 1830, but not until nearly a century later did worldwide mass production of cigarettes begin in earnest.

The booming cigar industry encouraged the Spanish to perfect the process of growing, fermenting, and curing a leaf flexible and strong enough to hold the *puro* together while, at the same time, blending in with the burning tobacco. Although the first cigars were not as smooth as they are today, their construction and manufacturing have undergone remarkably little change over the centuries. In time, new blends and superb wrappers have been developed.

By the late eighteenth and early nineteenth centuries, Spanish *puros* were lighting up the Continent. The Italian ports at Venice and Genoa became key spots for shipping cigars to central Europe and Russia. Tobacco escalated in value. Pirates seizing vessels often found that the cargo bays carried not gold and precious metals but a bounty of cigars and tobacco.

After George III of England's one-year occupation of Cuba in 1762, Israel Putnam, a British officer, came home to Connecticut with an aromatic collection of Havana cigars. They were treasured and could have contributed to the success of Putnam, who later became an American general in the Revolutionary War. By then, of course, Virginia and North Carolina tobacco fields had been established. George Washington and Thomas Jefferson, both Virginia plantation owners, received considerable income from growing tobacco. Cigars did not catch on immediately in the United States, where smoking tobacco in pipes was the norm, but the aroma and taste of Havana tobacco would soon play a role not only in the colonies but in international diplomacy as well.

Within Europe, Spain's manufacturing cartel was quickly challenged. By the mid-eighteenth century, Louis XV had pushed French industry into cigar manufacturing. In 1779 Peter Wendler, a German painter, was granted a five-year concession by the papal government in Rome to manufacture *bastoni di tabacco*—tobacco sticks, or cigars. By 1800 the Italian and German industries were manufacturing cigars. The New World joined the competitive arena when the British colonies in North America, specifically Connecticut, began rolling cigars in 1810. Furthermore, the Cuban brands had a strong allure for the growing number of connoisseurs across Europe, putting the island in a position to dominate the cigar industry.

CUBA'S *FÁBRICAS*

BETWEEN 1614, when the Spanish royal court authorized tobacco cultivation in Cuba, and the late eighteenth century, most Cuban leaf was sent to Spain to be made into cigars. When it was acknowledged that Havana cigars survived the transatlantic voyage much better than the leaf itself, the *fábricas,* or cigar factories, were born. They sprang up from the eighteenth-century tobacco plantations, each offering its own brand or brands of cigar, much as vineyards produce their own vintages.

The first names to be registered in Havana's trademark office, entered in 1810, were forerunners of a flourishing industry. An entry (preserved in the Cuban National Archives) for a permit issued for the establishment of one factory and shop reads: "Francisco Cabanas, born in Havana, single, has opened a shop in Jesus del Monte Avenue, which was previously operated at 112 Jesus Maria Street." In 1810 this *fábrica* had sixteen workers; by 1833, cigars made by Cabanas were being sold in a shop in London. These house labels identified the cigars being produced; each maintained its own distinct flavor through carefully guarded variations of plant types and processing techniques.

With Havana's emergence as a port of call, Cuban cigar makers, descendants of the Spanish colonists, gained easy access to markets not just in Europe but in the rest of North America. On June 23, 1817, Fernando VII of Spain signed a royal decree that allowed free trade for the island of Cuba. The subsequent boom in cigar sales filled the port of Old Havana with ships bound to distribute Cuban cigars the world over. The steamship ensured rapid distribution of Cuba's superior brands, further diminishing the predominance of the Spanish factories. So began the golden age of the Havana. Between 1830 and 1850 the great brands, many of which survive today, were founded: Por Larranaga, 1834; Ramon Allones, 1837; Punch, 1840; H. Upmann, 1844; La Corona and Partagas, 1845; as well as Vuelta, El Figaro, El Rey del Mundo, Romeo y Julieta, José Gener's Hoyo de Monterrey, Belinda, and Bolivar.

The *fábricas* of the nineteenth century accomplished two objectives. First, they created and established Cuban brands, familiarizing consumers with Cuban product and building the brand loyalties that the island would enjoy until the 1959 revolution. And, mostly in the latter half of the century, the *fábricas* refined their production techniques, improving the quality of cigars and allowing them to conquer foreign markets.

Cuban cigars finally gained acceptance in Europe during the Victorian age (1837–1901), when the cigar's aroma, convenience, and price gained

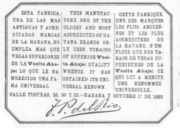

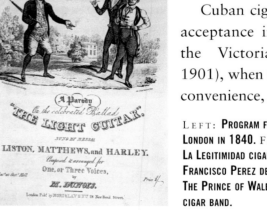

LEFT: PROGRAM FROM A PLAY PERFORMED IN LONDON IN 1840. FAR LEFT: A VISTA FROM LA LEGITIMIDAD CIGAR FACTORY, FOUNDED BY FRANCISCO PEREZ DEL RIO, 1882. RIGHT: THE PRINCE OF WALES HAD HIS LIKENESS ON A CIGAR BAND.

acceptance and respect among the aristocracy. To be sure, smokers risked the wrath of Queen Victoria, a formidable antismoking advocate. But despite Her Majesty's objections, between 1823 and 1840 the number of cigars imported into Britain alone skyrocketed from 15,000 to 30 million.

Even though smoking had caught on with a fierce passion, it still had its detractors. Victorian England presumed smoking to be impolite when practiced in public. In Great Britain municipal ordinances prohibited smoking on city streets, generally limiting the practice to smoking rooms and to men-only gatherings. In the 1840s British men's clubs became the principal havens of cigar smokers; in 1868 Britain enacted a law that trains would include smoking cars. Smoking in the Victorian era could be generalized by the statement "Men did it, women objected."

Queen Victoria's son Edward, Prince of Wales, was a passionate cigar aficionado. When, upon his accession to the throne in 1901, he spoke the memorable line "Gentlemen, you may smoke," cigars finally gained their rightful place in social settings.

By the 1860s and 1870s, the Cuban houses had invaded international exhibitions, winning medals and acceptance in every country. With this success the manufacture of Cuban cigars became an enterprise of unparalleled prestige and excellence.

At midcentury cigar workers themselves participated in an elevated level of culture. The practice of reading the great literary works became commonplace in Havana's *fábricas*. The rich aroma of the world's finest tobacco would mingle with the words of Victor Hugo or Charles Dickens, adding to the heady atmosphere of the *fábrica* and passing the hours more enjoyably for the rollers.

The United States also joined the production boom. After the Civil War one-man shops and full-fledged factories flourished in many states. Many American factories

were built along an east-west trajectory so that graders and leaf rollers would have northern light. In North Carolina the Duke family built an empire that would dominate the cigarette business within a generation. But the cigar industry really belonged to Cuba, where tobacco entrepreneurs continued to build the brands that made up the island's cigar empire.

In 1850 paper bands were introduced into the design of cigars as a means of distinguishing prestigious brands. They were created by Gustavo Bock, a Dutchman, who introduced them as a signature for his own cigars. Colorful and artistic, the bands around cigars and the boxes that stored them reflected a cigar's individual character, much as cigars themselves were crafted to have a particular taste, feel, and aroma. Power brokers, heads of state, kings and monarchs, presidents and dictators, companies and countries—all wanted a custom-designed band. This rush for cigars established the reputation of the Cuban cigar as an accoutrement of wealth, power, and prestige.

By controlling the growing, producing, and packaging of the product, Cubans such as Manuel Lopez, Alfredo Nogueira, and J. F. Rocha accomplished what their Spanish, British, and other European competitors had failed to achieve: They combined the art of cultivating tobacco with the craft of producing a cigar. As a result, the development of the cigar industry in Cuba was as much a story of the men and families that produced them as it was a story of the cigar itself.

THE CIGAR WARS

AT MIDCENTURY, as a key producer of sugar, coffee, and now tobacco, Cuba was the jewel in Spain's colonial crown, coveted by established and rising powers. In the United States the Monroe Doctrine had long designated Cuba as another star on the American flag. After Andrew Jackson's invasion, Florida was ceded to the United States; in the 1850s President Franklin Pierce attempted to acquire Cuba as well. But he failed to bring the island into the American fold.

In Britain the cigar craze continued. By the last quarter of the century, Britain was the leading market for Havana's cigar makers, with James Freeman leading the way. Financier L. Rothschild told

THE MONROE DOCTRINE

the Hoyo de Monterrey factory to develop a shorter cigar with a larger ring size, so that smokers could enjoy a richer taste without having to puff away at a full-length cigar. This opened up endless styles and sizes in cigar making.

As the nineteenth century progressed, Cuban supremacy in the cigar industry faced a serious challenge in domestic political unrest. Even before Cuba's abortive revolt against Spain in 1868–1878, many skilled laborers had fled the increasingly volatile island and settled in the Florida boomtowns. In Key West the Cuban population surged from a sleepy 3,000 in 1869 to roughly 18,000 by 1890. In the Tampa area, Ybor City and adjacent towns also saw growth, from 1,000 Cubans in 1885 to 20,000 five years later. The Tampa area would boast some five hundred cigar factories by 1898.

LEFT: THE TRADITIONAL *LECTOR* READING TO CIGAR WORKERS, A CUSTOM THAT IS FOLLOWED TO THIS DAY. RIGHT: AN AMERICAN CIGAR LABEL COMMEMORATED THE UNITED STATES' EXPANSIONIST POLICY.

The émigré communities arrived just as cigar smoking was booming in the United States. Cubans differed from other immigrants to the United States because they were largely homogenous and well capitalized. They had money to invest in a skill that would prove to be incredibly popular. Nor did their labor displace that of native workers, because they provided a new industry that served emerging markets and needs.

At the end of the nineteenth century, when Cuba struggled for independence from Spain, many of the island's premier cigar makers also left for Key West and Tampa as well as the Canary Islands and Kingston, Jamaica. These expatriates helped fund the revolt against Spain led by José Martí, Cuba's national hero, in 1895. Martí's order to fight was secretly sent from Key West to Havana in a cigar box. Eventually more than fifty companies in Ybor City were producing Clear Havanas. Soon the "Made in Tampa" stamp was considered almost as prestigious as "Made in Havana." Tampa could boast that its cigars were produced not only with Cuban wrappers and filler but by Cuban hands—hence the term *Clear Havana.*

After the 1898 Spanish-American War, the cigar industry saw another boom. The millions of dollars it brought to Florida competed with revenues from other sources such as citrus, tourism, and phosphate. In 1909 the cigar industry generated about $21.5 million worth of product and employed 12,280 people.

Expatriate Cuban labor was not the only source of professional expertise to boost American industry at the turn of the century. European immigrants, unsettled by Germany's expansionist rumblings, sought security in the New World, bringing their skills with them. The rising demand for cigars provided them with enough work to keep the country's seven thousand cigar factories at full capacity through the end of the Spanish-American War. This expansion helped the American cigar industry better its product by leaps and bounds. The Connecticut broadleaf soon enjoyed status as a fine wrapper. Price was also a factor: A good Havana cost fifteen cents, while American-made cigars were priced far lower.

Almost twenty years later, Vice President Thomas Riley Marshall further defined the cigar's role in American society. "What this country needs," Riley told the Senate, "is a really good five-cent cigar."

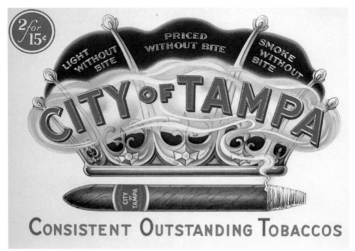

THIS PAGE: THREE VITOLAS FOR U.S.-MADE CIGARS MANUFACTURED FROM HAVANA-GROWN TOBACCO, KNOWN AS CLEAR HAVANAS. OPPOSITE: EARLY TWENTIETH-CENTURY AMERICAN LABEL TOUTED AFFORDABLE U.S.-MADE CIGARS.

THE TWENTIETH CENTURY

TECHNOLOGY PLAYED A major role in the way cigar making developed. Manufacturers soon realized that one reason Tampa cigars sold so well was that Florida's humidity helped preserve the taste and aroma. But since tobacco vendors and concessionaires usually kept their products in the open, the less humid northern air tended to dry them out. Electricity finally allowed tobacconists to store most of their inventory in humidified enclosures that kept the product fresh and desirable. One of the first to employ this innovation was Alfred Dunhill of London, who aged his cigars in cedar-lined rooms in his store. Later he sold the products in hermetically sealed tins.

World politics and conflicts continued to mold the cigar trade. The Spanish-American War had replaced Spain with the United States as Cuba's colonial guarantor. But the Platt Amendment (1901), which formalized Washington as Havana's principal supporter, was only a formality. *El Norte* had already acquired a lusty taste for Cuban sugar, coffee, and cigars. As American influence in Cuba increased dramatically, so did its desire for Cuban products, particularly its cigars.

The Great War in Europe once again jolted the global cigar trade. By damaging European industry, the conflict sapped the wealth of the aristocracy that had provided a ready market for the fine art of smoking. Some brands disappeared as a result. Even after peace and "normalcy" returned in other respects, the cigar industry was slow to recover. In the United States the frenetic popular culture of the 1920s gave rise to speakeasies, flappers—and the mass-produced cigarette. A generation of new smokers, many of them women, chose the jazzy and looser *papelito* as an accompaniment to their life style.

Despite the worldwide drop in cigar consumption, two groups of consumers held true. So fully had Spain inte-

LEFT: A TYPICAL LABEL FROM THE AMERICAN LITHOGRAPHIC COMPANY; THE EMBOSSING AND PRINTING PROCESS UTILIZED UP TO 11 AUSTRIAN LIMESTONE PLATES. ABOVE AND OPPOSITE: TWENTIETH-CENTURY AMERICAN-MADE LABELS FROM PHILADELPHIA AND NEW YORK.

grated the cigar into its culture that Spaniards did not give up smoking even in a severely depressed economy. And the United States' proximity to Cuba offered encouragement for American smokers to continue.

The 1929 stock market crash made matters difficult even for these loyalists, as they found themselves unable to afford the Cuban cigars they loved. The cigar trade remained quiet until the introduction of cigar-making machines helped lower costs while spurring production later in the 1930s. Some quality was lost, but the ingredients came from the same sources. The drop in prices came at an opportune time, and the cheaper cigars appealed to blue-collar laborers as much as to the affluent. Ultimately, however, the cigar's mass acceptance tarnished its reputation as a product for the elegant and rich.

A dramatic renewal came with World War II. The fight against fascism brought the cigar back in vogue—this time as a symbol of resistance. Winston Churchill, the quintessential emblem of perseverance, was rarely seen in public without either a cigar or his trademark V sign. After one ruinous Luftwaffe blitz over London, no less a figure than Alfred Dunhill was photographed taking orders outside what remained of his storefront. The war also realigned commercial markets. Britain, unable to buy cigars from Cuba because of freezes on the U.S. dollar, turned to Jamaica where the pound sterling could still be used. Even after the war ended, Britain did not resume im-

porting Cuban cigars until 1953. By then the Jamaican industry had matured, and brands such as Temple Hall, El Caribe, Flor del Duque, and eventually Macanudo had become competitive.

In America, postwar inflation drove up prices, pushing the cost of a cigar to a quarter. With increased production, overtaxed machinery began to tear wrapper sheets. A new, stronger wrapper was developed, making the fully mechanically produced cigar a reality. Even in Cuba, where hand-rolled cigars were a source of national pride, machines appeared. The move to machinery may have been painful to purists, but not for commerce. For the first time the cheaper brands of Havanas were accessible to the average working man, and their appeal rocketed again.

EXPOSITION UNIVERSELLE DE 1878.
LE JURY INTERNATIONAL DES RECOMPENSES
DÉCERNE
UN RAPPEL DE MÉDAILLE D'OR
A
Monsieur PARTAGAS

AFTER WORLD WAR II the cigar industry flourished again in Cuba and in Tampa, where Clear Havanas were made. But a shocking jolt came to the great Havana cigar makers in 1959, at the height of the renewed love affair between Americans and their Cuban cigars. Fidel Castro came to power on January 2, and the deposed dictator Fulgencio Batista fled to exile, followed by many tobacco plantation owners and cigar manufacturers. *Fábrica* employees, from farmers to scientists to rollers, put aside their duties in the face of the political turmoil.

After Fidel Castro's revolution, the cigar companies—many of which had been financed by American firms—were put under state monopoly. Castro's Marxist regime courted support from the workers—what he termed the proletariat—and the tobacco industry was a prime source. His appeal that the state, not the cigar companies, would

ABOVE: THE PARTAGAS FACTORY, WHICH PRODUCES ONE OF THE FINEST CIGARS IN THE WORLD, WAS FOUNDED BY JAIME PARTAGAS IN 1845. RIGHT: THE HAVANA CABANAS FACTORY HAS MADE CIGARS SINCE 1797. THE PLANTATION IN PINAR DEL RIO WAS CALLED HOTO DE LA CRUZ. IN 1810, FRANCISCO CABANAS FOUNDED ANOTHER FACTORY WITH MANUEL GONZÁLEZ CARBAJAL AND CREATED ONE OF THE FIRST CUBAN BRANDS, CABANAS Y CARBAJAL, IN 1848.

best serve the industry was geared at gaining their support. Cigar workers had always been at the forefront of social change in Cuba, playing a key role in the break from Spain in the 1890s as well as in a coalition that had ousted the dictator Gerardo Machado in 1933.

When Castro nationalized the cigar factories and eliminated individual cigar brands, however, he stunned the world. For one thing, the masterfully decorated cigar boxes and bands that had denoted the world's finest cigars were cast aside. Venerable labels such as Henry Clay, La Corona, Cabanas y Carbajal, Murias, and Villar y Villar disappeared. From the 960 brands of Cuban cigar that had flourished under his predecessor, only one new label emerged; the Siboney. Named after a legendary Cuban, the Siboney came in only four sizes of highly unpredictable quality. It was a serious disaster.

Cuban relations with the United States deteriorated at an alarming rate. In 1961, in response to Castro's expropriation of more than a billion dollars in American business, the United States imposed a trade embargo that eventually drove Havanas from American tobacco shops altogether. Cuban tobacco could no longer be imported into the United States.

Some American companies stockpiled inventories, which carried them through until the early 1970s. In fact, President John F. Kennedy, who signed the embargo order, asked a senior aide to purchase up to a thousand Havanas before it went into effect, so that he would have his own personal supply. Some canny manufacturers in Florida had stockpiled enough Cuban tobacco to be able to make new brands, such as the Tampa-made Bances, now licensed in Canada. Others tapped the Cuban tobacco supply by going through other countries, but even they saw the prices rise steadily, from $150 a bale to over $1,000.

To offset the price increases and the eventual supply problems, importers and distributors began searching for replacement sources. Early on, the focus turned to the Spanish Canary Islands. While these islands did not grow tobacco plants per se, they did offer a skilled workforce and advantageous tax and tariff situations that encouraged manufacturers to turn imported raw material into a connoisseur's delight. Other firms sought to replant operations in Jamaica and the Dominican Republic.

The disastrous effects of Cuba's nationalization finally forced Castro to backpedal. Partly because of the poor quality of Cuba's anonymous cigars, and partly in protest against the dismantling of a revered tradition, the world steadfastly refused to buy them. The regime decided to allow individual small landowners to keep their plots, and it broke up the larger plantations.

After consulting with Zino Davidoff, the most prominent cigar dealer and connoisseur in the world, the government reintroduced many of the great brands from Cuba's cigar heritage, eventually returning to 330 types and sizes. The 1964–65 tobacco harvest was the best in ten years. Gradually the Cuban cigar regained its exceptional quality and rebuilt its reputation.

By the 1970s, the Havana had completely regained its status as the best cigar in the world as connoisseurs in Europe accepted the Cohiba as a new symbol of Cuban cigar excellence. In part, this acceptance had come about because the Davidoff organization had continued its

relationship with Cuba, along with Dunhill's distributors, even as the state company Cubatabaco made demands for additional profits and percentages. But those relationships withered, and in late 1989 Davidoff pulled out of Cuba, seeking favorable terms and control in the Dominican Republic.

With the Cuban cigar industry in disarray, the door was open to competitors from other countries who were eager to take up the challenge of creating a premium cigar in the tradition of the Havana. Castro had unwittingly relinquished control of the international cigar market.

In 1975 the World Court ruled that exiled Cuban cigar makers had the right to use their former brand names. Many great cigar families, the Menéndez and the Cifuentes among them, had left their homeland, determined to resume production using their old names. These expatriates went on to develop their own tobacco, wrappers, and bands, so that in many cases there are now two versions of revered brands such as Partagas, Montecristo, Upmann, Hoyo de Monterrey, and Romeo y Julieta—Cuban and non-Cuban. Honduras had initiated cigar production in the late 1960s. In the 1970s the Spanish government cut state aid to the Canary Islands' cigar operations, a move that shifted almost all award-quality production back to the Western Hemisphere, benefiting Jamaica and the Dominican Republic.

With dedicated development, experience, and passion, many of the best-quality cigars are now manufactured not only in Cuba but in the Dominican Republic, Honduras, Nicaragua, and the Canary Islands. In these places the Cuban seed is grown, nurtured, and blended by families like the Fuentes and Olivas, who have contributed immeasurably to cigar making. With the contribution of the superior Connecticut leaf and Cameroon wrappers, cigars are once again being made in excellent quality with full-flavored taste, continuing a remarkable and romantic saga.

CUBA TODAY

THE 1990S HAVE NOT been kind to Cuba. The collapse of the Soviet Union was a severe blow, sending the country into an economic tailspin from which it is still recovering at this writing. Shortages of raw materials, such as fertilizers and packaging, have hampered the nation's efforts to revitalize its cigar-making industry. Cubatabaco, however, has been restructured and refinanced by Spain as Habanos, S.A., and is doing well.

The weather has been unpredictable, too. Heavy rains have limited harvests, and the regions that grow the *capa* leaf, used for the wrapper, have been hard hit, leading to a shortage. Many feel that Havanas have lost their balance and consistency. Still, the soil in Cuba is magic, and when a Havana is good, there is nothing like it.

> **"The most futile and disastrous day seems to be well spent when it is reviewed through the blue fragrant smoke of a Havana cigar."**
>
> *Evelyn Waugh*

A great debate is raging among connoisseurs on the subject "Which cigars are better, Cuban or non-Cuban?" Although the Cubans have been making cigars for hundreds of years, the expatriated experts have proven that a premium or vintage Dominican Partagas, Davidoff, or Dunhill, or a Jamaican Macanudo, or a Honduran Hoyo de Monterrey can be as beautifully made and measured to the highest standard. These cigars are as enjoyable and elegant and flavorful as any made in Cuba. Still, among tobacco makers from Havana to Honduras, there is a profound mutual respect. They share their knowledge and secrets in a fraternity of friendship that has as its charter to produce only the best, all handmade from the heart.

RIGHT: AN EARLY TWENTIETH-CENTURY LABEL CREATED BY LITOGRÁFICA DE HABANA FOR RÁMON FERNANDEZ WITH A ROARING TWENTIES INFLUENCE.

SANTA FELIPA

REAL FABRICA DE TABACOS
DE
Ramón F Fernández
HABANA

DE
RAMON FERNANDEZ
HABANA

SUN, SOIL, AND SKILL

LA CASITA CRIOLLA

CHAMBAS - CAMAGÜEY

THE PROCESS OF MAKING a cigar has not changed dramatically in five hundred years. To be sure, the machinery involved and the workplaces have been altered substantially. But the fundamental steps are much the same. So too are the criteria necessary for making the world's finest cigars: the proper seed and soil and, above all, the proper

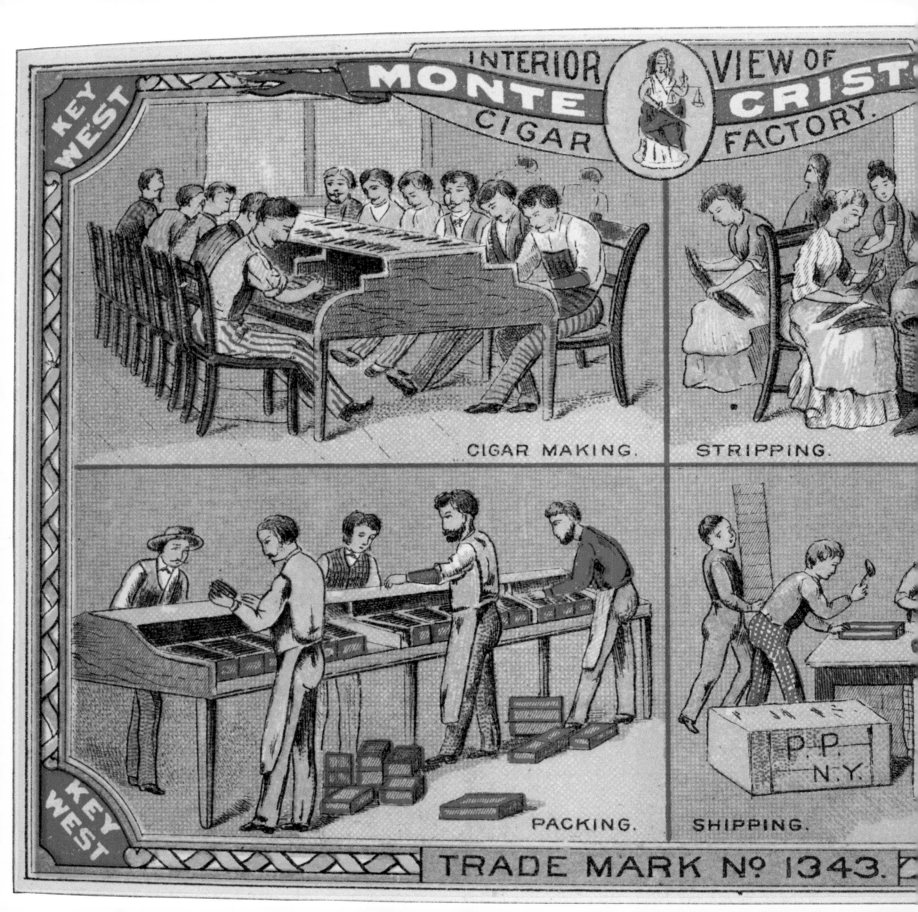

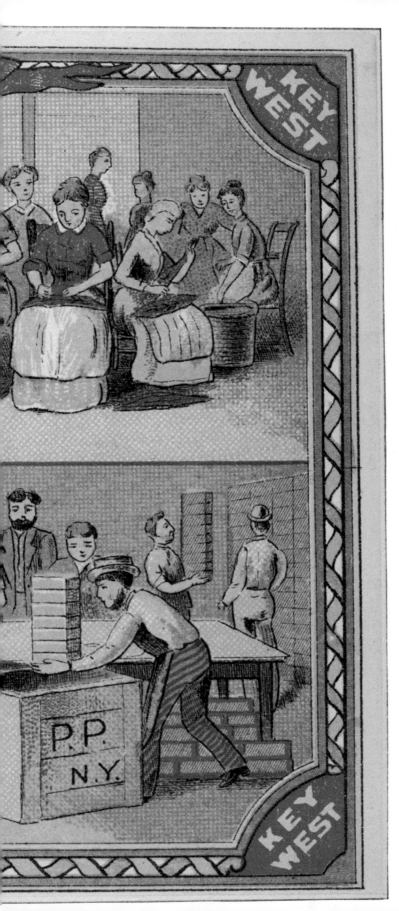

expertise to cultivate, cure, age, blend, bunch, and roll the leaves.

Despite the resurgence of interest in cigar smoking today, the subtle art of cigar making remains surprisingly intimate in scale and firmly rooted in its Cuban heritage. The unparalleled red earth of the Vuelta Abajo, a tiny triangle of land that represents a mere two percent of the land area of the island, produces what is arguably the best cigar tobacco in the world. From this fertile region, seeds for superior tobacco have found their way to other countries, where they flourish and help keep alive the great legacy of Cuban tobacco.

The *fábricas* themselves have changed little from the days of the great brands, and they hold a mystique all their own. Here cigar production, a prized skill learned over a

LEFT: A CLEAR HAVANA LABEL FOR MONTECRISTO DEPICTS SCENES FROM THE FACTORY.
ABOVE: SEVENTEENTH-CENTURY CUBAN VISTA FROM THE HAVANA MUSEUM OF FINE ARTS.

THE MANUFACTURING PROCESS OF CIGARS

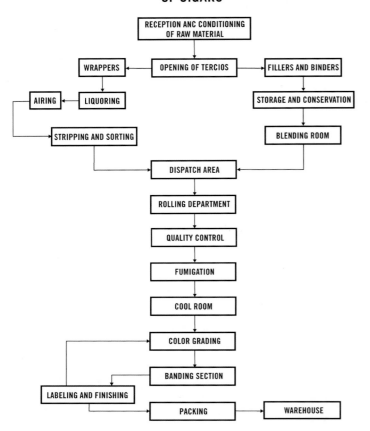

```
          RECEPTION ANC CONDITIONING
              OF RAW MATERIAL
                    │
   ┌──────────┬─────┴─────┬──────────────┐
WRAPPERS ◄── OPENING OF TERCIOS ──► FILLERS AND BINDERS
   │                                      │
   │                              STORAGE AND CONSERVATION
AIRING ── LIQUORING                       │
   │                               BLENDING ROOM
STRIPPING AND SORTING                     │
          │                               │
          └────► DISPATCH AREA ◄──────────┘
                      │
               ROLLING DEPARTMENT
                      │
                QUALITY CONTROL
                      │
                  FUMIGATION
                      │
                  COOL ROOM
                      │
                COLOR GRADING
                      │
                BANDING SECTION
                      │
  LABELING AND FINISHING
          │
          └──► PACKING ──► WAREHOUSE
```

lifetime, is done completely by hand. Contrary to myth, Cuban cigars are not rolled on the smooth thighs of beautiful women; the job of cigar rolling was traditionally held by men, although women have gradually replaced men in some of these jobs. Women are more likely to be employed as strippers, whose job it is to cut away the central vein from the leaves on a curved board, which is held to their thighs by tight-fitting wedges. This job is of lower status than that of the roller and is often accompanied by much raucous conversation. The rollers are, by far, the most highly skilled workers in the *fábricas,* and when working, they foster an air of solemnity and concentration. The skill of cigar rolling takes years to learn and a lifetime to master.

Only a few geographic areas on the globe, usually near the equator and in uneven landscape, provide the climate and soil conditions required to produce the aromatic and savory leaves of quality tobacco plants. Like Californian and French vintners, tobacco growers look for the perfect combination of elements. For the most part, these occur in the greater Antilles and Central America—specifically, the lush, humid valleys of the Dominican Republic, Cuba, and Jamaica.

Just as it was centuries ago, the harvesting and preparation of cigar tobacco remains a delicate operation. Timing is crucial: Each plant must be harvested on the exact day it is ready, and each leaf on the plant has a specific purpose. The nearer a leaf is to the sun and the longer it remains on the plant, the stronger the tobacco will be. Wrapper leaves and filler leaves come from two separate types of plant, each cultivated for its own specialized purpose. Good wrapper leaves must be strong and supple, yet thin enough to burn well and wrap neatly. For this reason, even today, superior cigars cannot be rolled by machine: Only the discerning touch of the human hand can work with the delicately thin leaves. Automated wrapping machines require sturdier leaves and even then result in sloppy wrapping.

The *corojo,* named for the famous plantation, El Corojo Vega, where it was developed, is used to produce only wrappers. By contrast, the *criollo* plant provides a potpourri of flavors for the filler and binder, giving Havanas their distinct aroma and flavor.

Seed selection is the primary determinant of the size, color, and texture of the leaf. The tobacco-growing season on the *vegas* (plantations) begins in late September and October, when the flat seed beds are prepared and the seeds are sown. After about forty-five days, the seedlings, now six to eight inches tall, are carefully winnowed; the sturdiest specimens are transplanted to fields that have

OPPOSITE: FIRST FAMILY FUENTE, CARLOS JUNIOR AND SENIOR, AT THEIR PLANTATION IN THE DOMINICAN REPUBLIC.

been plowed several times to soften the soil for the plants' delicate roots. Some are planted in shade and others in direct sunlight.

Shade-grown *corojo* plants receive filtered sunlight through translucent cheesecloth. Grown this way, their leaves can remain thin and develop the smooth texture needed for wrappers.

The *criollo* plants that provide the filler and binder are always grown in direct sunlight. The intensity of the sun's brightness and heat cultivates the abundant mix of flavors prized by connoisseurs. The farmer clips any flowers or side-shoots as soon as they appear—which allows the plant to concentrate its energies on producing the largest possible leaves.

After another forty-five days, the leaves are ready for picking. Harvesting, of course, has its own strict discipline. The leaf is generally considered ready when its arch folds downward and its principal vein turns white. The leaves are harvested two or three at a time by hand and with great care.

The *corojo* plant produces eight or nine pairs of leaves, destined to become wrappers, which are graded into six categories, from top to bottom: *corona, centro gordo, centro fino, centro ligero, uno y medio,* and *libre del pie*. (Sometimes the top leaves are further divided into *corona* and *semi corona* categories.) The *corojo* leaves

are harvested in six stages, working successively higher on the plant, at one-week intervals. The general principle is that the higher the leaf and the more sunlight it receives, the thicker, darker, and more flavorful it becomes.

By contrast, the *criollo* plant sprouts only three types of leaves: the *ligero, seco,* and *volado*. The *volado* leaves grow at the bottom of the plant and are very mild in taste but burn very well. The middle leaves, the *seco,* give mild to medium flavor and aroma and a steady burn. The highest leaves, the *ligero,* have a rougher texture and a stronger taste because they are more oily, and they burn at a slower rate. Harvesting always begins with the *volado,* which allows the *seco* and *ligero* extra time to mature.

By the time the last leaves are harvested, the tobacco plant will have spent about three months in the field and reached six to eight feet in height. Each plant produces between twelve and twenty leaves before late January, when the remaining stem is cut down. If the climate is supportive, some plantations attempt a second planting in a season that runs from December to April.

After harvesting, the leaves are moved to tobacco sheds for air curing. They are sewn in pairs with cotton thread, then draped over the *cujes,* long poles that allow them to hang near the roof of the barn away from sunlight. These sheds, with their rustic thatched roofs made of dried leaves from the *palmas reales* (royal palms) that tower over all, dot the picturesque tropical landscape of the *vegas*. They face east-west for exposure to the early morning and late

OPPOSITE: CUBAN TOBACCO PLANTATIONS ON THE VUELTA ABAJO, PRODUCING GREAT TOBACCO FROM A PERFECT SOIL AND CLIMATE. ENTIRE ACRES ARE SHADED WITH GAUZE TO PRODUCE THE RENOWNED SUNSHADE TOBACCO. ABOVE: HENDRIK KELNER, WHOSE OUTSTANDING TOBACCO IS GROWN FOR DAVIDOFF, GRIFFIN'S, AND AVO CIGARS.

afternoon sun; the temperature and humidity inside are carefully monitored and controlled by opening and closing the doors. The curing process takes 45 to 60 days.

Once brown, the leaves are ready for the natural, age-old process of fermentation. First fermentation, which is similar to composting, takes another 30 to 40 days. The leaves are arranged in three-foot stacks. Pressure and moisture generate heat, which must not be permitted to exceed 95 degrees Fahrenheit, within the piles of leaves. After first fermentation the leaves are cooled and moistened. Filler and binder leaves are partially stripped of their stems; wrapper leaves will undergo this process later at the factory. All are separated and graded by size, texture, and color.

Next comes the crucial second fermentation. The leaves are flattened and piled into huge stacks called *burros,* which range between four and six feet high and weigh as much as ten thousand pounds. Again, the air trapped inside the stacks heats up, this time to about 110 degrees, causing sap and ammonia to seep out of the tobacco. With this physical change the tobacco darkens, starch in the leaf turns to sugar, and each leaf acquires finesse and character. The stacks are rotated at regular intervals; as with first fermentation, if the interior temperature gets too high, they are broken down and restacked. Due to these careful

stages of fermentation, cigar tobacco contains less acidity, tar, and nicotine than cigarette tobacco.

Now the leaves are ready to be shipped to warehouses and factories. First they are aired out, then bundled in bales made of palm bark *(tercios)* and aged for as long as three years before they are made into cigars. The lighter tobaccos take less time to mature. Once a bale has been selected for processing, the leaves must first go through a *moja* (wetting), in which they are separated and rehumidified with a misty spray. The wrapper leaves receive pure water before they go to the stripper, while the binders and fillers are given a mixture of water and tobacco juice.

The next step is the blender, where the leaves are again categorized for taste, then blended according to an individual recipe—the cigar maker's most closely guarded secret. Blending tobacco leaves is somewhat similar to shuffling playing cards, which is why the blending department in a Cuban *fábrica* is often referred to as *la barajita,* literally "the pack of cards."

The cigar maker in charge of blending is the keeper of the keys and must know exactly what each leaf is capable of producing and how it will interact with others. The filler is the soul of a cigar for aroma and taste. A mild, smooth cigar such as a Macanudo will have a high percentage of *seco* and *volado* leaves in its blend, while a stronger, full-bodied cigar like a Partagas will have more *ligero.* Blending is an art that takes a lifetime of experience, knowledge, and passion to master.

When prepared filler goes to the roller (*torcedor,* liter-

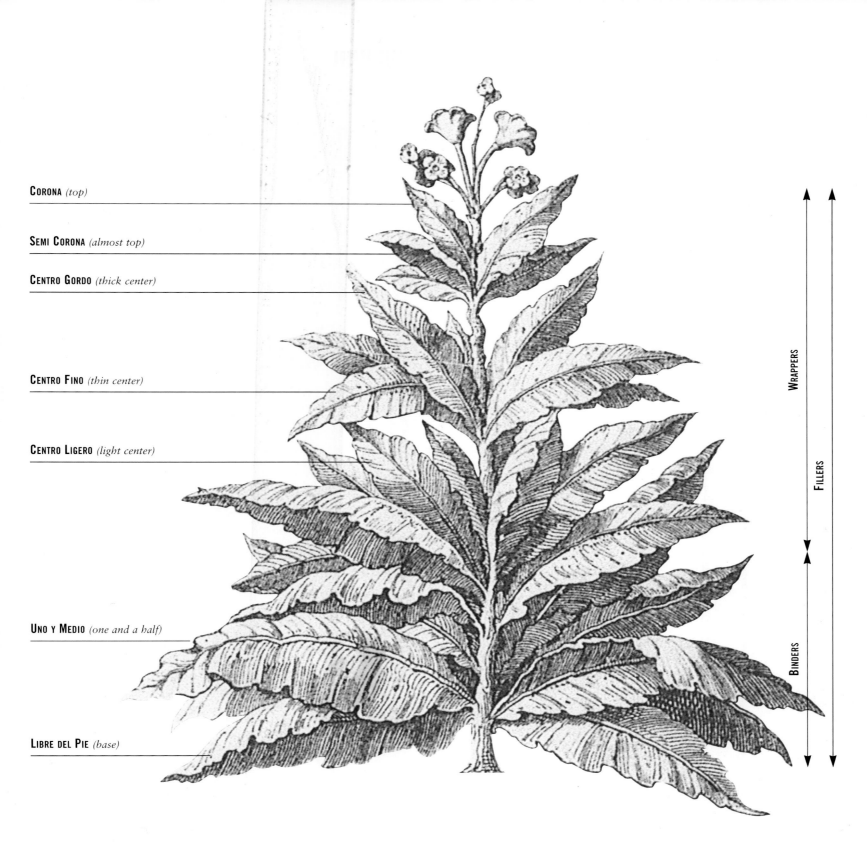

CORONA *(top)*

SEMI CORONA *(almost top)*

CENTRO GORDO *(thick center)*

CENTRO FINO *(thin center)*

CENTRO LIGERO *(light center)*

UNO Y MEDIO *(one and a half)*

LIBRE DEL PIE *(base)*

WRAPPERS

FILLERS

BINDERS

THE CONNECTICUT
CONNECTION:
AUSTIN MCNAMARA

Austin T. McNamara is president and chief executive officer of General Cigar Company, the only cigar manufacturer that grows, cures, and ages its own Connecticut shade wrapper.

On any summer day along Interstate 91 just north of Hartford, acre after acre of tobacco fields appear to be cloaked in a kind of unending snow-white veil of mystery. And well they should be.

While Connecticut tobacco farmers of the 1800s had few, if any, equals anywhere in the United States, they had yet to develop a cigar wrapper leaf to match those that were grown either in Cuba or Sumatra, lacking the tropical humidity and the low-hanging, sun-shading clouds that are most conducive to growing the finest wrappers. Then too, the Connecticut farmers had nothing in the way of wrapper seeds to approach the quality of those from Cuba and Sumatra.

In the last years of the nineteenth century, an attempt was finally made to grow world-class wrapper leaf in Connecticut using Sumatran seeds. To approximate the steamy Sumatran climate, the Connecticut Valley fields were meticulously covered with acres of tenting, similar to the polymer we use today to increase the humidity surrounding our tobacco plants by at least 20 degrees. Unfortunately, however, the Sumatran seeds were not at home in the Connecticut soil, and the leaves that resulted were much too thin to be of any value as cigar wrappers.

A miracle eventually arrived in the form of some precious Cuban seeds that were imported (not smuggled, as some people thought) from Cuba. The importer was none other than the U.S. Department of Agriculture, and the seeds, which have been refined considerably since those early times, remain the only wrapper seeds that have ever been grown with success in Connecticut. Just as curiously, no one has ever been able to grow Connecticut shade with any good fortune anywhere else in the United States.

As for the surprisingly fertile quality of the Connecticut Valley's sandy loam, some people believe that it is caused by the valley's tidal-river overflows, while others credit the rich nutrients contained in various glacial deposits. On the other hand, still others credit the nature and location of the valley itself, partly because its high summer temperatures are ideal for growing and its low winter temperatures are just as favorable for curing. One thing can be said for certain: The cultivation of Connecticut shade is very likely the most labor-intensive of all forms of agriculture. In contrast to a vegetable such as corn, a crop of which costs about $300 an acre to cultivate and process, Connecticut shade now costs $26,000 an acre.

The seedlings for each crop, the seeds for which are so minute that they must be coated with a greenish clay to make them clearly visible to the human eye, are grown in our greenhouses until they reach a height of from four to six inches. The small plants are then taken to carefully plowed fields, where they are planted at 16-inch intervals in long straight rows that are 34 inches apart. Under constant care to prevent pests from attacking them, the plants grow as tall as eight or ten feet in a matter of two months. Then, every seven to ten days thereafter, the plants are harvested, or "primed," until six or seven primings yield a total of 18 to 21 leaves from each plant. Our growers select only the longest, finest-grained leaves from the choice third and fourth primings.

After they have been moved to our curing sheds, the virgin-green leaves are sewn together then tied to wooden poles hung as high as 40 feet from the ground, to await the curing process that will dry and turn them to golden brown.

The leaves are then packed and sent by ship to the Dominican Republic, where they are slowly fermented or "mulled" to enhance their burn, taste, and color. In the process, the temperature of each "bulk" of wrappers rises every day. Then after twelve days, or when the thermometer registers 112 degrees, the hands (bunches of leaves) are shaken out one at a time for one hour in a room set at 75 degrees to give them fresh, cool air. The inner and outer hands of leaves in each bulk must be turned again and again, as the mulling is repeated three times every eight to ten days at increasingly cooler temperatures, until the initial mulling process is complete.

In early autumn, the leaves are baled and returned by ship to their original cool climate in Connecticut for "winter sweat"—an additional mulling process of seven months that enhances the characteristics of the leaves. Then, when spring arrives, the leaves are shipped back to the Dominican Republic, where we age them for twelve more months before they can be unbaled and moistened with fine mist to make them pliable enough to handle. All told, each leaf of our Connecticut shade undergoes three years of cultivation and processing as well as several thousand miles at sea before it can be used to wrap one of our premium cigars by hand.

The fact is, General Cigar is the only wrapper com-pany that still takes the time and effort to age its Connecticut shade wrapper leaves twice—something that the Cuban cigar makers used to do decades ago to give their cigars a smoother, mellower character. And at least one master Cuban cigar maker in Havana in those days would never want us to do otherwise. His name is Benjamín Menéndez, and he has been the overseer of all our Macanudo cigar production since 1984.

AUSTIN MCNAMARA'S TOP TEN

1. **Partagas Limited Reserve Royale:** "Strong and mellow. An after-dinner cigar that can be savored slowly."
2. **Macanudo Hyde Park:** "Full-bodied. A cigar that's great for weekend enjoyment."
3. **Cohiba:** "A great cigar for a special occasion."
4. **Macanudo Miniature:** "Small and sweet with the taste of a full-sized cigar."
5. **Partagas 150 Signature Series:** "A once-in-a-lifetime taste that comes from eighteen-year-old tobacco."
6. **Partagas Sabroso:** "Well-protected in a tube to stay fresh."
7. **Temple Hall Estates Maduro:** "A sweet, full-bodied cigar that's perfect with coffee and dessert."
8. **Partagas No. 10:** "True Partagas flavor. Sweet and full-bodied with a large ring gauge."
9. **Bolivar:** "A big cigar with a big taste."
10. **Macanudo 1988 Vintage Cabinet Selection No. 4:** "A great robusto-sized taste."

ally "twister"), it is bunched. This precise exercise requires a disciplined and steady hand to fold each leaf into the others. Next, the filler is placed on a binder leaf and rolled by hand. The binder is the so-called blanket that envelops the filler and holds it in place.

The crucial final stage of rolling is the making of the wrapper. Aficionados agree that the wrapper may provide as much as 60 percent of the taste and certainly 100 percent of the recognition factor for the cigar. To begin this all-important process, the bunch is pressed for proper form and shape using the wrapper leaf and the knifelike *chaveta*. Turning the leaf upside down, the cigar maker cuts it so that it perfectly covers the binder. Expert rollers are skilled enough to roll the wrapper so that the leaf tips end at either end of the cigar, which allows savory and aromatic oils and flavors to accumulate there, to the delight of the eventual smoker.

The most delicate step, rounding the cigar, must be executed perfectly; if the wrapper is too tight, the cigar will

not draw properly. Finally the cigar is capped with a small piece of leaf that has been cut with the *chaveta*. It is carefully attached with colorless, flavorless plant-based glue to cover the head of the cigar. On a few of the very best premium handmade cigars—the Cohiba Corona Especial, for example—the cap consists of the expertly twisted end of the wrapper, known as a flag cap.

An expert cigar maker rolls about 120 medium-size cigars per day; a star roller might make 200. The larger sizes are more difficult to make and take longer. Once the cigars are finished, they are bundled in groups of fifty (*medias ruedas*, or half wheels) and identified with key information: the name of the maker, the brand, the shape, and the type of tobaccos that were used.

Quality control and accountability are a critical part of the process. At any stage a cigar can be rejected if it is not up to the manufacturer's standards. The rolled cigars are weighed to make sure they contain the proper amount of ingredients, then passed through a ring gauge to make sure

of aesthetics, not taste. In each box the producer will place cigars that are identical in color. The banding process, done by an *anilladora*—usually a woman—demands a great measure of precision to ensure that the rings fit snugly. Finally the cigars are carefully placed side by side in their cedar boxes, silent and solemn testimony to one of humankind's great handicrafts.

Once the cigar maker's work is done, the product is the connoisseur's choice. Each brand is distinguished by its individual flavor and aroma, reflecting the painstaking, step-by-step process of manufacturing the world's finest cigars, from seed to smoke with sun, soil, and skill.

they are the proper diameter. Each cigar is scrutinized visually. Random samplings from each roller are blind-taste-tested by a professional smoker known as a *catador*. This is a serious matter for the *torcedores,* who traditionally are paid by the piece—a rejected cigar means less pay.

From there, the cigars go back into an aging room, where moisture is extracted and flavoring is enhanced by allowing the cigar's different tobaccos to marry and settle. This final aging generally lasts three weeks, though some are aged longer depending on the quality that the brand's loyal connoisseurs desire and demand.

At the end of the aging process, the cigars are again inspected for color: Aging can produce as many as five dozen shades of brown. At this point, color is a question

ABOVE: **A WORKER SORTS THE FINISHED CIGARS BY SIZE AND COLOR.**
ABOVE RIGHT: **THE FINAL AGING PROCESS CAN LAST FROM THREE MONTHS TO THREE YEARS.**
RIGHT: **THE NEWEST HAVANA CIGAR, THE CUABA, INTRODUCED IN 1997.**

RINGS AND THINGS

LIKE THE ARTISTRY that goes into the actual creation of a cigar, its packaging and presentation represent a long and rich tradition, which in turn reflects and enhances the prestige associated with an individual brand.

By the mid-nineteenth century, the Havana cigar had been established as the world's premier smoke,

NON PLUS ULTRA

and demand for this precious commodity skyrocketed. But soon, in various countries, counterfeit Cuban cigars, sometimes made from Cuban leaves, appeared on the market. Facing the challenge of controlling the quality of cigars, the Cuban industry looked for ways to identify the real Havanas. When the industry introduced cigar labels and individual cigar bands, Cuba was the first country to adopt these innovations.

With his artistic temperament and flair for marketing, cigar maker Ramón Allones first introduced boxed cigars at his shop, La Eminencia, in central Havana in 1845. The whole industry was quick to follow. This trend created a new position in the cigar

factories, that of *fileteador,* whose job it was to dress the cedar boxes, creating a beautiful case worthy of fine cigars.

The Dutch merchant Gustavo Bock was the first to put rings, or printed paper bands, around his cigars in 1850, in order to distinguish his own brand of Havanas from his competitors'. The idea caught on rapidly and became a wildly popular way to personalize special orders. Monarchs, heads of state, millionaires—everyone clamored for a personalized cigar with their name on the ring.

OPPOSITE: NON PLUS ULTRA WAS ONE OF THE FIRST EUROPEAN CIGAR LABELS.
ABOVE: THE LABEL FOR ALLONES, ONE OF THE OLDEST CUBAN BANDS.
RIGHT: A LABEL FOR HENRY CLAY PRODUCED FOR THE AMERICAN MARKET FEATURES THE PRINTER'S NAME AS WELL AS THE MAKER'S.

LORDS OF ENGLAND
Gustavo Bock
HABANA

Europe. The elaborate but generic images left space for the insertion of the brand name. Portraits now appeared on the *vistas* too. Like the boxes themselves, which are always made of cedar (the only wood that can properly preserve a good Havana), the *vistas* became an expected part of the cigar package, with a fascinating tale to tell.

Designers drew inspiration from the best that Western art had to offer; they were also at times influenced by the decorative arts of other civilizations. Country-specific themes were common. Some of those created for the American market depicted great moments in United States history, while the great Cuban brands proudly displayed in gold relief the medals they had won at the worldwide exhibi-

As printing techniques improved, portraits were added to the bands. Relatively plain lettering on the gold band, pioneered by Bock, gave way to intricate, colorful portraits of the world's wealthiest and most powerful individuals. For some, collecting these miniature works of art, which were said to inspire poets and artists, became a true passion, and collectors from around the world strove to acquire them.

Before long, the powerful patrons of the greatest Cuban cigars wanted more than custom-banded cigars: They demanded that entire brands be dedicated to their exclusive patronage. With the rise of the great cigar brands and the increasing demand for customized brands, *vistas* became essential. Cigar boxes had long been adorned with *vistas,* the decorative labels attached to the lids, often of dazzling complexity and artistry. Usually chromolithographs, *vistas* were sometimes manufactured in America or

5¢
FIRST FLIGHT-NEW YORK TO PARIS-MAY 20-21,1927-33¾ HOURS
NEW YORK
PARIS
ST. LOUIS
Spirit of St. Louis
LONG FILLER IMPORTED SUMATRA WRAPPER
REG. U.S.PAT.OFF.
AMERICAN LITHOGRAPHIC CO.,N.Y. U.S.A.
MAZER-CRESSMAN CIGAR CO. INC.
SPIRIT OF ST. LOUIS
DETROIT, MICH.

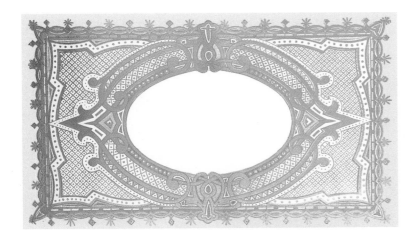

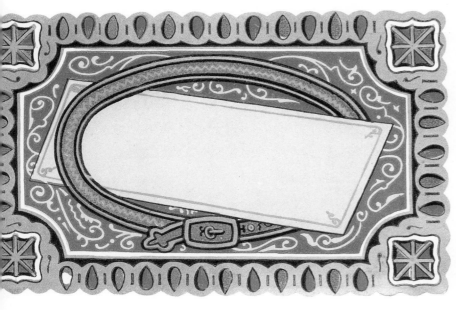

tions, often surrounding softly etched portraits of the owner, or the rolling green hills and red earth of Cuba.

Not all brands, or their distinctive artwork, have survived the years. Some disappeared after World War I, others during the Depression. By far the greatest assault on the tradition occurred when Fidel Castro abolished all brands in favor of his nationalized product. Despite his quick retreat, some of the most famous brands never returned to production. Today hundreds of bands and *vistas* survive as testimony to the glory days of Cuba's cigars, and to the extremely powerful individuals who commanded a personal signature for luxurious smokes. They are like windows into some of the greatest moments of the cigar's story: bright, intricate, colorful masterworks that strive to match the aromatic and flavorful artistry of the cigars themselves, and each one has a story.

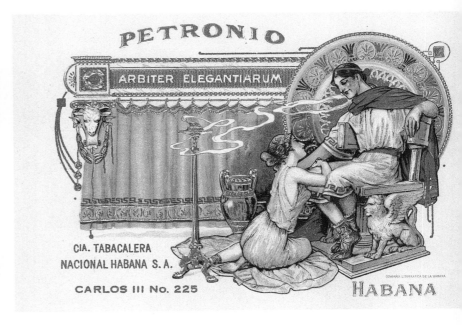

OPPOSITE: A LABEL FROM GUSTAVO BOCK, THE FIRST CUBAN MANUFACTURER TO USE DECORATIVE ART AND LITHOGRAPHY. A CLEAR HAVANA LABEL COMMEMORATES LINDBERGH'S HISTORIC FLIGHT. LEFT AND ABOVE: LATE NINETEENTH-CENTURY CUBAN LABELS SHOW THE INFLUENCE OF ART NOUVEAU. TOP: TEMPLATES FOR CUSTOMIZED LABELS CREATED BY GERMAN-AMERICAN LITHOGRAPHERS.

CIGAR LITHOGRAPHY

BEFORE CUBA'S TEN-YEAR war with Spain (1868–78), cigar *vistas* and bands had been printed by the stone lithography process, which was developed in Germany by Aloise Sene-felder in 1798. The superior limestone mined in Bavaria was to the lithographic industry what Vuelta Abajo tobacco was to the Havana cigar. Senefelder applied a mixture of soap and wax to the smoothly polished limestones, adding ink and then washing the image with a weak solu-

tion of acid to produce a relief design in the slightly lower etched surface. Paper was then applied and removed from the stone for a reverse copy.

In the early nineteenth century stone lithography was further developed into a multicolor art form, with gold leaf embossing. As many as ten colors could be printed and overlaid, using a different stone for each color. As Cuban tobacco became famous, the art form was advanced by Klingenberg, the most famous printer in Germany. A huge number of designers, engravers, and lithographers devoted their talents to the development of a whole new industry inspired by the cigar. They created a remarkable body of work.

The lithographic process quickly spread to the United States and England as well as to Cuba, where Luis Caire inaugurated the Havana Lithographic Workshop. Shortly thereafter the Royal Tobacco Company of Havana commissioned Litográfica de Habana to produce the array of labeling (*habilitaciónes*) used on every box of Cuban cigars. When Leopoldo Carvajal created Hijos de Cabanas y Carbajal in 1819, Ramón Allones used the *vista* on La Eminencia. Gustavo Bock used the first cigar rings for Golden Eagles at his factory, El Aguila de Oro. Two hundred years later, the Compañía Litográfica de Habana still continues to print labels.

After the unification of the German confederacies in 1871, many skilled lithographers emigrated to the United States, just as Cuban cigar makers were bringing their skills to Florida during Cuba's first struggle for independence. While Cuban émigré communities in Key West, St. Augustine, Ocala's Martí City, and finally in Ybor City in Tampa established cigar-production facilities, lithographers in Philadelphia, New York, and Boston worked hard to produce the art necessary to market the cigars.

Cuban cigars boasted images that suggested prestige and nostalgia with Spanish-sounding names. Anything associated with Spain was connected to status, and each image was worth a thousand puffs.

Not only did Cuba's early tobacco trade develop new markets around the world, it was a boon to the printing industry. In 1892 a trust formation of thirty-four lithographers came together as the American Lithographic Company, the beginning of a golden age in lithography.

Although Tampa's cigar-making industry flourished, the art of lithography declined after World War I, as fewer young people were interested in learning its skills. The post–World War II era adopted a mass-market economy, as war production was applied to peacetime goods, which further eroded the demand for those graceful printed pieces. Many of the Ybor City factories that had produced

OPPOSITE: THE DISTINGUISHED H. UPMANN LABEL FROM THE HAVANA CIGAR FACTORY FOUNDED IN 1844 BY HERMAN AND AUGUST UPMANN OF BREMEN, GERMANY. CAROL JULIUS UPMANN, HERMAN'S SON, ESTABLISHED A CIGAR FACTORY IN NEW YORK BUT NEVER USED HIS NAME FOR HIS BRAND. THIS PAGE: PRELIMINARY SKETCH AND ARTIST'S PROOF OF A LABEL CREATED IN 1882 BY LITOGRÁFICA DE HABANA; EARLY DUTCH TOBACCO TAX STAMP. OVERLEAF: DETAILS FROM THE EARLIEST EIGHTEENTH-CENTURY TOBACCO LABELS, PRINTED IN SPAIN.

hand-rolled cigars now converted to mechanized processes, while the development of photomechanical printing with color separations brought the demise of stone lithography. Seemingly overnight, inexpensive printing techniques transformed cigar art. Soon "The Loveliest Bosom of Old Castille" was replaced with slogans—"No hick can forget" and "It's a different business"—and memorable artwork was a thing of the past.

TOP: A PRINTER'S PROOF FOR A *VISTA* AND *PAPELETA*, THE OVAL, RECTANGULAR, OR SQUARE LABELS FIXED TO ONE END OF THE BOX AS A GUARANTEE SEAL, SHOWS THE ELABORATE PRINTING PROCESS. ABOVE: AN INTRICATELY SHAPED *CUBIERTA* FOR THE DUTCH MARKET. LEFT: ANOTHER EXAMPLE OF HERALDIC IMAGERY ON A CUBAN *VISTA*. OPPOSITE: A SAMPLE LABEL FROM THE ARCHIVES OF HARRIS LITHOGRAPHIC COMPANY IN PHILADELPHIA. HARRIS ADVANCED THE ART OF CIGAR LITHOGRAPHY IN THE U.S. WITH THE HELP OF GERMAN-BORN LITHOGRAPHERS.

FLOR DE TABACOS
DE
PARTAGAS
Y Cª
1845

CLARO
SELECTION

LA PREFERENCIA

LA GRAN
MANUFACTURA DE TABACOS
PREFERIDOS

DE EXQUISITOS TA
HABANA

LA GLORIA CUBANA
DE
C. E. G.
HABANA

LA IBERIA

FABRICA DE TABACOS

DE

M. A. y C.

HABANA

LA MAYOR RECOMPENSA OBTENIDA EN LA EXPOSICION DE PARIS 1878

LA ESPAÑOLA

FABRICA DE TABACOS.

CONSULADO 94 95

CONSULADO 94 95

HABANA

LA MERIDIANA

DE

P. M. y Cª.

HABANA

EXTRA.

VITOLPHILIA

INCLUDING THE BANDS, ten different individual trimmings (*habilitaciónes,* or qualifications) are used in the packaging of Havana cigars. Each is a unique collectible, in demand around the world and often selling for large sums—up to $100,000 for a single collection of original artwork. Those who collect and treasure cigar ephemera are known as vitolphiles, while the desire to collect them is called vitolphilia.

Dr. Orlando Arteaga, president of the Cuban Vitolphilic Association, is the world's most renowned authority on collecting cigar bands and labels from the eighteenth century to the present. His collection of *vitolas* is regarded as the most complete and authoritative of its kind in the world. A graduate of the University of Havana and a holder of advanced degrees in history and law, Dr. Arteaga began collecting just before the Cuban revolution. He is a close associate of and adviser to Litográfica de Habana, Cuban printers of cigar-related materials for over a hundred years. Examples from his collection are housed in the National Gallery in Havana and featured in these pages.

ABOVE: **A SELECTION OF** *FILETES* **FROM INTERNATIONAL BRANDS.**
LEFT: **AN AUTHENTIC CUBAN LABEL WITH ELABORATE USE OF GOLD LEAF.**

RINGS

Cigar smoking took on a more youthful and romantic image after 1960 with the elevation to the presidency of John F. Kennedy, who often appeared in public puffing on one of his favorite Havanas. This was when I, and some of my colleagues in the newspaper business, also indulged for the first time. From a journalist friend of mine who covered politics in Washington, I was able to obtain the best in Cuban cigars before and during America's lengthy embargo on all Cuban products; and I especially remember the gift box of Havana Churchills my friend sent me after the birth of my first daughter in 1964, and a second box after the arrival of my second daughter in 1967. Even more fondly do I recall in later years how my little girls would argue each night over whose turn it was to wear the "ring" after I had removed it from one of my after-dinner cigars—a ritual that I think not only introduced them to the blissful effluvium of a superior smoke but inculcated within them as well an appreciation and respect for the pleasure it brought me. That their loving response toward me and my cigars continues to this day, decades after their final fight over paper rings, makes me wonder if some women's repugnance for cigar smoking might have less to do with a cigar's smoke or smell than with their personal relationships with the first men in their lives who indulged in the habit.

Gay Talese

HABILITACIÓNES (TRIMMINGS)

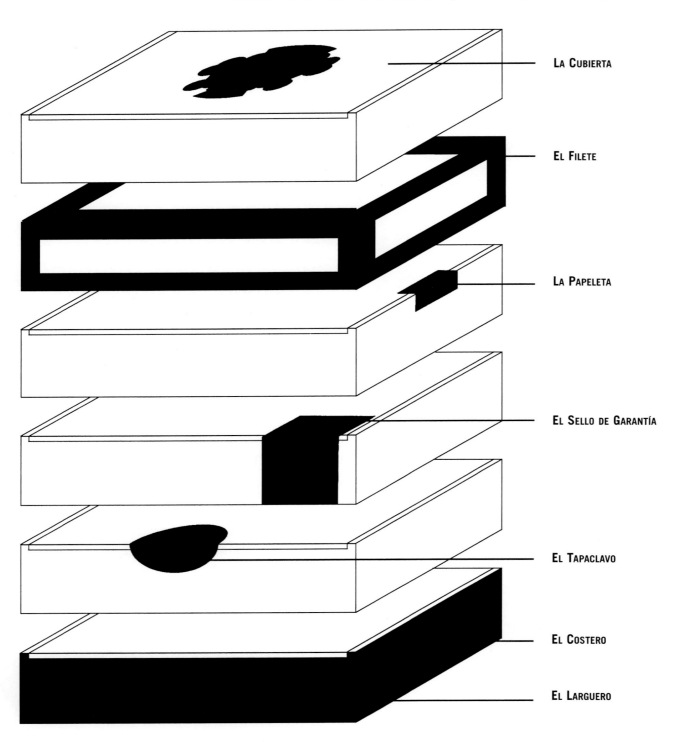

LA CUBIERTA

EL FILETE

LA PAPELETA

EL SELLO DE GARANTÍA

EL TAPACLAVO

EL COSTERO

EL LARGUERO

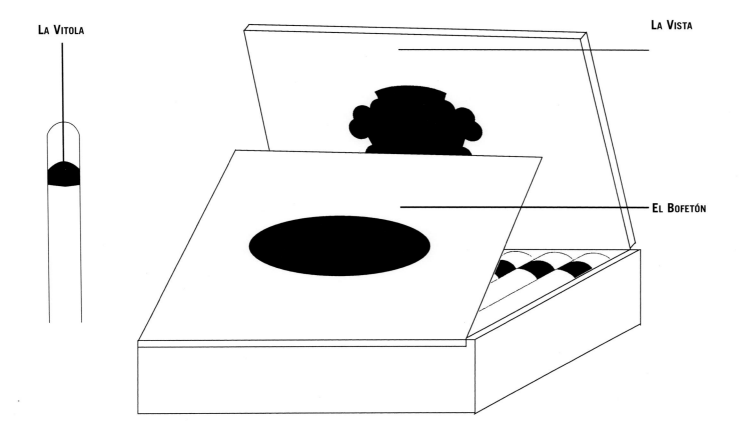

LA VITOLA

LA VISTA

EL BOFETÓN

- **LA CUBIERTA** is the image that covers the top of the box. Often the name of the factory in which it originated appears at the *cubierta*'s center as *el hierro* (the iron or brand), designed to imitate the mark of branding irons.
- **EL FILETE** is the long narrow ribbon of paper that seals the joints and edges of the box, preventing the aroma from escaping.
- **LA PAPELETA** is a rectangle, square, or oval of paper fixed to the short ends of the box.
- **EL SELLO DE GARANTÍA** is the official green government seal. Resembling a banknote, it runs down the front edge of the box. In Cuba, only a genuine Havana carries this mark of authenticity.
- **EL TAPACLAVO** is an oval label fixed over the clasp (or nail) that closes the lid.

- **EL COSTERO** covers the short sides of the box.
- **EL LARGUERO** covers the long sides.
- **LA VISTA** is glued inside the lid. It is decorated with information about the brand or its romantic history and is usually embossed.
- **EL BOFETÓN** is attached to the inside of the box by its lower edge. Designed in conjunction with the *vista*, it is a hallmark of the factory.
- **LA VITOLA** is the band—the spirit and signature of the cigar, appreciated by the smoker who selects it. It lends a certain nobility to the cigar's packaging design.

Note: On the bottom of true Havana cigars, you will find the following markings for identification: *Hecho en Cuba, Totalmente a mano,* and *República de Cuba.*

ABOVE: **DON QUIXOTE.**
RIGHT: **AN EARLY EXAMPLE OF A VISTA CREATED FOR THE QUINTANA BRAND.**
OVERLEAF: **DETAIL OF AN EARLY CUBAN VISTA.**

MAGNOLIA

HABANA

COMPAÑIA LITOGRAFICA DE LA HABANA

Subject matter for Cuban vistas ranges from naturalistic renderings of flowers and palm fronds to commemorative portraits glorifying the cigar maker, heads of state, and even characters from fiction, all in a framework of elaborately detailed artwork, as in these examples from Dr. Arteaga's collection.

CALZADA DE LUYANO Nº 100.

HENRY CLAY. HABANA

DEPÓSITO CALLE de O'REILLY Nº 9½

FABRICA

de TABACOS

MIEMBRO DE LA ACADEMIA NACIONAL DE AGRICULTURA INDUSTRIA Y COMERCIO DE PARIS

HECHO EN LA HABANA. CUBA

HABANA

MADE IN HAVANA. CUBA

LA INTELIGENCIA

DE ANTONIO V. COLMENARES HABANA

FLOR DE ALVAREZ

THIS PAGE AND OPPOSITE: *Vistas* DEPICTING DIFFERENT ASPECTS OF CUBAN LIFE.
OVERLEAF: EXTREMELY RARE OLD LABELS FROM THE EARLIEST SPANISH CIGAR BRANDS.

CIGAR-STORE INDIANS

AT ONE TIME a special nation of nineteenth-century Indians guarded tobacco's golden age, standing vigil in front of cigar stores from St. Louis to San Francisco. These silent and stoic sidewalk chiefs indicated to every passerby that cigars were sold within.

After the turn of the century, signposts on doors and buildings became a traditional form of advertising for doctors and lawyers. Indian chiefs joined the hallmark club, adding a measure of life-size stature to the visual parade of fortune-tellers, barber shops, locksmiths, and pawnshops along city streets. A symbol for tobacconists (after all, native Indians had introduced Columbus to tobacco), the handsome chiefs were intended to set their stores apart from those of other merchants. Sculpted by artisans who had learned their trade by carving decorative ship figureheads, they have since become valued collectibles.

Mark Goldman, New York's noted collector, has more than eighty works of art in his SoHo Reservation, some valued at more than $100,000. The value of each piece is determined by its condition and artistic integrity. Special colors of red, brown, and green paint that are now impossible to duplicate had a special ingredient that has held its rich patina through years of exposure to extreme weather conditions. These nostalgic artifacts are a powerful presence that recalls a time long gone by.

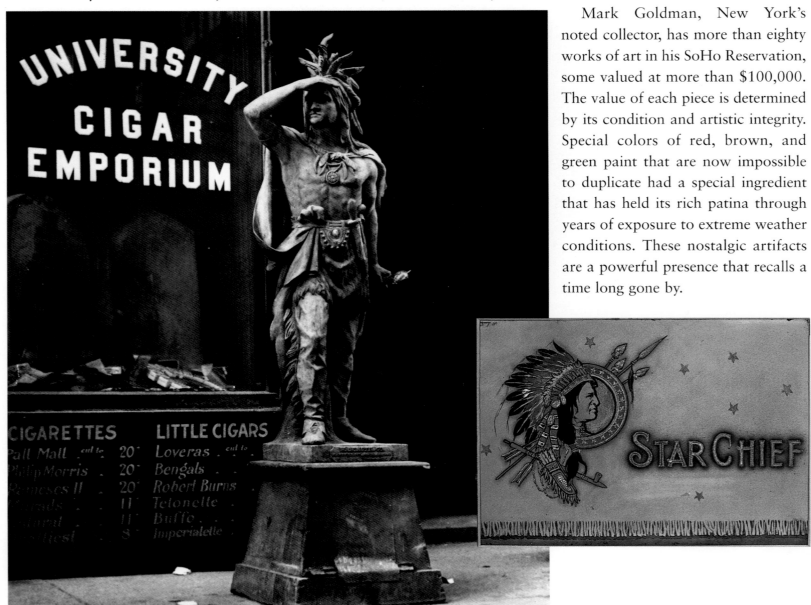

A Spectacular Vintage

For Sandy Perceval and his family, it was a struggle to maintain their ancestral home in the Irish countryside. Temple House and its surrounding 1,400-acre estate, in Ballymote, County Sligo, was in disrepair, faced huge taxes, and would have to be sold.

Then the Percevals remembered the cigars—more than six hundred vintage boxes in the cellar. A weekend guest took a hundred to be evaluated. Experts, including Simon Chase, pronounced them to be remarkably good, considering they had been bought in 1864.

No one was quite sure where they came from. The boxes had a stamp that read "Manila," which might indicate their origin or a brand. Some said Sandy Perceval's great-great-grandfather Alexander brought them back when he crossed the Atlantic to meet his bride-to-be in Boston and took a side trip to Havana. They had been exiled to the cellar by his wife, who was vehemently opposed to smoking. There they rested, in this natural humidor, for more than 130 years.

Regardless of their provenance, which may remain a mystery, the Perceval cigars are considered the oldest smokable cigars. Shortly after the Percevals went public with their cigars, they received an offer from an unidentified American investor of $1 million for five hundred of them. That translates to $2,000 per cigar or, assuming one puff a minute for the half hour it takes to smoke one, $66.67 per puff.

ABOVE: TWO EXTRAORDINARY EXAMPLES FROM THE VITOLPHILIC COLLECTION OF DR. ORLANDO ARTEAGA. OPPOSITE: A TWENTIETH-CENTURY AMERICAN-MADE LABEL COMMEMORATES CUBAN-AMERICAN COOPERATION.

MANY CUBAN CIGAR MANUFACTURERS MADE CUSTOM
CIGARS AND SPECIAL BANDS FOR CORPORATIONS AND
SPECIAL CLIENTS, AS WELL AS COMMEMORATIVE BANDS
GLORIFYING POLITICAL FIGURES.

CENTER: A BEAUTIFUL CIGAR RING PRINTED IN
GERMANY BY HERMANN SCOTT.

THE ARENTS
TOBACCO
COLLECTION

FOR A TRUE CIGAR LOVER, no visit to New York City would be complete without a stop at the New York Public Library's Arents Collection, one of the world's finest rare book and manuscript archives. It is devoted to tobacco.

Himself a nonsmoker, George Arents began collecting books on tobacco at the age of twenty, with the encouragement of his great-uncle, the tobacco magnate Major Lewis Ginter of Richmond, Virginia. Ginter offered the advice that as a person got older, he might need to moderate strenuous sports like mountain climbing and polo and turn to an equally captivating and challenging pursuit: book collecting.

Over dinner one evening the distinguished rare-book and autograph dealer William Everts Benjamin reinforced this advice. "You are young," Benjamin told Arents, who recalled the conversation in a speech more than forty years later. "Decide on one subject, stick to it, and one day you could have a great collection."

Young George Arents stuck to it.

The Arents family had been in tobacco for generations, and Great-Uncle Lewis headed the family firm, Allen & Ginter, which became part of the American Tobacco Company, James B. Duke's conglomerate. Arents earned degrees at Columbia and Syracuse, went to work for Duke in 1895, and shortly thereafter filed for a patent on a cigar-rolling machine. By 1905, Arents's machine was producing two-thirds of the cigars sold in America. The company he founded was called American Machine & Foundry (AMF).

His extraordinary fortune helped finance a collection of rare books focused not only on "literature about tobacco" but also on "tobacco in literature." From laws, regulations, commercial documents, and treatises on the medicinal value of the weed to manuscripts and letters, the requirement was simply that the item be rare and that it mention tobacco. For example, that the plot of Oscar Wilde's *The Importance of Being Earnest* hinges on a cigarette box was enough for Arents to acquire a manuscript of it.

Most of the collection consists of "print items" like pamphlets, manuscripts, autograph letters, original drawings, illustrations, sheet music, trading cards, and cigar-box labels. The collection resides in two rooms that were designed to replicate the library in Arents's Rye, New York, mansion. Arents gave the collection to the Public Library in the early 1940s, and the special rooms opened February 14, 1943. Its current curator is Virginia Bartow.

Long a quiet backwater of this prestigious and well-traveled institution, in the wake of the cigar renaissance, the collection now attracts many more visitors. It seems that, ironically, the backlash against smoking has made the collection all the more popular.

The catalogue to the collection comes in five volumes, with a ten-part supplement listing more than 2,000 manuscripts and 15,000 books. For students of tobacco history, the catalogue's annotated introduction is an invaluable resource.

Highlights of the collection include:
• Autograph letters of Elizabeth I and Sir Walter Raleigh; a George Washington autograph letter, 1762,

consignment of tobacco to London; letters of Thomas Jefferson, who was also a tobacco grower.

• *History and Natural History of the West Indies* by Fernandez de Oviedo, 1535, which contains an account of natives smoking as first seen by Columbus's colleagues Luis de Torres and Rodrigo de Jerez.

• *Cosmographiae Introductio* by Martin Wald-seemüller, 1507, the account of the voyages of Amerigo Vespucci based on his letters, considered the earliest known book referring to tobacco.

• A 1571 work by the Spanish doctor Monarde, which reported the Indians' use of the plant as an herbal cure and influenced Jean Nicot, who advocated tobacco as a panacea for all kinds of ills.

• Minutes of discussions before the Congregation of

Rites between 1718 and 1734 as to whether smoking should disqualify Joseph a Cupertino, a monk, from canonization.

• *Helps for Sudden Accidents* by Stephen Bradwell, London, a 1633 publication advising that a person accidentally poisoned can be prevented from falling asleep and presumably dying by blowing strong powdered tobacco into his nose with a quill to make him sneeze.

• *The Wonderful Deliverance at Sea,* 1674, the story of six shipwrecked survivors who subsisted for four days on a couple of pounds of tobacco.

• An original manuscript of Charles Lamb's "Farewell to Tobacco."

• A rare copy of Edmund Spenser's *The Faerie Queene,* which contains the first known reference to tobacco in English poetry, calling it "the divine weed."

• A manuscript of William Faulkner's early short story "Father Abraham," considered a seminal work, that begins, "He chews tobacco constantly and steadily and slowly, and no one ever saw his eyelids closed."

• A 1910 Honus Wagner baseball card, originally given away with a cigarette pack. Only about two dozen of these cards survive; one sold to hockey player Wayne Gretzky and friends for more than $450,000.

Arents, ironically a nonsmoker, included some items that protest tobacco. The most prominent is James I of England's *Counterblaste to Tobacco,* published in 1604. Many plays during his reign contained references to James's proclamation against tobacco, including Ben Jonson's *Every Man Out of His Humour.* Curiously, there is no Shakespeare in the collection—the Bard of Avon never mentioned tobacco.

2

Profiles in Smoking

THE GREAT CIGAR MAKERS

THE PREMIUM CIGAR BRANDS are created by master blenders, Cuban patriots and expatriates, who uphold a 150-year-old tradition in a circle of fellowship with a shared passion for cigars. We found these special people, and like their cigars they come in all sizes and shapes, from different and distant backgrounds. Each makes a unique contribution to the finest cigars in the world.

THE ULTIMATE CONNOISSEUR

ZINO DAVIDOFF

ZINO DAVIDOFF was born in 1906 in Kiev, the Ukraine, where his father had a shop that blended Turkish tobaccos into gold-tipped cigarettes. In 1911 the Davidoffs fled the czar's pogroms and settled in Geneva, where young Zino began working in the family business.

In 1926 Zino took a fateful trip to the great tobacco-producing areas of Latin America. In Cuba he fell in love with the Havana cigar. There, working in the fields, curing barns, and cigar factories, he learned about cigars, and Señor Palicio of Hoyo de Monterrey became his mentor.

In the 1930s Zino built a humidor in his father's shop at 2, rue de la Rive, Geneva. There he also built his cigar business. Soon he became known as the world's greatest cigar merchant and connoisseur.

Naming his Havanas, made by Hoyo de Monterrey, after fine French wines, Davidoff created an association between two proud cultures. Davidoff's Chateau series of cigars (Chateau Latour, Margaux, Haut-Brion, and Mouton-Rothschild) became a major market force.

When Castro's single-cigar nationalization program ran into trouble, the Cuban cigar chiefs appealed to Davidoff for advice on how to revive their industry. He encouraged them to reinstate the great old brands, and the industry was reborn. In 1967 Davidoff became the only non-Cuban with permission to have his own brand name of cigars manufactured in Cuba. Davidoffs were made at the temple of cigar making—the El Laguito factory, which now makes Castro's favorite, the Cohiba.

The international tobacco merchant company Oettinger, headed by Zino's great friend Dr. Ernst Schneider, became a majority shareholder in Davidoff & Co. in 1970 and helped Zino expand from his Geneva headquarters all over the world. There are now Davidoff SA stores in more than forty countries, in addition to the flagship Davidoff stores selling not only cigars but cognac and accessories.

In the late 1980s the Cubans moved to gain greater control and a 50 percent–plus share of the revenues from Davidoff's Havana cigars. He then moved his manufacturing operations to the Dominican Republic, forming an association with Hendrik Kelner's Tabacos Dominicanos. He forged new business friendships and continued to perfect the art of cigar making, always maintaining the highest standards for the eighteen sizes of cigars he produced.

"I was working with Cuba for sixty years," he said at the time. "Cuba was like a nice lady, but it was time for change. I have found a new lady, younger, thinner, lighter, so I have made a new marriage." He acknowledged that some customers prefer to continue smoking Havanas, so his shops continued to sell those as well, but not under the Davidoff name.

The great connoisseur passed away in January 1994. A man with a big heart, he made an indelible impression and still casts an imposing shadow over the industry that he lived and loved, the making and marketing of the world's finest cigars.

He once wrote: "When I was twenty, I fell in love with the great tobacco plantations in Cuba. This passion of my youth has never been spent. Today, I am able to say that my life has been placed under the sign of service to all those who are dedicated to the cigar—young or old. The cigar has been my life. I owe it everything: my pleasures and my anguish, the joys of my work as well as the pleasant leisure hours it affords, and if I have acquired over the course of the years some bit of philosophical perspective, it is again to the cigar that I am in debt."

Zino Davidoff was the ultimate connoisseur—elegant and charming, full of love, respect, and reverence for the cigar. He had an encyclopedic knowledge and shared it generously with aficionados everywhere.

ALFRED DUNHILL CONDUCTS BUSINESS AS USUAL IN FRONT OF HIS BOMBED-OUT STORE.

THE ESSENCE OF BRITISH EXCELLENCE

ALFRED DUNHILL

ESTABLISHED IN 1893 as a shop for saddles and harnesses, Dunhill's later branched out into other sporting items, such as a covered pipe that could be smoked in a motorcar. In 1907 Alfred Dunhill opened his tobacconist's shop in St. James's—convenient to the men's clubs of Pall Mall. The shop still stands, even though the building was heavily damaged during a German air raid in World War II. After the dust had settled, Dunhill moved his operations temporarily to Notting Hill Gate, but not before assuring his distinguished customer Winston Churchill that his private reserve of Havanas was intact.

After World War I, most significantly, Dunhill created the first humidor in Europe—a large cedar-lined, walk-in closet with air conditioning—in his Duke Street shop. There he kept his valued Cubans in perfect condition for his illustrious clientele, setting a standard that many international cigar merchants accepted. He opened shops in New York and Paris in the early 1920s.

Initially Dunhill imported tobacco from Cuba and manufactured his house brand in Britain; subsequently he contracted the manufacturing work out to Cuban factories. With the U.S. embargo in the early 1960s, however, North American outlets for Cuban-made Dunhills ended. He tried to continue with Cuban-made cigars—the Varadero, Mojito, Atado, Estupendo, and Malecon—but in the 1980s the Cubans were demanding unreasonable contracts and control, and like his longtime friend and competitor Zino Davidoff, Dunhill shifted production to the Dominican Republic. Although it is now part of the Rothmans International Group, Dunhill remains a family firm, Alfred Dunhill, Ltd., with Alfred's grandson, Richard Dunhill, as chairman.

EDWARD SAHAKIAN

THE PROPRIETOR OF the Davidoff shop at 35 St. James's Street, London, Edward Sahakian is another renowned figure among cigar aficionados the world over. A true cosmopolitan gentleman held in the highest esteem, he has proved himself over the years extremely capable of upholding the great Davidoff tradition. Sahakian was born in Iran to an Armenian family that was successful in the brewery business. They made and lost a number of fortunes due to the changing political climates of the countries in which they settled. Sahakian's family has lived in Russia, Iran, and Britain. "Cigar smoking is a conduit to friendship," he says. "There's a special allegiance with anyone who loves cigars, an affiliation, a bonding."

EDWARD SAHAKIAN'S TOP TEN
Davidoff Ambassadrice
Davidoff No. 2
Davidoff Double R
Cohiba Panetela
Cohiba Siglo IV
H. Upmann No. 2
Avo XO Intermezzo
Romeo y Julieta Churchill
Paul Garmirian Petit Bouquet
Arturo Fuente Hemingway Signa

THE NAMES CIFUENTES and Partagas have evoked images of superb craftsmanship and quality since the last golden days of the nineteenth century.

Ramón Cifuentes made his first Partagas cigar before he was allowed to smoke one. He watched the rollers in the factory, learning everything from his father before he could follow in his footsteps. He had wanted to grow up to be a cowboy, until his father taught him how to make a Partagas in the Havana of famous writers and silver daiquiris. It was a time and place where the whole world wanted to be—and Cifuentes never wanted to be anywhere else. The Partagas *fábrica* did a great business— since 1845 the great Partagas name had been consonant with a great cigar.

Then Castro came to power, and Ramón Cifuentes left his home with secrets locked in his heart. The Dominican Republic was receptive to his skilled hands, and its climate was ideal for the Cuban leaf. Partagas cigars are still made under the watchful eyes of the same man whose father and grandfather made them long ago in their native land.

Reflecting upon his life, this distinguished and lovely man says: "Throughout my life, people all over the world have depended on me to provide them with the greatest smoking pleasures. I could not begin to know them all, of course, but many of them have taken the time to tell me how much my cigars have meant to them. That is why I have never permitted even the slightest compromise at any stage of cigar making. To do so would be a betrayal of my trust.

"My father felt the same way, and when I was growing

CIFUENTES HABANA

LOS TABACOS QUE SE EMPLEAN EN ESTA MARCA, PROCEDEN DE LAS AFAMADAS VEGAS DE MI PROPIEDAD, EN VUELTA-ABAJO. Ramon Cifuentes

up in Cuba, I think I knew in my heart that cigars would one day become my life, just as they had become my father's. I was the first of three sons, after all, and I wanted to be as much like my father as I could. It was in this spirit that I assumed the responsibility of continuing to make Partagas a great Cuban cigar."

It was different in Cuba then—so full of life that when Fidel Castro took power in 1959, it was hard for him to

believe the changes. The new government soon nationalized his factory. Castro promised Ramón that if he remained in Cuba, he would be in charge of all cigar making in the country. But Cuba was not the same, and he left. "I lost my country but not my heart," he says. "I have never returned to Cuba. I love my country, as you might understand, but the making of cigars is a very personal thing to me."

THE PHILOSOPHER

BENJAMÍN MENÉNDEZ

"Listen to the cigar. It will talk to you and lead you to many secrets."

ON SEPTEMBER 15, 1960, at 5:50 in the afternoon, the offices of Alonzo Menéndez at Montecristo Cigars in Havana, Cuba, were sealed shut by General Francisco de la Cruz, Castro's cigar czar. Two days later, after a lifetime of passion for his Montecristos, Alonzo Menéndez took his son Benjamín and left Cuba with these parting words to the general: "I hope you have consideration for the cigar!" Like many fellow Cuban expatriates, he had never thought that Communism would take hold in Cuba. He had thought that Castro's days were numbered. He had been wrong.

With only five dollars in his pocket and one suitcase in his hand, Alonzo knew that the great Menéndez family's reign as kings of the cigar in Cuba had come to an end. It had all started in 1890 when Alonzo came to Cuba from Spain as a tobacco dealer. Later his cigar interests would take him to

RIGHT: A CERTIFICATE OF PERFECTION WAS PRINTED ON THE BACK OF ALL LABELS USED FOR PRE-CASTRO MONTECRISTOS.

Tampa, New York, Boston, and back to Havana again.

During the 1930s, along with their partner Pepe García, the Menéndez family made a great cigar, the Montecristo. (They later acquired H. Upmann.) The Montecristo is made from a special blend of all five cuttings of the tobacco plant. From the *centro ligero,* mild and smooth, to the last cutting of the *corona,* it is filled with flavor.

The first distribution was for Cuba, Spain, and the United States. After World War II Montecristo returned to producing cigars. (In England, Dunhill carried the Montecristo as an exclusive premium cigar, as it still does today, although the cigars are now made not only in Cuba but in the Dominican Republic.)

After leaving Havana, Benjamín Menéndez settled for a time in Madrid and made cigars in the Canary Islands. There, because of the U.S. embargo on Cuba and the scarcity of Cuban tobacco, he created and blended a new cigar, the Montecruz, with Pepe García.

Consolidated Cigar was very eager to produce great cigars and it acquired the rights to make Montecristo and H. Upmann brands in 1975. Meanwhile General Cigar acquired the rights to produce the Partagas from the renowned expatriate Ramón Cifuentes. Over the years,

Garantizamos que todas las vitolas de la marca "Montecristo" son de una sola calidad -la mejor-.

Los tabacos que utilizamos en la elaboración de esta marca, son seleccionados de la más alta calidad que se cosecha en la Isla de Cuba.

MENENDEZ Y GARCIA.

All sizes in the "Montecristo" brand are guaranteed to be of one quality only -the finest-.

The tobacco used in their manufacture being a selection and blend of the highest grade tobaccos procurable in the Island of Cuba.

MENENDEZ Y GARCIA.

COMPAÑIA LITOGRAFICA DE LA HABANA

two great names, Menéndez and Cifuentes, once strong competitors in Havana, have come together to oversee production of the Partagas in the Dominican Republic. They were always great friends, with the cigar creating a common bond. This year Partagas will make 81 million cigars in the Dominican Republic.

Menéndez and Cifuentes are wise and distinguished men who share their knowledge and experience with their colleagues and competitors in the circle of tobacco commerce.

Every once in a while Benjamín Menéndez lights up a Cuban Montecristo, and around the halo of blue smoke there is a meditative pause. After all, this is his cigar. Communist Cuba can never take the legacy away from him.

"It is still quite good," he confides. "There is always something special about the full-bodied flavor of a Havana," he adds wistfully, referring to the legacy that Castro had taken away from him. "But sometimes I am disappointed by the lack of consistency and the balance in the blend. It is always in the aging and the blend. That is what we learn in my land.

"There are hard times in Cuba today. But how amazing it is that even though we have lost something, we have also found something. We have developed from the seed of Cuba, the leaf, the cigar, the Partagas. It is the same, only made in a different place. You can never take away what we have learned from our fathers. New blends in new lands with knowledge and experience from all of us. I think we produce here a consistent and sometimes superior cigar. Now we have great tobacco and technology to choose from."

BENJAMÍN MENÉNDEZ'S TOP TEN

"A cigar always has its own time of day. The milder the taste, the more it can be enjoyed in the morning. The fuller the body, the more it belongs in the evening."

1. **Partagas Royal Limited Reserve:** "Strong flavor, very mellow. An exceptional after-dinner cigar."
2. **Macanudo Baron de Rothschild:** "A lighter cigar that never tires in taste."
3. **Macanudo Hyde Park:** "A larger ring gauge that allows for full-bodied blending."
4. **Partagas No. 4:** "A good small cigar."
5. **Macanudo Petit Corona:** "Small and sweet."
6. **Macanudo 1993 Vintage:** "Everything comes together, from the filler to the wrapper."
7. **Partagas Sabrosa:** "Well-protected in a tube. Stays fresh."
8. **Partagas No. 2:** "The same size as the Macanudo Hyde Park with a more robust taste."
9. **Macanudo Hampton Court:** "A shorter Baron de Rothschild in a tube."
10. **Partagas No. 10:** "A big cigar. True Partagas flavor. Sweet and full-bodied."

THE CONSOLIDATED MAN

RICHARD DiMEOLA

RICHARD DiMEOLA, executive vice-president of Consolidated Cigar, is an elegant and well-spoken man who, for the last forty years, has devoted himself to the finest cigars in the world. DiMeola is informed and decisive. With great pride, he would rather talk about his company than himself. "Prior to the Cuban embargo," DiMeola explains, discussing U.S. cigar-making trends and his company's role, "there were 185 million cigars per year sold in the United States, only eight percent of which were made in Cuba. Most Cuban tobacco was shipped to Tampa for Clear Havana—until the stock dwindled in the early sixties, with cigar sales falling below 50 million."

With the great Cuban families expatriated, Consolidated bought the U.S. rights to some of the Cuban trademarks, in partnership with such great names as Montecristo and Upmann—two of the company's flagship premium cigars today. They are now made with shade wrapper and broadleaf filler grown in the Dominican Republic, Indonesia, and Connecticut.

In 1975 Consolidated began the great Cuban comeback with Benjamín Menéndez and Pepe García of Montecristo and Upmann. General Cigar followed, with Ramón Cifuentes and Partagas soon after. Objective: to produce the great Havana cigars with the same care and experience outside Cuba.

It worked. In the mid-1980s cigar production reached 100 million and in the 1990s it reached pre-embargo heights, with 8.5 million cigars back-ordered at Consolidated.

The big cigar bang exploded in the mid-1980s, when one of the first cigar dinners was held in Boston at the Ritz-Carlton. As more dinners were organized, young men and women, fueled by the fashion industry, drove the market with personal enjoyment, conversation, and fellowship. *Cigar Aficionado* premiered in autumn 1992. Says DiMeola, "The new magazine jumped on a moving train just leaving the station. Then jet-set smokers took cigars into the stratosphere."

Now Consolidated has introduced a cigar originally conceived for owner Ronald Perelman. The Chairman's Reserve holds promise for excellence and taste, in keeping with DiMeola's vision. "You smoke with your eyes and feel and touch," he says.

"And the Connecticut wrapper," DiMeola muses, "is in my opinion the best in the world. With it, you have more taste from a perfect filler."

OPPOSITE: UPMANN'S ACCLAIMED CHAIRMAN'S RESERVE, CREATED IN THE DOMINICAN REPUBLIC FOR CONSOLIDATED'S CHAIRMAN, RONALD PERELMAN. RIGHT: THE ORIGINAL CUBAN H. UPMANN LABEL FROM THE HAVANA FACTORY FOUNDED IN 1844 BY HERMAN AND AUGUST UPMANN OF BREMEN, GERMANY.

ABOVE: Carlos "Carlito" Fuente Jr. personally created the label that is now the hallmark of A. Fuente.

First Family Fuente

Carlos Fuente, Jr.

"The cigar is the only companion that listens to your thoughts."

WHEN CUBANS FLEEING Havana after the Spanish-American War brought the "leaf" to Florida, they had the blessing of Cuban patriot José Martí. One of them was Arturo Fuente, who moved from Cuba to Key West in 1898. His first factory burned down, whereupon he moved to Tampa in 1912, building another to make Clear Havanas. His first cigar was called Tampa Sweetheart, and he later developed a special blended cigar that was the forerunner of the great Fuente. With another fire in 1920, Fuente lost his factory but not his vision; he began making cigars again from his home in Ybor City, Tampa's great Cuban cigar community.

In 1954 Arturo's son Carlos assumed the Fuente legacy, and shortly thereafter the current heir to the legend, Carlos Jr., was born. When the stock for making Clear Havanas dwindled after the embargo in 1961, the Fuentes considered Jamaica, Mexico, and Puerto Rico, then settled in Nicaragua, where they remained until the 1977 Sandinista revolution caused them to pull up stakes again. After moving on to other Latin American countries, they finally came to rest in the Dominican Republic, where they have achieved remarkable success with the Montesino, Arturo Fuente, Hemingway, Chateau Fuente, and Flor Fina 8-5-8. The Flor Fina— "Finest Flower"—is Arturo Fuente's personal blend of four different tobaccos. Made in a 47 ring gauge, it celebrates his eighty-five-year heritage. It is a wonderful cigar.

Perhaps the Fuente family's finest achievement is the Opus X, the triumphant culmination of a mission to create a new world-class wrapper.

Inspired by Angel Oliva, the brilliant pioneer of Cuban seed who traveled from country to country in search of perfect soil and climate where a superior leaf could be cultivated, the Fuentes began Project X, an enterprise that many experts thought could never succeed. Tobacco men felt that a superior wrapper could not be developed outside Cuba, Cameroon, Ecuador, and Connecticut. Many had tried but failed at great expense. Eventually on a riverbank in the Dominican Republic, a new leaf was born.

The *rosado* wrapper, organically grown at Château de la Fuente, provides a richer-tasting tobacco with greater combustion. It is grown in conditions gracious to soil, climate, and seed. The Fuentes believe that their leaf, aged in Courvoisier cognac barrels, has the familiar taste of a Havana, for a cigar that is aromatic, rich, and complex. The beautifully made cigar is carefully matured in cedar vaults for a year before being boxed. Fuente produces more than 34 million cigars a year, but only 750,000 will be the richly flavored Opus X. Recently a dispute over the Opus name arose between the Mondavi/Rothschild Winery, which produces the very fine Opus One wine and has announced their intention to produce an Opus One cigar, and the Fuentes. But to rephrase the Great Bard, "A cigar by another name would be just as sweet."

The Fuentes believe that time is the secret to producing a great cigar. "From the seeds of hope to the birthplace of a dream, the Fuentes carefully grow, blend, and age their tobacco, never rushing the hands of time." As they like to say, "With small drops of water on a stone, in time a canyon is created."

OVERLEAF: **CARLOS FUENTE AND CARLOS JR. AT THEIR DOMINICAN PLANTATION.**

The Poet

Hendrik Kelner

"TOBACCO WILL TELL YOU what it needs, and you must learn to listen to it," says Hendrik Kelner, the poet of tobacco. An engineer by training, a cigar *conocedor* by trade, and a romantic by nature, Kelner is of Dutch descent. Born in the Dominican Republic, he carries on the distinguished tobacco heritage passed down by his father.

> *El tabaco es como la mujer.*
> *Para conocerlo hay que comprenderlo.*
> *Para comprenderlo hay que amarlo.*
> (Tobacco is like a woman.
> To know her, you have to understand her.
> To understand her, you have to love her.)

When Zino Davidoff decided his firm had to leave Cuba, he and Ernst Schneider looked to Kelner, whose company had been making cigars in the Dominican Republic for many years, to meet their demands for taste and quality. Now a new generation of cigars has been created. Better made, with higher standards than the competition, they are a milder, consistent cigar with a beautiful wrapper.

Davidoff knew the difference between great and excellent, and Kelner is an alchemist who can produce a cigar near to perfection. Using three different leaves from Cuban seed grown in the province of San Vicente, and a Connecticut shade wrapper, the delicate and elegant Kelner cigars are like paintings, each with a varied composition. Each brand—Davidoff, Avo, and Griffin's—has its own demands and expectations.

Kelner follows a design, charting each objective to determine and influence the smoke. Consistency and balance are considered. He grows his tobacco from six different types of soil in the Yaque valley alone; these influential factors, along with the agricultural protocol of variety and climate, are adapted. Time and weather change from crop to crop. Growing, curing, fermentation, aging, making, and maturing all demand control and care.

Hardworking yet easygoing, Kelner knows as much about tobacco as anyone in the world and, in some instances, maybe more. From five different cuttings he selects the secrets of the *ligero* for punch, the *seco* for balance and percentage of blend, and the *volado* for combustion.

Kelner's chart includes all tobacco characteristics and combinations, containing the secrets of experience that combine into his blends. Often there are twenty-five different blends to choose from for filler and binder, and with the new Dominican wrapper Kelner has created, the perfect cigar is achievable.

"Airflow creates synergy of taste," Kelner says. "Taking into account the *dulce* [sweet] in front of the mouth, the *salado* [salty] at its sides, and the *amargo* [bitter] and *paladar* [sour] in the back, tobaccos are mixed to stimulate these different locations, eliciting a fascinating combination of tastes, just as a chef concocts blends of spices and special ingredients." With these careful considerations and controlled events, the leaves are grown in outstanding soil and climate, blended for flavor and aroma, and matured for four years to produce a cigar that is rare, robust, and revolutionary. This is the poetry of Hendrik Kelner. And, of course, the legacy of Davidoff.

HENDRIK KELNER'S TOP TEN

1. **Davidoff 1000:** "Small with good body. Easy for work."
2. **Grand Cru Series No. 3 and No. 1:** "A good cigar to enjoy with time."
3. **Double RR:** "An after-dinner cigar. At least an hour to smoke it."
4. **Paul Garmirian Petite Bouquet**
5. **Avo XO Intermezzo:** "Full body with spice."
6. **Davidoff Torpedo:** "Complex with discovery. Made with five different tobaccos."
7. **Macanudo:** "Good Connecticut shade wrapper."
8. **Griffin's 300:** "Cuban flavor. Stimulating, with a more direct smoke."
9. **Partagas:** "For the Cameroon wrapper."
10. **Kelner Blend:** "Not for sale. A wonderful corona."

VILLAZON & CO.

FRANK LLANEZA

FOR MORE THAN a hundred years, Villazon of Tampa has produced some of the best premium cigars in the world, with their Hoyo de Monterreys, Excaliburs, and Punches leading the pack. Headed by straight-shooting Frank Llaneza, Villazon factories today produce 60 million cigars a year.

When the Cuban embargo was imposed in 1961, Llaneza decided to move production elsewhere and looked around for a suitable location. They ruled out the Canary Islands, because there the cost of cigar production was high since Spain's Tabacalera controlled it. He and his partner Dan Blumenthal, as well as Angel Oliva of Oliva Tobacco, were familiar with tobacco grown in the Dominican Republic and even owned a tobacco plantation there (which was eventually sold to Carlos Fuente). But they favored the climate and conditions in Honduras. Together they inaugurated

Honduras farming and production, using the name Villazon. Having become friends with Fernando Palicio, who owned Hoyo de Monterrey in Havana, Llaneza and Blumenthal eventually acquired the rights to make the famous cigar outside Cuba.

In Honduras Llaneza literally founded a tobacco school, teaching farmers how to grow virgin Cuban-seed Honduran tobacco for aroma and body and how to make cigars from it. Adding an imported Connecticut shade wrapper that came from a big, bright leaf, they produced a quality blend and a superb cigar.

What cigars does Frank Llaneza like? He prefers the mild Excalibur No. 4, with its Connecticut shade wrapper, and the Punch Corona, with a richer body, in a Sumatra wrapper made in Ecuador.

FRANK LLANEZA'S TOP TEN

1. **Hoyo de Monterrey Excalibur No. 4:**
"A smooth, flavorful cigar."
2. **Punch Double Corona EMS:** "Robust flavor."
3. **El Rey del Mundo Flor de Llaneza:**
"Heavy, very flavorful."
4. **Hoyo de Monterrey Excalibur No. 1:**
"Long-lasting, very smooth."
5. **Macanudo Baron de Rothschild:**
"A beautiful wrapper; a mild, very
smooth smoke."
6. **Partagas No. 10:** "Excellent smoke;
a flavorful EMS wrapper."
7. **Belinda Breva a la Conserva:** "A wonderful
everyday smoke, with a very tasty wrapper."
8. **Hoyo de Monterrey Churchill:**
"Robust, very good taste."
9. **Hoyo de Monterrey Rothschild Maduro**
10. **Punch Rothschild Maduro:**
"Robust taste, excellent burn."

FRANK LLANEZA'S PRE-CASTRO FAVORITES

1. **Montecristo No. 1:**
"Fine flavor."
2. **Partagas Derby:**
"Shorter smoke, fine flavor."
3. **Montecristo No. 2:**
"Robust, heavier smoke."

THE MAN AT PARTAGAS

JORGE CONCEPCIÓN LUNA

ALONG A QUIET STREET in Old Havana lies the original Partagas factory. The *fábrica* is the same one where Jaime Partagas began production more than a century and a half ago. Passing through the large oak doors just inside the entrance, one enters a large humidor room filled with the aroma of cigars and Cuban coffee. Along the walls are boxes of Havanas that I long to have: Cohiba, Hoyo de Monterrey, Romeo y Julieta, Montecristo, Partagas—beautiful and inviting, they are all there. Here is the smoking ground of Jorge Concepción Luna, who invites me to join him in his "cigar library."

Luna is vice-director of Partagas in Havana, and as his name implies, he was conceived to be part of the land. His father arrived from the Canary Islands and cultivated tobacco in the Las Villa province. Under his tutelage Jorge became an expert in the geography of the leaf. Even

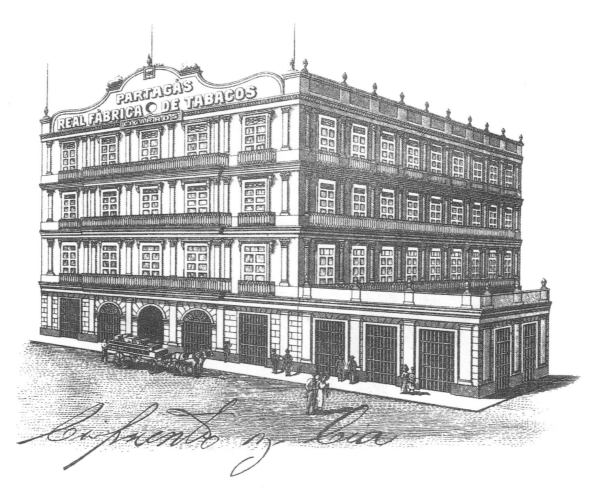

though the Dominican Partagas uses some filler grown from Cuban seed, he believes it can still be distinguished from the Cuban Partagas. "You can never achieve exactly the same environment," he says. "It can never be the same."

Concepción oversees much of the tobacco growing in four different regions of Cuba. The Vuelta Abajo, he explains, grows the best *capa* (wrapper) as well as superb filler known as *triepo*. In the nearby Semi Vuelta the tobacco is also sun-grown for filler, under a cheesecloth covering. Other tobacco is grown in Remedios, in the cen-

ABOVE: THE ORIGINAL PARTAGAS FACTORY, FROM THE REVERSE OF A CUBAN LABEL.

tral part of Cuba, following the mountains east. "This is the land of Partagas," he says with great confidence.

"Any smoker," he continues, seated at a long polished table and offering friendship with a generous smile, "who likes a good aroma, with strength, should consider a Partagas because of its consistent stability and quality, which only come with years of experience—part of our tradition."

The growing season for tobacco in Cuba is September to February, but Concepción confides to me that he has been experimenting with remarkable new techniques that could extend the season by five additional months in order to achieve production of 140 million cigars annually. A terrific concept, to be sure.

The Tobacco Angel

Angel Oliva

As long as man has smoked tobacco, he has appealed to higher powers to safeguard his crop. In Cuba the mystical god of tobacco is Hatuey, while in the Dominican Republic Princess Anacaona, a beautiful Indian goddess, protects the tobacco crop. Many would add Angel Oliva to this list. He is held in awe by most knowledgeable cigar people. Lew Rothman of JR Tobacco calls him "the Albert Einstein of tobacco; nobody else even comes close."

When Angel Oliva came to Tampa, Florida, over seventy-five years ago, he had a dream that the dirt roads leading to Ybor City would one day be lined with lush green tobacco plants. His father, Juan Francisco Oliva, was foreman of a 2,500-acre farm in Pinar del Rio, and Angel himself had been a tobacco farmer in Cuba. He thought of America as a land filled with opportunity not only for a better life but for tobacco factories and fields. He was not far from wrong. Still, as he knew, great tobacco was grown in Cuba.

When Angel set up the Oliva Tobacco Company in 1932, he supplied not only a great Cuban wrapper leaf for fifty tobacco companies making Clear Havanas in Tampa, but binder and filler as well. His warehouse had an inventory with thousands of tobacco bales, hand selected by the Angel. His business was run on a handshake, built on trust and faith—until his suppliers in Cuba broke their word.

Up until the time of the embargo, Tampa had relied

The Olivas' Top Ten

1. **Fuente Opus X:** "We enjoy any cigar in this line. The rich wrappers make them absolutely splendid smokes. A texture like no other cigar."
2. **Ashton Vintage Cabinet No. 2:** "A beautifully made, smooth cigar. We save them for special occasions."
3. **Bering Plaza:** "Affordable everyday smokes: an example of a good cigar that doesn't cost an arm and a leg."
4. **Cuba Aliados Valentino:** "A great medium-bodied smoke with a gorgeous wrapper. This is a big cigar that is as good in the middle of the day as it is after a big meal."
5. **Cuesta-Rey 1884:** "Always a consistent, light-bodied cigar, perfect to start the day with."
6. **Hoyo de Monterrey Excaliburs:** "Once again, a wonderful line of cigars. The hallmark cigar of Honduras, always a wonderful complex smoke."
7. **JR Ultimates:** "Another fantastic line of cigars. Full-flavored, powerful smokes that make us think of Cuba."
8. **La Gloria Cubana Wavell:** "A cigar well-deserving of its excellent reputation, with its own richly distinct character."
9. **Punch Grand Cru Superiors:** "Absolutely one of our favorites. The beautiful EMS wrapper makes it a classic."
10. **Tabacos San Jose Torpedo:** "A little-known gem made in Miami, one of the best-made and most flavorful torpedos in the business."

Oliva Tobacco Company
PACKERS OF DOMESTIC AND IMPORTED TOBACCOS

on Cuban tobacco. After 1961 Angel set out to develop a replacement supply. He worked with farmers in Florida, Connecticut, and Honduras, gambling time, energy, and his savings, starting tobacco-growing projects, to develop a leaf as good as his father had grown in Cuba. Fueled by missionary zeal, he worked endlessly with his brothers, Martin and Marcelino, to foster the tobacco business. Everyone—his friends and other cigar makers—looked to him for guidance and assistance. With his own money he brought his family and friends over from Cuba, offering them a better life. Even today, the Oliva Tobacco Company is a sanctuary that helps many Cubans ride out hardship, always providing hope as well as opportunity.

Angel finally proved that Connecticut farmers could grow superior wrappers—a *candela* wrapper, fire-cured within seventy-two hours to preserve its color and taste, a leaf preferred for top cigars.

Even with the wrapper problem solved, Oliva's inventory of Cuban filler had dwindled. Angel took the initiative again, this time making extensive studies of soils and climate in countries with geographical conditions similar to Cuba's. His first experiment, with fifty-three acres of land in Honduras, was a marked success. Encouraged, he cultivated another seven hundred, producing the natural and sun-grown fillers that the cigar industry needed to survive. Cigar makers were amazed and astonished at the results.

Not content to rest on his laurels, Angel, with his sons and grandson, Angel Jr. and Johnny and John Jr., ventured elsewhere in Latin America, planting Cuban seed in other promised lands. They weathered war and political upheaval in Nicaragua. They endured tough climates and changing conditions. They designed barns and trained farmers. They cultivated soil and engineered seeds. They shared their knowledge and experience, everything they knew, always with courtesy and respect, supplying tobacco for such brands as Fuente, Hoyo de Monterrey, Punch, Belinda, and La Gloria Cubana.

Today the Oliva family develops great tobacco for premium cigars not only in Honduras but in Ecuador and the Dominican Republic. They were originally responsible for Château de la Fuente, a farm they sold to the Fuentes for the development of his extraordinary wrapper. Loved and respected, there is not another family like them.

"If the embargo ever ends," Johnny Oliva says, "we'll go back—not to live but for the tobacco. It's where we came from, and it is great tobacco. Cuba has promise in many ways. Maybe we'll even plant some Dominican seed. It's pretty good."

History and Elegance

NICHOLAS FREEMAN

THE COMING TOGETHER of the cigar world's brightest lights in Havana to celebrate the thirtieth anniversary of Cohiba afforded an unprecedented opportunity to meet some of the most amazing tobacco traders. Among them was Nicholas Freeman, CEO of Hunters and Frankau, the United Kingdom's sole importer of Cuban cigars, with total sales (including Swiss, German, and Dutch brands) upward of 25,000,000 per year. Like the Cullman family of Consolidated in America, the Freemans have traded in tobacco for five generations. Nicholas Freeman is no stranger to Havana; he knows the business and he knows a good cigar.

Freeman's great-great-great-grandfather, James Rykers Freeman, established the firm after learning the tobacco business in Holland, and he soon had three cigar factories in England. For a period of time he owned H. Upmann, which gave him a strong presence in the Cuban market and a relationship with Habanos S.A. that continues today.

Though the company's primary concentration has always been Cuban tobacco, England's currency restrictions during World War II resulted in an embargo on Cuban cigars from 1939 to 1953. During this period the family forged a market for Jamaican cigars in partnership with Alonzo Menendez, and though their business flourished, the family returned to Havana as soon as conditions permitted.

Today, the smart and elegant Nicholas Freeman has

contributed to the tobacco industry's continued growth with pride and dedication. He says, "Tobacco has been an amazing leaf for five hundred years. For a while, I feel that the industry was devalued by the cigarette. But now there is a return to tobacco's true tradition and properties. I should think that in two hundred years' time the cigarette will be just a page in history, and the pleasure of the cigar will continue to be recorded and enjoyed in volumes."

A Proud Patriarch

ROLANDO REYES

BEFORE THE REVOLUTION in Cuba, the Aliados factory in Havana was making more than 6 million cigars a year. The family business was headed by patriarch Rolando Reyes, a man with a great passion for perfect cigars. For thirty years Reyes had worked for Upmann, Partagas, and Romeo y Julieta. Then, with zeal and excitement to apply all he had learned, he opened his own factory.

But in 1970, after the government nationalized the company, Don Rolando left Cuba, finally settling in Honduras, a place he feels is the best country for making hand-rolled cigars. "The climate is good, the people are hardworking, and the government very encouraging," Reyes says. There the Aliados factory started producing its famous hand-rolled cigars again.

Not long ago, Cuba Aliados introduced the Puros Indios at its Danlí factory. The new cigar is distinguished by blends of "ultra-premium" tobaccos and is made in a variety of shapes and sizes. Of the 5 million cigars that the

Aliados factory makes annually, only half a million are the increasingly popular Puros Indios. Like so many premium cigars, they are on back order.

Reyes, who personally supervises every step of the cigar-making process, owes his success to attention to detail and quality control. He uses only aged Dominican-grown Cuban-seed filler and Ecuador-grown Sumatra-seed binder and wrapper. Recently he has been growing filler in Jalapa, near Nicaragua. The business has several million dollars invested in good tobacco.

"All tobacco is processed and aged according to my specifications," Don Rolando says. "And if tobacco is not aged for the proper time, the cigars will not be good. Let's face it, cigars are only as good as the tobacco in them."

Davidoff's CEO

Dr. Ernst Schneider

CONSISTENCY. Excellence. Organization. The man behind the legend.

With an intensity that would melt the alpine snow near his Basel home, Ernst Schneider has always loved the good life. His philosophy of pleasure: "Eat less, but eat the best. Drink less, but drink the best. Smoke less but only the best. And smoke only Davidoffs."

Over twenty-five years ago he bought Davidoff & Co. for more than $1 million and remained a silent partner while the legendary Zino Davidoff served as spokesman and ambassador for the marvelous line of cigars he had created. Davidoff, a gentleman with impeccable taste, was truly a great connoisseur. Together they made a formidable team. Combining Davidoff's cigar-making experience and charismatic personality with Schneider's skill as a business strategist, they successfully expanded the company into a sophisticated marketing and distribution operation that exhibits its style and pride worldwide. There are now elegant Davidoff stores in London, Geneva, New York, Hong Kong, Taipei, and Singapore, with new ones opening in Shanghai and Moscow. "Davidoff started with a tree and now it's a forest," Schneider says.

After World War II, Schneider was a member of the Swiss Red Cross and arranged medical help for displaced persons and victims of the Dachau concentration camp. He joined Oettinger, which was headed by his father-in-law, in 1949, having learned the import-export and distribution business with Loens & Company.

Schneider has built the Davidoff brand with core stores, showcases like the ones in Geneva and London, surrounded by what he calls "depositaires," smaller franchises or satellite stores that help the network branch out. Three points serve as the governance charter at Davidoff: First, the complete shop. Quality and price must always be in order; and a complete line of premium cigars, Davidoff and otherwise, must be carried, always kept in perfect condition. Second, always follow vision with a sound concept. Third, create outstanding and selective distribution.

> "A true connoisseur loves cigars just as he loves music, wine, and life."
>
> *Ernst Schneider*

Davidoff has four cigar brands. Special-quality tobacco is reserved for the mildest, the Nos. 1, 2, and 3. They lead the parade, followed by the 1,000 and 2,000. The Grand Cru marches next, and then come the special initials R and T. Soon the new Connoisseurs will join the ranks. The Griffin's, Zino, and Avo are all special cigars for special markets, all with their characteristically superb blends. They are formulated, along with the main Davidoff line, by expert cigar maker Hendrik Kelner of Tabacos Dominicanos.

When Davidoff and Schneider reached an impasse with Cuba, like other cigar makers they looked for a place and a partner to make their cigars. After considering Haiti, Nicaragua, Brazil, and Java, they found in the Dominican Republic not only the best climate and soil but the Kelner family business, which had been built with years of care and experience in true cigar-making tradition. So impressed were they with the superior quality and taste of Kelner's Griffin's that they contracted him almost immediately. It has been a good marriage. With the exception of the Zino, which is made in Honduras, Davidoffs are now manufactured exclusively in the Dominican Republic—more than 10 million per year.

Ernst Schneider likes to compare the Havana to a fine burgundy wine. "A burgundy essentially uses one grape, the Havana one tobacco," he explains. "The Davidoff is more like a Bordeaux wine, created from a mixture of different grapes. We use a blend of different tobaccos, which I believe gives a fine, aromatic, and softer smoke that is not as strong as a Havana."

On my last evening in Geneva, at a dinner party given by Dr. Schneider, the Davidoff CEO offered cigars to a few friends, remarking that he had recently returned from Cuba. "Ah," his fellow aficionado replied, "there is nothing like a good Havana." But these cigars were from the Dominican Republic. And in this context, I asked the head

of Davidoff if he would ever return to Cuba, to reinstitute production of Davidoff's famous Chateau line.

"No," he replied, "I think we will stay in the DR, but if Cuba opens, then my mind will open, too. In some ways we may go back to Cuba. I do think it would take four or five years to achieve the consistency and quality we would be looking for. There is great tobacco in Cuba but also great inconsistency."

COHIBA'S FIRST LADY

EMILIA TAMAYO

EMILIA TAMAYO, like her exquisite and *especial* cigars, exhibits a robust spirit that she applies vigorously as managing director of Cohiba. Over half the 185 people working under her are women. When Castro introduced the new cigar thirty years ago, he also introduced gender equality, both in management and production, breaking the traditions of what had always been a men's club.

For twenty-one years Tamayo has produced a cigar that

In the past, Cuban cigar production has been criticized for lack of consistency—especially Cohiba's Lanceros and Esplendidos. Tamayo has vowed to take total control, with responsibility for quality. A limited number of Montecristos are made at El Laguito, as well as the legendary Trinidad, a treasured cigar that is made to order for Castro and his secretary of state for diplomatic gifts. Only a few boxes are produced each month, with a specially designed gold label. Executives at Habanos, S.A., are thinking about making the Trinidad more widely available.

THE TRINIDAD

THIS MYSTERIOUS CIGAR, which is not for sale to the general public, is made only with the approval of Cuban president Fidel Castro and his secretary of state, for honored guests. The Trinidad, named after one of Cuba's most beautiful and historic cities, comes from the El Laguito factory in only one size, *vitola de galera* Laguito No. 1, which is $7\frac{1}{2} \times 38$, the same size as the Cohiba Lancero. It is a medium-to-full-bodied smoke and is rated by Simon Chase as the best, according to his personal taste. Made from the finest tobacco selection, many experts put it right at the top of the list of the finest cigars in the world.

many aficionados consider unequaled in quality and flavor. One of the secrets of her success is her personal humanity. She loves her workers and her factory, which is situated in an Italianate mansion in the El Laguito district of Havana; for two decades it was home to the Davidoff cigar. It is a beautiful setting, near embassies and consulates, which is only appropriate since the Cohiba is an ambassador to the world, carrying a portfolio with well-regarded credentials.

The scene at the El Laguito factory might have come straight out of *Carmen*; hundreds of women are sitting at row after row of old polished tables rolling cigars.

Cuba produces about 65 million cigars each year, and 1.6 million of them are Cohibas. Most of the tobacco for what some consider the world's finest cigar comes from the Vuelta Abajo, whose ideal conditions many experts believe can never be duplicated. It is home to tobacco.

I asked Tamayo why the Cohiba is so extraordinary. She replied behind a warm smile, "We have the *volado* for combustion, the *seco* for aroma, the *ligero* for strength. Cohiba is the only cigar that undergoes three fermentations. But our biggest secret, you see, is that you must love the cigar when you roll it."

Maybe it is not rolled on the thighs of beautiful Cuban women, but certainly the Cohiba is made with the tremendous care and appreciation of Emilia Tamayo.

The Tobacco Troubadour

Avo Uvezian

"I have always loved beautiful music. Then I found the cigar. A good cigar is like music. Now I have two loves."

There he is at his piano with a grand cigar, the great Avo—composer, musician, lover. With his good friend Hendrik Kelner of Tabacos Dominicanos, he orchestrates the Avo cigar in much the same way that he does his music. The four best cigar makers in the world, according to Avo, are Hendrik Kelner of Davidoff, Daniel Nunez and Benjamín Menéndez of General, and the Fuentes.

Avo was born in Beirut of Armenian heritage and at sixteen formed his own jazz ensemble. After studying at both French and American universities and then at Juilliard, he was invited by the Shah of Iran to play at his palace in Teheran. He became the personal pianist to the Shah and Queen Soraya and a creator of the song "Strangers in the Night." Then it was on to New York to continue his studies under Teddy White.

To his surprise, he was drafted into the U.S. Army, but he improvised a place with the U.S. First Army Band. Playing each evening at the officers' club, he soon learned that the commandant at Fort Dix was from Fort Wayne, Indiana. Each evening he played "Back Home in Indiana" for the general, a rendition that probably kept Avo from being shipped off to Korea.

Years later, at his daughter Karyn's christening in Switzerland, he was outraged when a tobacconist charged him twenty-five dollars for a cigar and a bad one at that. With great style and flourish, he waltzed into the offices of Hendrik Kelner in Santiago, who blended and produced a cigar to his liking. So good was it that Avo gave them to his customers in his piano bar in Palmar del Mar, Puerto Rico. His first order was sold through J&B in England. Eventually fans all over the world were requesting his cigars, including Zino Davidoff himself. Did Zino like the music or the cigar? Probably both. Davidoff and Ernst Schneider bought the Avo cigar for Davidoff, Ltd.

In the beginning, Avo produced only 20,000 cigars per year. From Michel Roux of Carillon Importers, he learned something he never forgot: "Take care of your smallest client just as you would take care of your biggest."

With Davidoff, Avo now produces more than 2 million cigars a year. A new blend is currently being made, the Avo XO Quartetto. It will be available in the same four sizes as the Avo XO and will be called the Allegro, Serenata, Notturno, and Fantasia.

Avo believes that his cigars have taste and harmony and discovery, like notes and themes in a musical composition. "The taste of the Avo," he says, "can be likened to preludio, intermezzo, and maestoso." Music to the ears.

BRAVO AVO

After dinner one June evening with Hendrik Kelner, Benjamín Menéndez, and Avo Uvezian at the Grande Almirante in Santiago, Avo presented me with a cigar.

"You will now smoke another wonderful cigar," he pronounced with a stunning musical fanfare. "I want you to try it."

"What is it called?"

"No name. Just enjoy it."

It was late after a superb supper, with the forging of new friendships. The conversation had been good. Now before me was a new blend with an extraordinary new Dominican *capa* that had been developed and crafted by Kelner. Within a few moments I knew that this was truly the best cigar I had ever smoked. Like silk.

"Bravo, Avo!" I said.

A moment passed, and he smiled. "Yes, that's it. Thank you, Nathaniel."

But I should be thanking you, Avo, I thought, and gave him a puzzled expression.

"'Bravo Avo,'" he repeated. "You have given me the name for my new cigar."

LEW ROTHMAN

JR TOBACCO SELLS about 40 percent of the premium cigars bought in the United States. For someone who wields this kind of market power, Lew Rothman remains a remarkably down-to-earth fellow.

Rothman's empire includes a 70,000-foot warehouse in North Carolina; the world's largest cigar store, which is actually the world's largest walk-in humidor, in suburban New Jersey; and a nationwide mail-order operation that offers great prices and quality to a huge following of loyal customers.

The man who has been called "the Robin Hood of cigars" originally had thoughts of going to law school, but due to his father's illness he wound up carrying on the family business. Rothman realized he was operating in a very price-sensitive environment—even his most loyal customers were willing to go elsewhere for a better deal. So he vowed never to be undersold.

In a relatively short time, Rothman was among the top five cigar merchants in the New York metropolitan area. As the business grew, JR had the clout to create its own brands, and in 1980 Rothman built a 3,000-square-foot "supermarket" in Manhattan.

"People would come into our store and see thousands of cigars all stacked up in boxes," he says. "We would display a thousand boxes of our brands right next to a thousand boxes of Macanudos, which gave our brands legitimacy.

"We always provide our customers with the same quality merchandise as our competition, but at a much better price," Rothman says. "We could sell cigars for a lot more than we do, but we have a formula. It's worked for twenty

LEW ROTHMAN'S TOP TEN

1. **El Rey del Mundo Flor de Llaneza:** "The best cigar I ever saw."
2. **Macanudo Vintage No. 2:** "Day in and day out, the most consistently made cigar in the industry."
3. **El Rey del Mundo Cedar:** "A unique taste; I'm a particular fan of its size, 7 × 42, which is longer than usual for a cigar of that ring gauge."
4. **Dunhill Samana:** "A mild, clean-smoking cigar with no aftertaste."
5. **Casa Blanca Bonita:** "At 4 × 36, the only little cigar that tastes like a big cigar."
6. **El Rey del Mundo Rectangulares:** "About as close as you're going to get to a Cuban cigar; a square, hard-packed, knockout heavyweight."
7. **Marsh Wheeling Virginians:** "Machine-made in Wheeling, West Virginia, with a Connecticut broadleaf wrapper; it's my car smoke."
8. **JR Special Jamaican Bonita:** "Just as good as any of the more expensive torpedo-shaped cigars."
9. **Santa Clara Premier:** "A tubed cigar, it transports well. I don't often go for the Mexican taste, but this one I find very palatable."
10. **Don Diego Privada No. 4:** "The most consistent of the whole Don Diego line. Very mild, but very flavorful."

years, and we're not about to change it: The better I buy, the better my consumer buys."

Rothman likes to recount some of his most memorable sales. "We once sold a thousand boxes of Te-Amo Meditations to a customer from Argentina, a rancher by the name of Oliveros. He came into our store on a Saturday and asked how much was a box of Te-Amo Meditations. It was $19.95 at the time. He asked, 'Okay, how much is a thousand boxes?' and I replied, 'A thousand times $19.95.' He said he was going to shop around and he'd be back. I said, 'You don't have to shop around because no one sells them for less, and nobody's got a thousand boxes of Meditations.' He came back later that day and bought the cigars with cash."

Another memorable sale for Lew Rothman was when he sold a box of cigars to Fidel Castro. It was 1961, and he was a teenager working for his father. Castro was in New York to visit the United Nations, staying at the Hotel Theresa, across the street from the Rothmans' store.

"He came in with a bunch of guys in combat outfits," Rothman remembers. "The best cigar we had at the time was La Corona Corona. It was thirty-five cents, or three for a dollar. He bought a box of fifty for $17.50. It was the largest sale I had ever made in my life. When I was a kid, if somebody walked up to my father's counter and asked for three Corona Coronas, conversation would stop and everybody would look up to see who was the guy who could afford to buy three La Corona Coronas.

"Castro asked the price in very broken English. There were cops on horseback everywhere, and huge crowds. I never saw so many cops in my life. I thought Fidel was a hero at the time, the guy who freed Cuba."

JR has counted among its valued customers most of the great cigar personalities, including Milton Berle, Doc Severinsen, Jack Paar, Jack Lemmon, Carroll O'Connor, Cary Grant, Walter Mondale, Bill Cosby, Alan King, Mario Puzo, Gay Talese, Joe Pesci, and Robert DeNiro. Rothman sold cigars to most of the actors who starred in *The Godfather,* and he even supplied the cigars for the wedding of John Gotti, Jr.

Rothman moved his company to New Jersey in 1985, where he still operates the world's largest cigar store, then to North Carolina in 1990. But the services of Robin Hood are never farther away than the nearest telephone.

THE AFICIONADO'S ALTERNATIVE

CUBAN CIGARS HAVE BEEN prized for their full-bodied, earthy taste and aroma for more than two hundred years; legendary smokes have been celebrated in song and story in the poetic verses of Kipling and Byron. From Churchill to Kennedy, Hugo to Hemingway, Whitehall to the White House, Havanas have always been associated with power and prestige.

After Cuban cigars were made illegal in the United States in 1961, the innovative Lew Rothman of JR Tobacco decided to do something about it.

The Jamastram valley, lying between Nicaragua and Honduras, comes very close to duplicating the climatic conditions of Cuba's Vuelta Abajo, the source of all great Havana tobacco.

In early 1989 Rothman gathered samples of many great Cuban cigars and sent them to F. Palicio & Co. in Honduras. There he assembled a team including Frank Llaneza, the world-famous cigar maker; Estello Padron, a Cuban expatriate cigar master; and John Oliva of Oliva Tobacco, one of the world's foremost authorities on the tobacco leaf. These four set about to duplicate the style, shape, and taste of several famous Havana brands, such as Montecristo, Bolivar, and Partagas.

After successfully realizing that goal, the team moved on to create alternatives to Jamaican, Dominican, and Honduran cigars. Altogether, JR has duplicated more than 175 famous cigars, making the taste of expensive cigars an affordable pleasure.

This is one reason Rothman has been called a one-man cigar-marketing phenomenon and the Robin Hood of the cigar world, among other epithets. Available by mail order, JR Alternatives are for sale at a fraction of what the cigars that inspired them cost. For example, the Hoyo de Monterrey Epicure No. 1, which would cost about $370 for a box of twenty-five, is sold by JR for $20.95 for a box of twenty; that's about $1.05 per cigar versus $14.80! Rumor has it that most smokers, in a blind taste test, would be hard-pressed to tell the difference between a JR Alternative and the real thing.

PERSONALITIES, PRIVILEGE, AND PRESTIGE

A CIGAR IS MORE than a good smoke—it is the focal point of an event. And the personalities who smoke it are as distinguished and different as the brands and rings. From century to century the cigar has heralded the greatest triumphs and dignified the most bitter defeats. It has been there to celebrate

BUCKINGHAM PALACE

the victor and to restore a measure of integrity to the vanquished. The Brazilian proverb, "Every cigar goes up in smoke," holds true. But the enormous effort that goes into cultivating and rolling cigars enhances the overall enjoyment.

The cigar has always been associated with romanticism, art, and idealism. After all, it was first introduced in Europe's cultural cradle and grew in stature in the nineteenth century, an era of passions, of love, war, and literature.

In both the New and Old Worlds, cigars were always connected to the few privileged personalities. At the beginning, in the Aztec civilization, cigars were reserved for the enjoyment of high priests and nobles. Those that were smoked in Montezuma's court for religious and medical

purposes were laden with vision-inducing hallucinogens. With the arrival of the Europeans, the focus on tobacco remained as tight as the band encircling a cigar. John Smith achieved as much celebrity as the first tobacco planter in the New World as he did for marrying the Indian princess

Pocahontas. Later on, in Spain and Portugal, its enjoyment was reserved for people in high places.

The connection between cigar and celebrity, the best and the brightest, historians and aficionados agree, evolved during the nineteenth century, the golden age of the cigar. Havanas fueled romantic values held by heads of state and monarchs, actors and writers. From Victor Hugo to Otto von Bismarck, the cigar embodied the fortunes and misfortunes of crusades and crusaders.

Monumental men and modern women smoked cigars, reflecting an air of nobility and power. One day in 1870,

THIS PAGE: GENERATIONS OF BRITISH ROYALTY WERE HONORED WITH COMMEMORATIVE CIGAR LABELS LIKE THESE CREATED BY LA CORONA FOR THE BRITISH MARKET. OPPOSITE: A NINETEENTH-CENTURY ENGRAVING CELEBRATES THE PLEASURES OF A GOOD CIGAR.

while riding through the Bois de Boulogne in Prussian-occupied Paris, Bismarck heard some angry shouts coming from behind him. Not protected by his customary escorts, the Prussian chancellor was in danger. Most men would have acted rashly. But Bismarck, with an easy calm, pulled out one of his finest cigars and requested a light from a passerby. Although the citizen may have wanted to deny the chancellor's request, he thought better and acted diplomatically. To have denied a man a smoke, even if he was the enemy, would have been bad form. The shouts quieted as the flame was lit. Perhaps Bismarck had quelled a potential rebellion, not with sword and fury, but simply with smoke.

DEFIANCE AND CONFIDENCE

DEFIANCE HAS LONG BEEN a key ingredient in the cigar smoker's attitude. One of the earliest recorded expressions of this link between cigar and cause célèbre was in 1815, as Napoleon's Marshal Ney faced a firing squad. Granted his last request, Ney chose a cigar, which he smoked until the last puff was sent heaven-bound. Even the deferential Don Juan, when confronted by Satan, produced a cigar and demanded a light from the Devil, who to his amorous delight offered a flaming torch.

Self-confidence and self-assurance also seem to be shared by cigar personalities, qualities that bring power and pleasure to the smoke. Lenin was a famous customer of the Davidoff shop in Switzerland. Zino Davidoff remembers, "My father's store . . . was a small one . . . not like any other. From time to time, bizarre gentlemen with conspiratorial looks would gather there. They *were* conspirators. And just as the liberator of Cuba, José Martí, exiled in Florida, used to send messages rolled in cigars, so the enemies of the czars in Kiev carried out their plans behind a cigar-smoke screen. Eventually the conspiratorial ring was discovered, and I, with my family, left Russia in a covered wagon.

"In Geneva my father opened a small workshop and began again to build up a trade. Other exiles came to the shop. They were feverishly preparing for the revolution. One of them greatly impressed me. He had a thin face and brilliant eyes and spoke in a loud voice. He also took cigars and didn't pay for them. My father never tried to recover the money. On a bill that I have kept as a souvenir are stamped the words *Not Paid* and the name of this customer— Vladimir Ulyanov."

The nineteenth-century French poet Auguste Barthélemy gave this advice on smoking and leadership: "It is necessary to know how to smoke so that one knows how to choose. The true smoker abstains from imitating Vesuvius. He demonstrates the requirement that for three-quarters of an hour a cigar can rest in his hand without going out." To be sure, the great figures knew when to think and when to draw.

"Tobacco is the plant that converts thoughts into dreams."

Victor Hugo

ARTISTS AND WRITERS

THE CIGARS PRODUCED IN nineteenth-century Seville provided inspiration for writers, composers, and painters. Byron and Hugo, Bizet and Ravel, Renoir and Van Dongen—all enjoyed the cigar as much as artistic creation. In the nineteenth-century Manet portrait of Stéphane Mallarmé, the poet sits pensively reviewing his work, cigar calmly in hand.

Amandine Dupin, better known as the novelist George Sand, is recognized as the first woman to smoke in public, with a "cigar that fills the solitary hours with a million gracious images." Except for Sand and other women who smoked in private, the cigar embodied mannered machismo. Perhaps it was best exemplified by Casanova, who was known to smoke on occasion. The strength of the aroma, the power of the taste, the tough texture of the wrapper all reflected his sense of adventure.

A certain drama was associated with smoking. Edward VII gave the following counsel to a young lord in his court: "Pierce the cigar with a lance and, after lighting it, wave it in the air."

Sigmund Freud, the father of psychoanalysis, always smoked a cigar as he listened to his patients relate their dreams. To this quintessential cigar smoker, the practice

of lighting up could sometimes differentiate the genders.

Like their counterparts in the previous *siglo,* writers and artists of the twentieth century were loyal to their smokes. Ernest Hemingway was devoted to his Havana-made Coronas. He presented Ava Gardner with a band as a token of their meeting. Paradoxically, Graham Greene's *Our Man in Havana* made no mention of the cigar. Virginia Woolf and her husband, Leonard, hosted the smoke-filled meetings of their literary Bloomsbury group. Pianist Artur Rubinstein, who owned a tobacco plantation in Cuba, chose his cigars as carefully as he chose his notes.

VICTORIAN VISIONS

LINKING CIGAR SMOKING with the veiled sexuality of the Victorian Age, critic Mark Alyn notes that "the cigar smoker, like the perfect lover or the bagpipe player, is a calm man, slow and sure of his performance." Mallarmé remembered that when his father opened boxes of Valles, Clays, and Upmanns, it "evoked visions of dancing girls, and I removed the bands because that is what is to be done." Prosper Merimée, who authored *Carmen,* said he was captivated by the girls who worked in the cigar factories of Seville.

SILVER SMOKE AND THE SILVER SCREEN

PRINCE AGA KHAN, the Barons Élie and Edmond de Rothschild, the banker Gérard Perèire, and the great American industrialists J. P. Morgan and Andrew Carnegie were lavish consumers of cigars. Some went through a thousand each month. Never passive smokers, they were well versed in the process of making and caring for their cigars, watching their humidors and nurturing their collections.

For a time in the twentieth century, mass manufacturing changed the way cigars were made, especially in speed and volume, and it altered the dynamics of cigar smoking as well. Still, the best smokes were the domain of wealthy industrialists, political leaders, and movie stars.

In *The Gold Rush* Charlie Chaplin gives an unforgettable performance as the little tramp who picks up a cigar butt thrown away by a millionaire, chewing it and mimicking the haughty tycoon. Audiences loved Chaplin's tweaking of the privileged class. In a poetic twist of fate, Chaplin, W. C. Fields, George Burns, and Groucho Marx—all cigar aficionados—introduced the art of the cigar to their audiences.

HOLLYWOOD

Hollywood has had a seventy-year love affair with the cigar. Coburn and Coppola smoke them; DeNiro and DeVito do too. Among the greats of the past who smoked cigars are Edward G. Robinson, John Wayne, Orson Welles . . . the list goes on. Here are a few current aficionados.

Milton Berle: "The Davidoffs are just made so well. I'm finding the domestic cigars are getting better and better. And I'm also finding there are a lot of inconsistencies with Havana cigars. But still, when it comes to my favorite, Havana wins. I'd rather smoke a figurado, Montecristo No. 2, than any cigar. I love its shape.

"When I heard about the embargo, I went to every store I could to stock up on cigars. I needed my supply to last me until this thing was over. Store after store, Dunhill's, Davidoff's.

"There I was, asking a salesman if he had any Upmanns, and he had a few left. He asked me if I'd like to sample one, and of course I agreed. I lit up and savored the smoke for a couple of puffs, but this wasn't an Upmann. I complained to the very nice salesman, who assured me it was an Upmann.

"'No, this is definitely not an Upmann.'

"Just then a little man with a moustache sitting nearby on a couch interrupted me. 'It's an Upmann,' he said.

"I got a little annoyed with this intrusion. 'Who are you?' I asked. 'I'm an expert on Upmanns, and I'm buying the cigars.'

"Then he said, 'It's an Upmann.'

"'Will you shut up? Who are you anyway?'

"He turned to me and said in a most diplomatic and assured way, 'My name is Upmann, H. Upmann. My family started the company.'"

Whoopi Goldberg prefers small cigars, even though she has been known to share a Cohiba Corona Especial with friends. Her favorites are the 80 Anniversario, a difficult-to-find Cuban Davidoff especially made for Zino Davidoff's eightieth birthday.

Gregory Hines: "I love the taste. I love the ritual. Clipping off the tip. Rolling the cigar in my fingers. Looking at the wrapper. Lighting it up. The aroma. I love that it takes a long time. It really relaxes me. Lately, I've been smoking Zinos and Davidoffs. They are beautifully made."

Lauren Hutton: "It's like an agreement you make with yourself to take the time to relax and smoke a cigar. Smoking cigars makes you feel worldly. And getting them gives you someplace to go. One of my favorites is the Dominican H. Upmann in a 41 ring size."

Jack Nicholson: "When I was making *The Last Detail*, I wanted the petty officer character I played to be a cigar smoker. So I smoked cigars while we were filming the picture. Real Cuban cigars, which, of course, are the best. The only cigar, in fact, I could get them in Canada where we shot the picture. And that started me smoking cigarettes again, until about four years ago, when I took up golf.

"I'm so nervous when I play that I found I was smoking a half a pack of cigarettes during a round. So in order to cut down, I got in the habit of lighting a cigar around the fifth hole and smoking nothing but cigars for the rest of the round. That succeeded in calming me. And now I'm down to a 12 handicap."

Arnold Schwarzenegger: "I was introduced to 'real cigars' in 1977, when I met Maria Shriver at a celebrity tennis tournament. Her dad, Sargent Shriver, gave me one after dinner at the Kennedy compound in Hyannisport. That's a big advantage in life, when your wife can't complain about your cigars. I can always say, 'Look, honey, your father wouldn't have introduced me to something that's bad.'

"I enjoy Cohibas, Punch Punch, Hoyo de Monterrey, and an occasional Romeo y Julieta or Davidoff."

TOM SELLECK'S SELECTION

Montecristo No. 2
Hoyo de Monterrey Double Corona
Punch Double Corona
Ramon Allones Gigante
Cohiba Robusto
La Gloria Cubana (U.S. made)
Davidoff Special R
Davidoff Special T
Davidoff Special Double R

GENÈVE *Davidoff* GENEVA

REEL TO REAL

THE IMAGE OF THE CIGAR in the twentieth century was, in large part, shaped by the movie industry. In 1949 U.S. cigar importers named Edward G. Robinson "Mister Cigar." That legendary screen personality advanced cigars to new heights. But whether the cigar was smoked by Robinson's gangster characters or by John Wayne's cowboys, it was a reflection of the widespread popularity of a good smoke.

In real life, however, the good guy was usually the one who lit up. It is hard to imagine Adolf Hitler calmly smoking a cigar, but his challenger, British prime minister Winston Churchill, was identified with the cigar. The prime minister was such a beloved figure that Zino Davidoff said he was willing to forgive Churchill's greatest transgression—holding the cigar between the index and middle fingers instead of between the index finger and the thumb.

In fact, hardly a photograph of Churchill exists without his trademark cigar, documenting his very real passion for smoking. After a German blitz damaged the Dunhill store, Churchill anxiously waited to learn whether his cigars had escaped harm, especially his favorite Havana Double Coronas. At another time, Field Marshal Montgomery was claiming to be in 100 percent good shape because he did not smoke or drink and got plenty of rest. Churchill shot back, "I drink a great deal, I sleep little, and I smoke cigar after cigar. That is why I am in 200 percent form."

Churchill usually smoked no more than half his cigar, but he chose all sorts of the finest Havanas, in dark tobacco, sometimes double coronas, also Lonsdales and the occasional panatela, often with a band bearing his picture. Certain Havanas were named Churchills in his honor. A constant supply of cigars was provided to him by his col-

leagues and admirers, and he sent many of his extras to the Finnish composer Sibelius.

At one time there was a plan to erect a monument to Churchill on the cliffs of Dover, a massive statue of him holding a cigar. The lit cigar ash would serve as a revolving lighthouse beacon for ships at sea. It was never built, but there are numerous statues and images of Churchill with a double corona.

In World War II cigar iconography, Churchill was not alone. There are lasting impressions of the American GI on top of a tank with a cigar in his mouth. GIs smoked cigars in movies like *The Longest Day*, where Robert Mitchum sports a panatela all the way from D-Day to V-E Day.

Rebels of the twentieth century also smoked cigars. Pancho Villa, the Mexican revolutionary and outlaw, advised his men to smoke a cigar before breakfast. Fidel Castro emerged from the Sierra Maestra mountains sporting not only a beard but a cigar. Thirty years later, his announcement that he was giving up smoking cigars caused barely a ripple. Revolutions and revolutionaries have their time.

OPPOSITE: PANCHO VILLA AND HIS COMPADRES. ABOVE: CHURCHILL WITH HIS NAMESAKE CIGAR.

AFICIONADAS

MEN AND CIGARS—that's usually the way it is. Think of great historical personages like Sigmund Freud, Victor Hugo, Mark Twain, Winston Churchill, Fidel Castro. Groucho Marx's wife told him he'd have to choose between her and his cigars. Faced with giving up his precious smokes, Marx quipped to her, "No, but we can remain good friends."

As the age of chivalry gave way to the sexual revolution, the cigar, in some ways, remained at the epicenter. It still embodied some of the sensual characteristics that it had acquired in the Victorian Age—signifying power, affluence, chivalry, stature, and machismo. While she was living with the composer Chopin, George Sand was reprimanded by the Russian nobleman W. de Lenz: "In no salon, Madame, have I ever seen a woman smoking a cigar." Women who lit up were walking a confrontational high wire. But that is slowly changing.

Though they are still a minority—about two percent of the cigar-smoking set, according to the Cigar Association of America—female puffers have gained acceptance as well as notoriety. In fact, women cigar smokers seem to be everywhere: in trendy nightspots, on the covers of magazines, and in the private and public eye.

After all, the twentieth century has been the age of suffrage and women's rights. Women have occupied key positions in the political, social, and cultural arenas and serve comfortably as company presidents and labor union leaders, as white-collar professionals and blue-collar workers. Many have started their own companies, while others occupy other nontraditional roles. True, the glass ceiling exists, but it is higher than it has ever been. So with more and more women

in boardrooms, in business, politics, and entertainment, it is only natural that increasing numbers are lighting up.

As a celebration or simply for enjoyment, many women have turned to cigar smoking and as such are riding into the final frontiers of gender segregation. Comedienne Whoopi Goldberg, actresses Demi Moore and Lauren Hutton—even the guardian of femininity, Helen Gurley Brown, has admitted to taking a puff, although she is not an aficionada. But many more women off the spotlight are also enjoying tobacco.

Women are attending cigar seminars and Big Smokes in increasing numbers. There are special ladies' only gatherings. Most who attend these informational lectures are bankers, corporate execs, realtors, and small business owners. Women are now recognized as part of the cigar-smoking lobby. Cigar smoking is as much a bonding experience for women as it has been for men. For example, when one midwestern steakhouse hosted a power dinner for businesswomen, it had a full house—Smoking Room Only. Cigar smoking is no more a "guy thing" today than golf, painting, hunting, jogging, or tennis.

Yet while cigar aficionadas may now be trendy, they are not an entirely new phenomenon. In Victorian times women were advised to choose a man as they chose a cigar. In *Gigi* Colette wrote, "Remind me to teach you how to select cigars. If a woman knows a man's preferences, including his preference in cigars, and if a man knows what a woman likes, they will be suitably armed to face one another." Catherine the Great, Annie Oakley, Greta Garbo, Marlene Dietrich, and even Bonnie Parker were all ardent smokers.

It is hard to generalize about why women are

> "A thing that has always baffled me about women is that they will saturate themselves with a pint of perfume, a pound of sachet powder, an evil-smelling lip rouge, a peculiar-smelling hair ointment and a half-dozen varieties of body oils, and then have the effrontery to complain about the aroma of a fine cigar."
>
> *Groucho Marx*

choosing to smoke, and it is just as difficult to classify women smokers demographically. But experts claim that if there is a typical aficionada, she is an affluent professional, well educated, and ranging in age from the mid-twenties to the late forties. She is a genuine connoisseur, just as interested in the fine aspects of taking a puff as in the mechanics and mystique, in everything from cutting the tip to lighting the cigar to deciding whether to remove the ring.

ELEGANT PREVENTIVE OF THE CHOLERA.

While it is clearly the shock value that attracts some female smokers, that is by no means true for all women who light up. Cultural historian Camille Paglia, herself a smoker, says women "feel they belong to the power structure in certain ways, and they are recognizably female, and they are not in any way compromising their heterosexuality or their femininity by employing the iconography of the cigar. They understand that it kind of enhances their desirability."

CIGARS IN THE WHITE HOUSE

FROM THE SMOKE-FILLED back rooms of Boston to the elegant gatherings of the powerful in Washington, cigars have always been part of the pomp and circumstance of the American political tradition.

The demise of the White House cigar may be near, but during many terms of presidential office it was held in great esteem. The White House legacy was established early. Madison and Adams smoked. Andrew Jackson and his wife, Rachel, sat in rocking chairs before a fire and enjoyed cigars. Ulysses Grant, whose campaign slogan was "A Smokin His Cigar," smoked more than twenty a day. William Howard Taft brought his humidor to the White House. Calvin Coolidge, who developed the persona of "Silent Cal," dramatically punctuated it with his cigar. Richard Nixon, although not a cigar smoker, enjoyed taking a ceremonial puff with world leaders.

More recently, Bill Clinton has comfortably adjusted to the First Lady's White House smoking ban—he has stopped lighting up. But sometimes in his office or during a briefing in official chambers, he will hold an unlit cigar, giving credibility to the statement that he "never inhaled."

Shortly after Pierre Salinger became press secretary for John Kennedy, the president called him into his office. "I need about a thousand Petit Upmanns." Salinger, a bit astonished, asked the president when he might need them. "Tomorrow morning," came the reply. "Let me know as soon as you have them. It's important."

Salinger left the Oval Office, hoping he could find the cigars. With the help of a few diplomats and some contacts at State, he was able to complete his mission. A few hours later, the U.S. embargo on Cuba was announced, but the president had his supply of Havanas.

William Styron's reminiscence of Kennedy and Nathaniel Lande's own encounter with LBJ are treasured White House recollections.

THE PRESIDENT AND HIS PARTAGAS

After the ice cream and coffee, the president passed out to the men Partagas cigars, made in Havana and encased in silver tubes. I rolled mine around between my fingers

delightedly, trying not to crack too obvious a smile. I was aware that this was a contraband item under the embargo against Cuban goods and that the embargo had been promulgated by the very man who had just pressed the cigar into my hand. Therefore, the Partagas was all the more worth preserving, at least for a while, in its protective tube, as a naughty memento, a conversation piece with a touch

of scandal. I watched as the president began to smoke with pleasure, displaying no sense of the clandestine. I palmed the Partagas into my pocket while Kennedy wasn't looking, resolved to smoke it on some special occasion, and lit up one of my Canary Island coronas. Soon afterward, however, I began feeling a certain odd, fugitive sadness I couldn't quite fathom, though it may have been only the same poignant regret that prompted me to write, later on, when I remembered the boat trip, "of irreconcilable differences, the ferocious animosity that separated Castro and Kennedy. Of all the world's leaders, the Harvard man and the Marxist from Havana were temperamentally and intellectually most alike; they probably would have taken warmly to each other had not the storm of twentieth-century history and its bizarre determinism made them into unshakable enemies."

I saw Kennedy again the following November at a crowded, elegant party one Friday night in New York.... Rose and I, entering the dinner, discovered him at the bottom of a flight of stairs looking momentarily lost and abandoned. As if arrested in an instant's solitude, he was talking to no one and pondering his cigar. . . . He asked me how the novel was coming. . . . Finally someone distracted him and he disappeared into the crowd. Sometime later, on his way out, he caught my eye and, smiling, said, "Take care."

They were words I should have spoken to him, for exactly two weeks later, on another Friday, he was dead in Dallas. I smoked the Partagas in his memory.

William Styron

H. Upmannship

It was a great evening. After a formal state dinner in the East Room, Jack Valenti, the president's press secretary, invited me to join the president and a few guests upstairs. I was a very young man and had been at the White House staging the musical *Salute to Congress,* celebrating the accomplishments of the Great Society. The show ended with a stirring epic narration taken from Thomas Wolfe's *You Can't Go Home Again.* Ferde Grofé's original score played softly in the background.

So, then, to every man his chance . . . / To every man, regardless of his birth, / His shining, golden opportunity— / To every man the right to live, / To work, to be himself, / And to become / Whatever thing his manhood and his vision / Can combine to make him— / This seeker, / Is the promise of America.

The president liked the words.

Sitting in the Lincoln bedroom with Vice President Humphrey, Gregory Peck, and Jack Valenti was an extraordinary experience indeed. Not so much for the august company as for the situation itself. The president, just getting ready to retire, was having a massage.

We sat in a circle near the president, not sure what to say or do. Then someone passed out Havanas. They were contraband H. Upmanns in medium silver tubes, something to divert and redirect our attention.

A good cigar with good company and good conversation added to what might be called a unique bonding experience. I had heard of historic backroom cigar smokers, and here I was, a nonsmoker yet.

"Those were fine words tonight, Nathaniel," the president said. "You write 'em?"

"No, sir," I replied. "It was Thomas Wolfe."

"Those cigars—they're not Cuban, are they?" The president turned, looking suspicious.

"Oh, no, sir," we all replied in unison.

"Yep, fine evening tonight," the president intoned with a Texas smile.

With that pronouncement, the president jumped off his massage table and went over to a tall Chippendale dresser, opened the top drawer, took out a few small boxes, and passed out gold cuff links with a replica of the presidential seal. He was stark naked.

All of us stood in respect, stunned but pleased by the unusual impromptu ceremony. Hopping back on his table, the president asked again, "Sure those aren't Cubans?"

"Oh, no," we again chorused, following the blue smoke curling heavenward and feeling a bit guilty.

The president returned to his back massage, occupied with reading files from folders. The evening passed into memory.

Several weeks later the president stood at the foot of the Statue of Liberty for a ceremony. A new immigration bill had just passed the Eighty-ninth Congress. LBJ concluded his speech dramatically, looking off to a distant shore.

"So, then, to every man his chance . . . to become whatever thing his manhood and his vision can combine to make him— This seeker, is the promise of America."

The president had liked those words. In fact, he'd liked them so much, he'd made them his own. I thought of that evening, the night of the cigars. H. Upmann, the president, and the cuff links. Who would believe it?

One-Upmannship indeed.

Nathaniel Lande

PUBLISHING FOR PASSION

Marvin Shanken, Editor and Publisher, Cigar Aficionado

WHEN IT DEBUTED IN 1992 with an anticipated initial circulation of 20,000, Marvin Shanken's *Cigar Aficionado* was met with a chorus of cynical hoots from the advertising and publishing community. But as the magazine escalated to a print run of 400,000 copies within four years, the hoots turned to enthusiastic hoorays.

"They said it couldn't be done," Shanken says, "but then, *they* always say that."

Cigar Aficionado finds its niche as a quality men's magazine that includes not only cigar-related subjects and ratings but features on travel, dining, the arts, and collecting. The magazine was ignited by Shanken's love of and appreciation for premium cigars.

His offices are a repository of art, wine, and cigars. Here, for every dreamer, are the good things in life, and here are some of the things Marvin Shanken loves best. On one side of his reception room is a glassed wine cellar filled with hundreds of extraordinary rare vintages, including a Margaux bottled for Thomas Jefferson. Along the crisp white walls is a stunning lineup of original Belle Epoque gold-framed posters, which lead to a series of walk-in humidors filled with five thousand cigars, including pre-embargo Havanas. Nearby is a box of Churchill's cigars, along with JFK's humidor, recently acquired at auction. It's not a bad place to spend your day, and pretty good for a man who started poor. But Marvin Shanken has always been rich with promise.

Unconventional in business but traditional in values, he has done more to accelerate the cigar business than anyone in the world today. A defender of the cigar, a Renaissance man, a hero to smokers everywhere, a product of the American Dream, he is a publisher and editor whose pages are devoted to his readers.

The idea for *Cigar Aficionado* came to him after a trip to Havana, where he was working on a story for his previous magazine, *Wine Spectator*.

"After visiting the great factories and farms, I was in tobacco heaven, and I knew I had to start a magazine about cigars," says Shanken. "I've discovered that cigar smokers have the same emotional interest and passion that wine lovers feel about a great vintage."

His vision is limited only by his imagination. And through cigar smoke, he clearly sees forever.

ABOVE: MARVIN SHANKEN'S FIRST SOLICITATION FOR SUBSCRIBERS TO HIS FLEDGLING CIGAR PUBLICATION. OPPOSITE: HEAVYWEIGHT CHAMPION JACK DEMPSEY ENJOYS A CIGAR AT A DEMOCRATIC FUNDRAISER IN 1934.

GREAT CIGAR PERSONALITIES THROUGH THE YEARS

At the Legal Seafood Restaurant in Boston, an item on the menu reads: "No cigar or pipe smoking except for **Red Auerbach**." **Honoré de Balzac** did not care for cigars, unlike some of the great characters in his novels. Colonel Chabert (in *Le Colonel Chabert,* 1852), on his return from exile, spent the first few moments of his new life purchasing cigars. **Otto von Bismarck,** the Iron Chancellor of Germany, was a cigar lover and believed that the cigar had a role in diplomacy. Legend has it that when he once gave a dying soldier his last Havana, he said, "I have never enjoyed a cigar so much as that one I never smoked." **Lord Byron** was the first poet to write an ode to the cigar, "Sublime Tobacco." It was inspired by the 1789 mutiny on the ship *Bounty* and ends with the line, "Give me a cigar!" **H. de Cabanas y Carbajal** is one of the oldest names inscribed on the registry of trademarks in Havana (1810). The same registry reads: 1827, Partagas; 1830, Mi Fama por el Orbe Vuelta, José García; 1834, Por Larranaga; 1840, El Figaro de Julian Rovera; 1844, H. Upmann; 1845, La Corona. **Casanova** was one of the first Europeans to evoke the cigar in a literary work, his *Histoire de ma vie.* He gave *cigaritos* to his colleagues and said since it didn't offend the ladies, it didn't offend him. **Bartolomé de las Casas** was the first chronicler of the discovery of the cigar and of the Spanish conquest of the New World. In his *Istoria de las Indias,* he paid tribute to the cigar: "If you smoke too much, you will become drunk as with strong wine. . . . I found this out for myself." **Sir Winston Churchill** discovered cigars during the Spanish-American War, when he was no more than twenty years old. According to historians, he smoked more than 300,000 in his lifetime. Churchill's cigar smoking played a role in his political life. During the electoral campaign of June 1945, Labour politicians rebuked him for smoking expensive cigars when the common man had to queue up just to buy a pack of cigarettes. In 1947 Lord Chorley, a Labour MP, proposed that Churchill be punished for his severe denunciations of the majority Labour leaders by being deprived of his cigars for two years. The motion was defeated in a voice vote. **Cigar,** a six-year-old Thoroughbred racehorse, tied the great Citation's record of sixteen consecutive victories in 1996. In his seventeenth race to break the record, he ran hard but lost by three and a half lengths. Close, but no . . . **Bill Clinton** celebrated the dramatic rescue of downed flyer Capt. Scott O'Grady in Bosnia by smoking a one A.M. cigar with National Security Adviser Anthony Lake on the Eisenhower balcony of the White House in May 1995. **Raoul Dufy** bartered many of his paintings for cigars. **Edward VII** of England assumed the throne after sixty years as Prince of Wales, uttering these words in Court: "Gentlemen, you may smoke." He thereby broke the ban imposed by his mother, Queen Victoria. His royal preference was the double corona, and his personal band is decorated with three white plumes. **Edward VIII,** who abdicated the throne in 1936 to marry the twice-divorced American Wallis Warfield

Simpson and was thereafter known as the Duke of Windsor, was a great cigar aficionado. **King Farouk of Egypt** was a famous cigar smoker and lover of large cigar shapes. **Sigmund Freud,** the founder of psychoanalysis, smoked continually while interpreting the dreams of his patients. Despite the advice of doctors, he was never able to do without them. **Oscar Hammerstein I,** a theatrical manager whose son was the famed Broadway lyricist, had forty-two tobacco-related patents, including one for an adjustable cigar case. When his Olympia Theater failed, taking the rest of his empire with it, he met a friend on the street and said, "I have lost all my theaters, my home, and everything else. My fortune consists of two cigars. I will share it with you." **Ernest Hemingway** was a devoted smoker of Havanas; for him, the smoke from a Havana had the importance of Proust's sugar cake. **Victor Hugo** is still known in the cigar factories of Cuba, where his works have long been favorites to read aloud. Poet Robert Desnos, upon his visit to Cuba in 1928, was delighted to discover that some of the workers knew lines of Hugo's poetry by heart. **Rudyard Kipling** placed a high value on the cigar. Referring to his daily cigar, he wrote, "If Maggie does not wish to have a rival, then I do not wish to marry Maggie." He is also the author of the celebrated sentence, "A woman is only a woman, but a good cigar is a smoke." The **Duc de la Rochefoucauld-Liancourt** is the author of the oldest-known French paean to the cigar. **Franz Liszt** always traveled with a supply of Havanas in a special three-tiered wooden case. Later in life, when he retired as a monk, he received a special papal dispensation to smoke whenever and wherever he pleased. He said, "A good Cuban cigar closes the door to the vulgarities of the world." **Amy Lowell,** poet and critic,

was a formidable woman of great talent, author of "Patterns" and "Lilacs," and scion of the famous Boston family. She was sometimes seen smoking a cigar. **José Martí,** the great Cuban patriot, was once a reader in a *fábrica.* He built a political base among tobacco workers—an alliance that continued until Castro's revolution. **Groucho Marx,** the longest-lived of the great Marx brothers, was seldom seen without his trademark cigar, though in his films they were never lit. **W. Somerset Maugham** was a devoted student of the cigar: "A good Havana is one of the best pleasures that I know. At the time when I was young and very poor, I only smoked cigars which were offered to me. I promised myself that if I ever had some money that I would savor a cigar each day after lunch and after dinner. This is the only resolution of my youth that I have kept, and the only realized ambition which has not brought disillusion." **Herman Melville** claimed that the Cuban climate gave tobacco grown there the best aroma in the world—and the Cubans the most beautiful complexions. **H. L. Mencken** began smoking cigars at sixteen at the suggestion of his father, who reasoned that the boy was going to spend the rest of his life in the family tobacco business and might as well learn how. Mencken learned to roll cigars with the best Havana leaves that his father had in his factory. A fierce defender of freedom of speech and the civil liberties of every American, Mencken believed that one should have the right to smoke a cigar whenever one pleased. **Napoleon III** was a cigar lover who received one

of the greatest gifts in cigar history: 20,000 Havanas, gold-tipped, stamped with his monogram. They were worth $50,000 at the time. **Aristotle Onassis** shared with his friend and frequent guest Winston Churchill a liking for Havanas. His yacht *Christina* was outfitted with a humidor. **Prince Rainier** of Monaco is a true connoisseur of the cigar. He has always loved the Davidoff Chateau-Margaux and also the Rafael Gonzalez Lonsdales. He is said to have told Onassis, then a business associate, that while the Greek magnate judged cigars by their length, he chose them by their band. **Sir Walter Raleigh,** if one believes the chroniclers of the year 1618, smoked a cigar on the executioner's block. His name is often linked with tobacco, particularly tobacco from Virginia. **Dan Rather** received a cigar as a gift from Castro but held on to it for a special occasion. He wanted to light it with the mujahideen in Afghanistan but couldn't because they were in war-zone blackout conditions. **Maurice Ravel** was a great lover of Havanas. He claimed that smoking cigars inspired him to compose. **Edward G. Robinson** chewed his cigars a little too far on-screen, especially in gangster movies, but offscreen he smoked them with elegance and decorum. **"Pepin" Fernandez Rodriguez,** one of the greatest cigar entrepreneurs of all and the visionary who made Romeo y Julieta into one of the greatest cigars in the world, tried to buy the Capulets' house in Verona to convert it into a cigar store. Eventually he received permission to set up a booth in front of the house, where he gave a free cigar to each visitor who wanted one. The **Rothschilds** have traditionally appreciated great cigars. Baron Élie, of the French branch, ordered two thousand of Davidoff's Chateau-Lafites every year. **Artur Rubinstein,** the famed pianist, gave out cigars banded with his own design. **Babe Ruth,** while he played for the Yankees, manufactured his own brand of perfectos called Babe Ruth. **Stendahl,** in his journal dated April 10, 1838, wrote with respect of the young businessmen of Marseilles "who earn eight or ten thousand francs a day . . . and who carry cigars in their pockets." Stendahl smoked the Toscani, manufactured in Italy. "On a cold morning in winter," he wrote, "a Toscan cigar fortifies the soul." During his time Cuban-leaf cigars made in Seville were forbidden in Italy. **Mark Twain** was a celebrated cigar smoker. On the Mississippi he very quickly learned from the poker players the difference between a Havana cigar and those from Tampa. He preferred the Havanas. **Two German spies** in World War I posed as cigar merchants and toured the British ports reporting on the presence of warships. When they ordered six hundred double coronas, it meant they had spotted six battleships; one hundred demi coronas meant a submarine. They were eventually caught and executed. **Vladimir Ilyich Ulyanov** was a cigar customer at Zino Davidoff's family tobacco shop in Switzerland who didn't pay his bills. Later, he returned to Russia as **Lenin** to lead the Bolshevik Revolution. **Queen Victoria** hated cigars and forbade smoking in her presence or by her entourage. She reinforced the stiff edicts of her predecessor James I, one of the fiercest nemeses of tobacco. **Jack Warner,** the famed head of Warner Bros., preferred light tobacco. He smoked a panatela of Hoyo de Monterrey on the day he held, at the Palm Beach casino in Cannes, his famous *banco* of a hundred million francs. To remember the run, he preserved the cigar in a silver box. **John Wayne** was a great Hollywood cigar smoker. For his Westerns he had a special cigar made, one longer than usual. **Orson Welles** always demanded that one open a cigar box before buying it. He never complained about his purchases, and his favorites were the Montecristo and Por Larranaga. **Darryl F. Zanuck,** the famous film producer and connoisseur of the cigar, owned interests in the plantations of the Vuelta Abajo. He never bought fewer than five thousand cigars at a time.

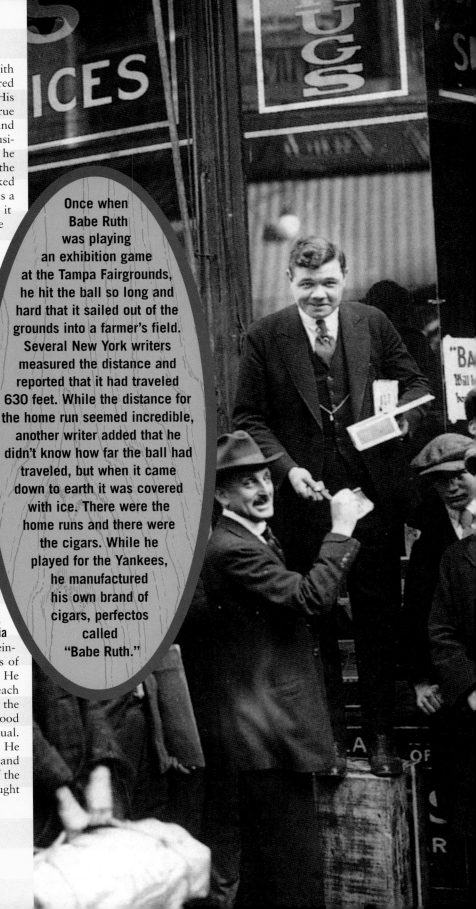

Once when Babe Ruth was playing an exhibition game at the Tampa Fairgrounds, he hit the ball so long and hard that it sailed out of the grounds into a farmer's field. Several New York writers measured the distance and reported that it had traveled 630 feet. While the distance for the home run seemed incredible, another writer added that he didn't know how far the ball had traveled, but when it came down to earth it was covered with ice. There were the home runs and there were the cigars. While he played for the Yankees, he manufactured his own brand of cigars, perfectos called "Babe Ruth."

ANA - J. CUESTA - HABANA - J. CUESTA - HABANA - J. CUESTA - HABANA - J. CUESTA - HABANA

The Connoisseur's Companion

3

6

ENJOYING YOUR CIGAR

NURTURING A LOVE of cigars is the key to getting the most out of the smoking experience. Enjoy the experience of choosing your cigar and the ceremony of lighting it, as well as the smoking of it. There will always be new and different cigars to smoke and plenty of room to expand your knowledge and refine your taste. It's an ongoing process that never really ends.

HOW TO JUDGE A GOOD CIGAR

ALTHOUGH FINDING THE CIGAR that best pleases your palate is a subjective endeavor, there are nonetheless objective standards to which all fine cigars can be held. The three criteria for appreciating a fine cigar are similar to those applied to fine wines: flavor, body, and aroma.

Flavor. Taste can discern four basic categories: sweet, bitter, salty, and acid. Bitter and sweet are the easiest to detect, the others a bit more difficult, and they are subjective. Connoisseurs use terms like *fruity, nutty,* and *herbal, spicy,* and *floral,* to refer to the combination and balance of tastes. They identify such flavor notes as pepper, wood, nut, cream, coffee, nutmeg, cinnamon, citrus, cedar, chocolate, and leather. The classifications mild, medium, and full refer to the degree of flavor.

Body. The *body* of the smoke refers to the strength of the tobacco, its overall effect on the smoker. Its degrees are light, medium, and heavy.

Aroma. The *aroma* of a cigar is one that pleases you.

Learning to discern the differences in these three categories is the first step on the road from aficionado to connoisseur. To gain some perspective on the finer points of selecting a good cigar, we drew on the expertise of Richard DiMeola of Consolidated Cigar, whose guidelines offer considered criteria for the cigar smoker.

"There are two crucial elements in making a fine, all-natural-tobacco, long-filled, handmade cigar: *quality tobacco* and *quality construction,*" DiMeola says. "Beyond that, the single most important factor for distinguishing a fine cigar is *consistency*, and that is key. The sports world provides many examples. Basketball players are measured by accuracy and consistency. Par golfers are judged by consistency. Baseball players are valuable because of consistency. A standard of performance, time after time, is a measure of excellence.

"Any producer of premium cigars can make an occasional smooth-burning, rich-tasting product. But a truly excellent maker will develop a way to do it every time."

Assessing the quality of a brand takes some time, DiMeola points out. You can't simply smoke one cigar, remark on its quality, then immediately apply that measure of excellence to the entire brand. If a cigar producer makes

a hundred out of a hundred great cigars, then it probably has achieved world-class status. But that's a lot of cigars to smoke in order to make a final assessment; a more practical gauge is a box of twenty-five. The best place to start is by considering the cigar's appearance.

Before buying a box, take the measure of the cigar. Any good merchant will allow you to open it and examine the cigars. Make sure they're supple and elastic, that their wrappers are in good shape, that their aroma is pleasant. Make sure your tobacconist has kept them properly. Then you'll be able to enjoy them fully.

Always buy from a respected merchant. Trust his advice, then make your own choice.

OSCAR BORUCHIN'S TOP TEN

Oscar Boruchin, president of the stunning Mike's Cigars of Miami Beach, is an important force in cigar retailing. Mike's Cigars, founded by Michael Mersel, now in his eighties and still a consultant to the business, has established a large mail-order operation. Boruchin, who came from Cuba thirty years ago, has created several brands including Bauza and Licenciados, both made in the Dominican Republic.

1. **Arturo Fuente Opus X:** "Full-bodied, solid manufacturing, a perfect draw."
2. **Partagas 150 Anniversary:** "A wonderful, medium-bodied taste with a very smooth draw."
3. **Dominican Montecristo No. 2:** "Medium body with a nice woody finish."
4. **Arturo Fuente Don Carlos Robusto:** "A nice peppery flavor."
5. **Licenciados Toro:** "Medium body with all kinds of flavors. I smoke it down till it burns my fingers."
6. **La Gloria Cubana Torpedo:** "Not as great as it used to be three years ago, but still an excellent cigar."
7. **Fonseca 2-2 Maduro:** "A mild to medium smoke with lots of spice. Burns beautifully like any MATASA product."
8. **Bauza Robusto:** "Like anything Fuente makes, you can take it to the bank. It has a sweet woody note."
9. **Macanudo Vintage No. 4:** "It has the great taste of aged tobacco, mild with beautiful construction."
10. **Dominican Partagas No. 1:** "A very smooth, medium to rich smoke."

ON CONSTRUCTION

THE CIGAR'S APPEARANCE is an important indicator of care and craftsmanship. The cigar should look good and feel smooth when you roll it in your fingers. The color of the different cigars in each box should be consistent from one to the next; if they are not, then the manufacturer did not do his color selecting properly. Wrappers, even from the same crop, can vary over twenty or thirty shades of color. Variation in color is not bad in itself, but the manufacturer who pays attention to detail makes sure that, in a given box, all the color shades are similar.

The wrapper should be smooth with a slight shine, no blemishes or rough stems, its leaves all spiraling in the same direction. The cigar should not be too dry or too firm. (Note: Cigars that come in tubes are convenient to carry around, but they tend to dry out faster, since the tubes are not totally airtight.)

> **"A good cigar closes the door to the vulgarities of life."**
> *Franz Liszt*

Give your cigar a gentle squeeze. It should be spongy to the touch and resilient enough to hold its shape where you have pressed your finger to it. Beware of any soft or hard spots that are inconsistent with the cigar as a whole; this is an indication of poor construction. Take a whiff of its rich aroma; if there isn't any, it's not a great cigar.

While *draw* and *burn* are the most important factors affected by construction, the aesthetics of construction can provide early warning signs regarding quality, taste, and aroma. Is it reasonable to assume that a company that places little importance on aesthetics places *any* importance on quality? Pride goes a long way toward ensuring a premium product, and a beautifully constructed cigar unquestionably enhances the smoker's experience. Think

about it: Does a fine wine taste better from a paper cup or from a beautiful crystal glass?

Construction is always the most essential factor. You can use the best, most expensive tobacco made by the most creative and knowledgeable blenders, but if the cigar is not constructed properly, the tobacco's intrinsic quality will never be brought home to the smoker.

If a cigar is loosely rolled, or constructed with an inadequate number of filler leaves, it will draw very easily. While that is often considered a benefit, a too-easy draw is offset by hot-burning harshness and air pockets that cause a fast burn.

If a cigar is tightly rolled, it will be difficult and sometimes even impossible to draw. This is a common complaint of premium-cigar smokers. A hard-to-draw cigar gives a much lower volume of smoke, with less taste and aroma.

While taste and aroma are important attributes for the consistently well constructed cigar, there are other indicators as well. When a cigar is properly lit, it should burn evenly all the way down. An uneven burn is a sign of an improper roll. The ash should be relatively firm, remaining intact for an inch or more without difficulty (with the exception of small ring-gauge cigars). A falling ash is not necessarily a sign of a poorly constructed cigar, but if your cigar develops a firm, even ash while you're smoking, it's an indication that it is well made.

A cigar should have good mouth feel. While it is never really recommended to chew the end, the cigar should feel firm and resilient in the mouth. If the cigar is soft, it's another sign of poor construction. It won't feel good either, and you won't enjoy it.

ABSOLUTE UNIFORMITY AND CONSISTENCY OF COLOR AND CONSTRUCTION ARE THE HALLMARKS OF A FINE HAND-ROLLED CIGAR, LIKE THESE MADE BY DAVIDOFF.

ON TOBACCO

WHEN CONSIDERING THE QUALITY of a good cigar, it's only natural to think first about the tobacco that goes into it. But too often that's the only thing considered. For that reason, we put *construction* first in this inquiry. But certainly *tobacco* is of great importance. When inferior-quality filler is used, the cigar will produce a harsh, rough, musty taste with an unpleasant, penetrating aroma.

Here again, consistency is of critical importance. To deliver good taste and aroma, a producer must be able to ensure a constant supply of the same tobaccos that make up his distinctive blends from year to year. Since crop yields vary constantly, the maker must be able to buy a sufficiently large stock of a particular leaf when the availability presents itself, in order to protect against short supply due to drought, heavy rains, too much or too little sunshine, and political upheaval. Unless a manufacturer has the resources for quality tobaccos, the taste and aroma of his cigars will vary from year to year. Random leaves make

a uniform blend impossible. Consequently, significant resources are required for quality and consistency.

With experience, a manufacturer gains the expertise to know good tobacco from bad. The best tobacco men today have loved and appreciated tobacco for decades. They travel the world buying leaf stock for their companies, returning to their particular trusted farmers year after year.

Not only must the tobacco be superior, it's imperative that it be properly processed. All the elements—filler, binder, and wrapper—must complete the entire fermentation process before they are ready to be rolled.

If you experience harshness or bitterness in a cigar or find it goes out easily, chances are the leaf has not been

OPPOSITE: **A HISTORICAL ALLONES LABEL.** ABOVE: **ORIGINAL ART FOR A CUBAN CIGAR LABEL FEATURES A TOBACCO PLANT IN THE FOREGROUND.**

HOW MUCH OF YOUR CIGAR'S TASTE COMES FROM ITS WRAPPER?

Some experts reply authoritatively that it's 60 percent, some more, some less. But the real answer to this and other important questions about flavor is not so simple.

"It really depends on what point in the smoke you're talking about. Even before you light up, there is a taste sensation, and that is a hundred percent wrapper. You might very well like a maduro cigar, but you might be put off by the initial spiciness from its wrapper. The first taste sensation of a maduro is strong. Although you might really end up liking the cigar, a lot of people never give it a chance. It takes time and a cultivated taste.

"Once the cigar is in progress, the taste of the filler starts to blend in. The binder is a special tobacco that shouldn't interfere with the taste of the wrapper or filler. Cigar makers have experimented to find a binder that complements the other two parts of their cigar.

"The cigar changes over its smoking time. In the first half, the length of the cigar itself and the tobacco inside acts as a filter, giving a very clean smoke. Then the tar builds and starts to produce a more powerful aroma and taste. I never smoke the second half of a cigar. A lot of people smoke it down, saying it keeps getting better. Not in my opinion."

Lew Rothman

fully fermented and aged. If this happens with a few cigars in your box but not all of them, the manufacturer is not consistent in his use of tobaccos. If it happens with a majority of them, he is not making the investment in fully aged leaf and is using tobacco before its time. No amount of aging or maturing in the box will solve the problem of unfermented tobacco. Cigar tobacco, like wine, ages and gains new complexity with time. (For more on fermentation, see Chapter 2, page 30.)

Whenever you smoke cigars from one box, see if you can determine any significant variation in taste and aroma. But remember, a cigar will taste different depending on when it's smoked: morning or evening, after a meal, with coffee or cognac, indoors or outdoors. Slight variations are acceptable. It's the wide swing in quality and taste that you must watch for. Remember, the worst cigar in a box costs the same as the best one. You're entitled to assured value for your investment.

LIONEL MELENDI'S TOP TEN

Lionel Melendi and his son Ron represent the third and fourth generations of a family with Cuban roots in the cigar tradition. Since 1963 their fine shop, De La Concha, has stood at 1390 Avenue of the Americas in New York City. Lionel's father, José, a cigar manufacturer, came to New York from Cuba in 1924 to ply his trade; his grandfather was a veguero in the Vuelta Abajo.

1. **Cuban Montecristo No. 2:** "Full-flavored but not heavy; an extremely well made torpedo shape."
2. **Arturo Fuente Opus X Double Corona:** "A nice colorado wrapper; one of the few hundred-percent Dominican *puros*."
3. **Arturo Fuente Don Carlos Grand Reserve Robusto:** "A full-bodied Cuban-style blend with excellent craftsmanship."
4. **Bolivar Belicoso Fino (torpedo):** "Great tobacco taste, good body, outstanding workmanship."
5. **Dominican Montecristo Churchill:** "A mild smoke for a change of pace."
6. **Puros Indios Piramide No. 2:** "Made in Honduras, medium strength with an Ecuadoran wrapper that has a nice oily texture; burns very well with a solid white ash."
7. **Avo Belicoso:** "A distinctive peppery taste, medium strength, and consistently good."
8. **Cohiba Esplendido:** "When they're running, they're one of the best anywhere; the Cubans make excellent marble heads."
9. **Ashton Double Magnum:** "Another mild change-of-pace smoke made by Fuente, good after a light dinner. The individual cedar wrapping gives it a nice taste."
10. **Don Lino Havana Reserve Churchill:** "A medium-strength Honduran, fine flavor and very well made."

ON PRICE

THE BIGGEST COST COMPONENT of a fine cigar is the tobacco. Elaborate presentation and packaging, however, can add greatly to the overall cost. Individual aluminum or glass tubes, polished and beveled cedar and mahogany boxes, special gift selections of five or ten cigars—all significantly increase the price of an individual cigar.

Often prices vary greatly. Some cigars cost ten times more than others of the same size. It's a smoker's dilemma to judge their relative worth. Sometimes the price of an object influences us, prompting us to assume that if it costs more, it must be better. A high price alone does not guarantee a good cigar. You should smoke at least ten cigars from a brand in order to determine its consistency. Handmade cigars are subject to the same idiosyncrasies as other such products.

So when considering how much you're prepared to pay for a cigar, be a smart smoker. Whatever you pay in your pursuit of the perfect smoke, use your own criteria to determine just how good a cigar is. It's a matter of personal choice and taste.

SIZES AND SHAPES

THE WORLD'S FINEST CIGARS vary in size from about a 9 × 64 (which is one inch *wide*) down to approximately 4 × 30. The first number refers to the cigar's length, in inches; the second is its ring gauge, or the thickness of the cigar, measured in sixty-fourths of an inch. The world's largest commercially available cigar is a Santa Clara Magnum, which is 19½ inches long, with a 66 ring gauge. It appears in *The Guinness Book of World Records*.

Most cigar smokers gravitate to a particular size, so when considering the quality and consistency of taste and aroma of a cigar, your sense of comparability can be confused and it will be difficult to judge fairly unless you're smoking the size you're accustomed to. In other words, the same cigar blends in different sizes taste different, sometimes vastly different, because of the different ring sizes and lengths. A big ring gauge, 50 or 52, produces an immense volume of smoke compared with a 28, 36, or even a 42 ring.

Naturally, taste and aroma are strongly influenced by size as well. Generally, the larger the cigar, the more full-flavored and less harsh and hot-burning it is. Larger ring-gauge cigars tend to draw more slowly and yield a bigger volume of cooler, rounder, and less bitter smoke, but they tend to have less flavor. The thinner cigar has a harder draw. It is sometimes harsher and hotter-burning. One reason is that in a thinner cigar there simply isn't enough width to blend enough different types of tobacco to produce a subtle, smooth smoke.

To a lesser extent, length also influences taste. For example, the 7-inch cigar, when smoked an inch or so, will taste a little different from one that is actually 5½ inches.

Thus, if a manufacturer excels at making a great cigar at 6½ × 42 ring, it does not necessarily follow that the same brand in other sizes will be as good or as consistent. You'll have to try a box of each. In the

THE EXOTIC CULEBRA.

final analysis, choose the size of your cigar according to what's comfortable and aesthetically pleasing to you. But always bear in mind: Size affects taste.

Through the history of the cigar, a thousand different sizes and shapes have been made in the *fábricas* of Havana. Today there are forty-two classic *vitolas de galera*—Cuban factory names—each indicating a different cigar. Traditionally, there are about thirty basic shapes. Beginning on page 174 you will find an illustrated guide to each of these sizes and shapes and a listing of the brands that produce cigars of that size.

Here are the terms commonly used to describe different sizes.

CLASSIC SIZES with standard shape, a square-cut foot and rounded head:

Churchill: Named in honor of the great British statesman; the traditional size is 7 × 48 or 49.

Corona: The classic shape, with a ring gauge of 42 (about ⅔ of an inch) and a length of 5½ inches.

Corona gorda: A "long robusto" format with measurements of 5⅝ × 46.

Double corona: A large cigar with dimensions of 7½ to 8 inches × 49 to 52.

Petit corona: A smaller cigar, 4½ inches long × 40 to 42 ring gauge.

Lonsdale: 6¼ to 6½ inches × 42 to 44; another classic shape that bears the name of the British aristocrat who first smoked it.

Panatela: 5 to 7½ inches × 33 to 38; a longer and thinner cigar that was popular in the 1960s and 1970s.

Robusto: A "short Churchill" format that is growing in popularity in the 1990s; traditionally 5 to 5½ inches × 50.

RIGHT: EL REY DEL MUNDO OFFERS A SUPERIOR SELECTION OF SHAPES AND SIZES, INCLUDING THE TORPEDO-SHAPED FLOR DE LLANEZA AND A PYRAMID (LEFT AND SECOND FROM LEFT). OPPOSITE: CIGARS FROM DON DIEGO RANGE FROM MADURO (FOURTH FROM LEFT) TO CLARO CLARO (SECOND FROM LEFT), WITH SELECTIONS IN BETWEEN.

SHAPED CIGARS (or *figurados*) Those whose body is some other shape besides a straight cylinder with parallel sides reaching its rounded head:

Belicoso: Traditionally a shorter version of the pyramid, 5 to 5½ inches long × 50 or less, belicosos are now often simply coronas or coronas gordas with tapered heads.

Culebra: The most exotic of all cigar shapes, it is really three panatelas of about 5 × 38 size braided together.

Diademas: Another old-time favorite, it is essentially a large torpedo, at least 8 inches long × 40 at the head and 52 to 54 or more at the foot.

Perfecto: A shape that was popular in the nineteenth and early twentieth centuries. Cartoons of the era often show tycoons smoking them. The cigar is fatter in the middle, closed at its head, and tapered or closed at its foot, with a length of 4½ to 5 inches × 38.

Ideales: Longer versions of the perfecto shape, up to about 6½ inches long.

Pyramid: Tapered evenly from the foot to the head, it has a length of 6 to 7 inches and a ring gauge of about 40 near the head and about 52 to 54 at the foot. Rare in today's market, it is really a marvel of cigar-rolling handiwork.

Torpedo: Similar to the pyramid except it has a closed foot.

COLOR CHART

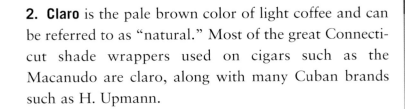

THE COLOR OF A CIGAR'S wrapper, the *capa*, is generally the key to its flavor. The darker the wrapper, the more full-bodied and sweeter a cigar is likely to be, although the true determinant is the color of the filler.

A few important variables affect the final flavor and quality of wrapper leaves: their location on the plant; when they are harvested; and how they are fermented or dried. The longer a leaf stays on the plant and the more sunlight it receives, the darker it will be. As in the production of wine, where the longer the grape is on the vine, the sweeter it is likely to be; extra exposure to sunlight produces a leaf with more oil and sugar content.

Although scores of shades are used in the subtle color-gradation process at the *fábrica*, the following seven general categories are the accepted norm among experts.

1. Double claro (or claro claro), also known as *candela*, is greenish brown and very mild with very little oil. Before the leaf reaches maturity, it is picked and then dried very rapidly, often with help from a fire. In the past this color was very popular in the United States, which is why it is also referred to as American Market Selection (AMS). More recently, however, the U.S. market has embraced a wider variety of colors.

2. Claro is the pale brown color of light coffee and can be referred to as "natural." Most of the great Connecticut shade wrappers used on cigars such as the Macanudo are claro, along with many Cuban brands such as H. Upmann.

3. Colorado claro is a tawny medium brown, also called "natural." Claros are sun-grown, many of them in Cameroon, for cigars like the Dominican Partagas.

4. Colorado is aromatic and reddish brown and embraces rich-flavored, well-matured cigars. This and other brown wrappers are also known as English Market Selection (EMS), although they have become equally popular in the United States.

5. Colorado maduro is dark brown and medium strength, a little more aromatic than the maduro, with a rich flavor. It is found on many premium cigars from Honduras.

6. Maduro is a very dark and rich brown, a color for seasoned and experienced smokers. It offers less aroma and more flavor than the colorado maduro. It is sometimes considered a traditional Cuban color and is also referred to as Spanish Market Selection (SMS).

7. Oscuro is almost black in color and very strong, with little bouquet. These sun-grown wrappers are not in demand today and are produced in small quantity in Nicaragua, Brazil, Mexico, as well as Connecticut (the broadleaf as opposed to the shade).

Smoker's Bill of Rights
by Gay Talese

While the aroma of superior smoke has historically circulated in high circles—hovering over Winston Churchill's library, over Dr. Sigmund Freud's couch, and in the closet of President Clinton's Oval Office (where he was rumored to have exhaled on a Macanudo Portofino while his wife met with male-bashers and antinicotine lobbyists at the international women's conference in Beijing)—citizens such as myself with a fondness for excellent cigars are encountering increasing amounts of hostility whenever we attempt to light up after dinner in our neighborhood restaurants and in the homes of our otherwise liberal and pro-choice friends in New York and elsewhere in this supposedly democratic republic.

I am even lawfully prohibited from smoking outdoors in the vast and virtually incombustible steel-and-concrete stadiums owned by Major League corporations, whose ineffective control over their own drug-abusing, steroid-scarred athletes is no secret to most locker room intimates. And I cite this not out of rancor toward top athletes, whose high salaries I think blind us to their relatively brief and injury-prone careers of servitude in a subculture of franchised inhumanity, but rather to emphasize the absurdity of banning smoking in open areas like Yankee Stadium, when the real health danger to society dwells beyond the grandstands within the urban blight and poverty that spawns high quotas of drug-dependent criminals that I fear I'll face some evening while walking my dogs and my cigar in the carcinogenic streets that are becoming my last refuge—and even there my smoking prompts disapproving stares from priggish joggers, and drunken doormen, and cruising cokeheads, whose wavering olfactory sensibilities are never predictably cigar-friendly.

Indeed, as I stroll through the night, I see my burning cigar clenched between my teeth as my lodestar, my lance, my badge of courage in a badgering world that seeks to eradicate all vestiges of male pleasure and pride, returning us perhaps to the more temperate times of the early twentieth-century American mistress of discipline, Ms. Carry Nation, the Bible-quoting, hatchet-wielding, saloon-smashing antinicotine priestess who helped to inspire the passage of the national Prohibition law of 1920. Earlier this year the "21" Club in New York revealed that it was prohibiting smoking of every kind in its dining area, surrendering to the lawmakers who had earlier surrendered to the antismoking lobbyists that had probably included a number of disenchanted and divorced second wives.

Lighted cigars at the dinner table are similarly no longer allowed in most steakhouses and private clubs in New York and around the nation that were once the domain of men, although such places often retain humidors and (like "21") allow cigar smoking in the lounge or bar or other isolated areas—but this means, of course, that the noble fraternity of cigar aficionados must mingle with commoners who indulge in cigarettes.

Exchanging cigars is a male courtship ritual, a peace offering between pals who've had a falling out, a potency totem bestowed by new fathers, an indication of altruism by doddering old patriarchs. The cigar can also represent an eleventh digit on the hands of men, giving a finger to the contemporary codes of correctness, and it can as well be a tribute to a handmade craft that brings honor to tobacco leaves that are born of a special soil and sun and that follow a slow-aged growth toward binding ties and lasting memories.

Whenever I go out in the evening, I carry in my pocket at least one extra cigar, not only because I welcome co-conspirators but because I think that a cigar smoker who has not brought provisions for a companion is, to put it mildly, small-minded and miserly and never to be fully trusted.

Whenever I try to analyze the contemporary American trends that have induced our present-day government to become our governess—a meddlesome nanny who scolds us not only for smoking but for making passes at girls who wear glasses, and for various other transgressions against myriad special interest groups' Storm Troopers of Virtue—I am reminded of a Joyce Carol Oates comment that I read a few years ago and that I quote often: "When America is not fighting a war, the puritanical desire to punish people has to be let out at home." This is a most perceptive observation in my view, for the propensity for punishment remains constant in our tradition, despite whatever influences are infused through immigration and diversity.

Angry at being ostracized from most restaurants and public places, and having the money and the will to counterattack, cigar advocates are now investing in speakeasies for smokers. However, in recent months there are indications of change. A small group of resolute males, they are banding together to take back the night.

SMOKING YOUR CIGAR

A CIGAR CAN PROVIDE a great deal of enjoyment, and it should not be rushed. Allow yourself time to appreciate the whole experience, from choosing and cutting to lighting and smoking.

The pleasurable ritual of smoking a cigar begins with cutting it. Most modern experts agree that the best way to cut the head of your cigar is with a guillotine-type cutter. Never use your teeth, a knife, or your fingernail. The cut should be careful, clean, and crisp, without any damage to the cap. Be sure to leave enough of the cap, about an eighth of an inch or more, so that the wrapper does not unravel. Make a hole big enough to provide a volume of smoke. The old-fashioned lance method (piercing) and V-shaped cutters are not recommended because the openings they make don't deliver the optimum volume of smoke and can become clogged.

In offering his essential advice on smoking technique and etiquette, Zino Davidoff was against piercing the cigar, even though Alfred Dunhill recommended otherwise. Piercing was apparently common among British aficionados, including Edward VII. While most "experts" recommend cutting a hole in the end of the cigar just a bit

narrower than its full diameter—that is, leaving a fraction of an inch of the cap so the wrapper doesn't come apart—Zino preferred a much smaller hole. His advice on cutting: "The opening should be small, reasonable, in proportion to the cigar, and made so that an appropriate amount of smoke will be produced. The opening ought to be clean."

Lighting a cigar is a ritual with plenty of potential for theatricality. It can often be a moment of excitement, the crescendo of anticipation, especially if it is your after-dinner cigar or that special double corona you've been saving for so long.

As with all cigar-related matters, the point is to have fun and suit yourself. But you should also follow a few rules of practicality. The first is to light the cigar with an odorless flame from a butane lighter or wooden match. Hold the foot of the cigar close to the flame, about a quarter-inch away, rotating the cigar until it's evenly charred. This is called "toasting." Only then, still without the flame touching the foot, puff gently, making sure the cigar is evenly lit. Blow on the end if you like, checking for an even glow.

There is a range of opinions about whether to remove the cigar band. Arthur Schlesinger, Jr., the great Harvard historian and adviser to President Kennedy, likes to tell an anecdote about a dinner that took place at the house of Alfred Knopf, the publisher: "At the end of the dinner, the great Knopf collection of cigars was produced. We were all puffing away, and I noticed that [Artur] Rubinstein had not removed the band from his cigar, which I had always been taught to do before you start smoking. I said to him,

'Mr. Rubinstein, I know you're a great connoisseur of cigars, but I'm struck by the fact that you have not removed the band from your cigar. Is that your practice?' He replied, 'Every time that you drink a glass of wine, do you soak the label off the bottle?' So thereafter I've never bothered to remove the band from the cigar." The final word seems to be, if you're going to do it, wait until the cigar has heated a bit, and remove it carefully without causing damage to your wrapper.

There are various ways to smoke a cigar. An individual's preference will determine how much smoke is drawn into the mouth, and how often. Some people like to savor small puffs, while others like to take long, steady draws that fill their mouths with the cigar's flavor. Most connoisseurs take about a puff a minute, holding the smoke in, swirling it in their mouths, enjoying it. How long you keep the smoke in your mouth is less important than how slowly you exhale. By exhaling slowly, you allow your palate to discover fully the cigar's flavor. Like a glass of fine wine, a superior cigar is meant to be luxuriously savored. Just remember that smoking too quickly will cause the cigar to burn hot, while not drawing on it often enough will allow it to burn out.

Another captivating question is how much of the cigar to smoke. Most connoisseurs will recommend no more than half to three-quarters, but most aficionados also have their preference. After you enjoy its beautiful, rounded, mellow flavor, a great cigar is hard to relinquish.

A good corona should take about fifty minutes to burn down to the band. At this point the flavor has intensified and the smoke has become hotter. A cigar will go out on its own. Don't grind it out in an ashtray; it doesn't dignify the cigar.

There's a widespread prohibition against chomping or chewing a cigar or even holding it in the mouth for the entire length of the smoke. But suit yourself; many of the ultimate *conocedores,* Havana's cigar makers, have done it for years.

If your cigar goes out, simply relight it by toasting the charred end. It's not always necessary to puff on it; it should reignite easily on its own.

Cigars at Various Times of Day

Whether different cigars are suitable for different times of day is again a matter of preference. Usually an aficionado will smoke small, mild cigars during the day before enjoying a large, rich cigar in the evening. Smaller cigars don't require as big a time commitment. In the evening, when one usually has more time, a larger cigar is more easily managed. As for strength, if you start the day with a rich cigar, you may not appreciate later cigars, full and mild, because the palate has already been given the maximum amount of flavor it can receive.

Cigars and Beverages

A wide array of beverages can complement cigars. Cognac, a traditional companion, can add greatly to the smoking experience. Single malt Scotches, whiskeys, ports, Armagnacs, brandies, and finely crafted ales, porters, and lagers can also work well. Some nonalcoholic drinks pair well with cigars, including fine coffees (cappuccinos and espressos) and, surprisingly enough, a quality root beer. Experiment with different drinks while smoking, and decide what's most enjoyable to you.

A FEW FINAL WORDS ON CHOOSING YOUR CIGAR

LIKE ANY OF LIFE'S great pleasures—eating, drinking, smoking—the final word on cigars is, to each his own. Experts might make general pronouncements—for example, that a certain size or strength must be smoked at a certain time of day: a mild cigar in the morning, a medium one after lunch, a stronger one after dinner. Some even say that people with round faces should smoke short cigars, while those with long faces should smoke longer, thinner cigars. But that is truly a matter of taste and appearance.

The great Zino Davidoff offered the last word on choosing a cigar: "What is most important is to be sure of your taste. You can understand now why my response to the usual question, 'Monsieur Davidoff, what do you suggest?' is always so evasive. After all, you select according to color, shape, brand name, and eventually you will be attracted to one or two cigars that seem right.

"If you are a beginner or an occasional smoker, you will probably stay with the fine cigars, the light ones—a panatela for example. Later, you might want to make the acquaintance of heavier cigars, thicker and longer ones. If you smoke too much already, you should not choose a cigar of more than four inches. If you are a man who smokes one cigar a day (or two), a Havana of five inches (a corona, perhaps) is perfect. If you are very sensitive to smoke, you should stay with light cigars. If you are a heavy smoker and your taste buds are already conditioned, you can choose a maduro—heavy, fragrant, and musky.

"In the midst of all these *ifs* is one sure thing: Whatever your tastes, your habits, your needs, there is a cigar that will be right and in harmony with your mood."

OPPOSITE: A SAMPLE LABEL FROM THE AMERICAN LITHOGRAPHIC COMPANY'S CATALOG DISPLAYS A NUMBER FOR INVENTORY PURPOSES.

The Gentle Art of Smoking

by Alfred H. Dunhill

On Offering and Choosing a Cigar

Boxes should be opened carefully with a special blunt-bladed tool that cannot damage the cigars. Penknives are dangerous for this purpose. Cigars in bundles should be lifted from and returned to their boxes by means of the paper encircling the bundle, or when placed flat in a row, they should be taken out individually by pressing lightly on the rounded head, thus raising the opposite end. The amateur who attempts to lift them straight from the box with finger and thumb is likely to damage the wrapper.

The only sure test for a cigar is to smoke it, but experience makes it possible to conjecture what it is one is about to smoke. Although the wrapper should be smooth, firm, without prominent veins, and neatly finished at the head, it is only one part of the cigar. Its paleness does not necessarily mean that the filler is mild also, although, as a general rule, darker leaf always tends to be stronger. A few light spots (sometimes caused on the growing wrapper leaf by dew that has been dried in the sun) are of no consequence, and there is little to be learned from the popular practice of sniffing at the cigar, or of placing it close to the ear where even gentle pressure on an immature cigar will produce a faint crackle. The novice who wants to enjoy a cigar should select one that is not too big—a half corona size is suggested—and after examining the wrapper, the only other test is to press it gently with the fingers. It should feel even and firm throughout its whole length; if it feels soft, it is probably immature or badly filled; a brittle crackling is an obvious sign of dryness.

On Preparation

After pressing the band lightly with the fingers and thumb all the way round, it should be torn off carefully so that the wrapper is not damaged.

Although there are various ways of piercing the butt end, some of them may damage the wrapper and produce an unsatisfactory aperture. Much depends on the condition of the cigar. In the United States it is customary to bite off the end of "green" (or fresh) cigars. When handling mature cigars, some smokers crack open the end by squeezing it between finger and thumb, but unless the cigar is in excellent condition and the butt perfectly made, this can be disastrous. Many prefer to use a cigar pierce and take care to tap out any broken fragments of leaf; although, by exposing the minimum amount of filler, this method helps the wrapper to keep tobacco tar away from the tongue; the smoke and moisture concentrate in one narrow passage and may result in a bad draw.

Perhaps the most satisfactory method is a clean V-shaped cut made by a cigar cutter, because this ensures the removal of broken leaf and provides a passage for the smoke that does not concentrate all of it upon a small area of the tongue. It is unwise to blow through a cigar in order to remove particles of broken leaf because this injects moisture from the breath. The top of a pointed shape should be removed with a straight cutter or turned against the blade of a sharp knife and cut straight across. Some experts like to prepare cigars of every shape in the same way.

The broad flame of a match or spill is the most satisfactory for lighting, and this should be done carefully and without hurry. Some smokers prefer to hold the tip in the flame until it glows evenly and then gently to draw in enough smoke to fill only the cigar. If this is expelled through the cigar, no smoke made harsh by lighting can spoil the palate. Whatever method of preparation may be preferred, there is no doubt that careful lighting and slow smoking are the only ways to ensure that the cigar burns evenly; if it does not, the only remedy is to smoke as slowly as possible until the shape of the ash becomes uniform. The retention of the ash helps to keep the smoke cool, but although it should not flake, the length of the ash will depend on the cutting of the filler and not necessarily on its quality. White ash does not denote the best cigars, for Havanas produce an ash that is steel-gray in color.

A cigar in good condition should not go out during smoking. If, however, relighting is necessary, it is advisable to rub off the charred end with a match until it is level and then, as the flame is applied, to draw very gently in the way that has already been suggested. This will ensure that rank fumes contaminate the palate and the rest of the cigar as little as possible.

The Care and Keeping of Cigars

Choice and expensive cigars, which are made with such skill and labor, require far more attention than they often receive. On account of the sensitive and absorbent quality of the leaf, they should be bought and stored in small quantities and in a constant temperature of 60 to 65 degrees Fahrenheit; they need protection just as much from drafts and smells as from the quick-drying effects of central heating. They can even become contaminated by the smell of soap from the hands. Since too much heat spoils their quality and damp produces mold, humidors, designed to keep them in perfect condition, are always a wise investment. In a room where a number of boxes are to be stored, a cedar wood cabinet is essential, for this wood affords the best protection and yet allows the process of maturing to continue. Thus the lids of boxes should be firmly closed after each cigar has been removed. "Green" (or moist) cigars should be kept in aluminum tubes, cellophane wrappings, or glass jars in order to preserve their freshness.

Those which have been allowed to become dry should never be moistened, and cigars that, through excessive damp, have begun to smell musty have been spoiled irreparably and should be thrown away. There is no remedy for a failure of this kind. To give the care and attention that avoids such disasters is to understand the delicate nature of cigars and the immense pleasure they offer to those who treat them well.

Since every smoker of experience has his own fads and foibles, in the matter of smoking it is dangerous to be dogmatic. So much is a matter of taste and opinion. Nevertheless, there are a few important points that give the cigar a chance to offer its best.

BUYER BEWARE: COUNTERFEIT CIGARS

"Ninety percent of the Cuban cigars sold in the U.S. are counterfeit."

Oscar Boruchin

THERE ARE FIVE HALLMARKS of authenticity on each box of Havana cigars. To avoid counterfeits, make sure your box has all five:

• *The warranty seal.* This green sticker, printed in the style of a banknote, has graced the Havanas' boxes since it was adopted in 1912.

• *The hallmarks.* Three of them are stamped into the box: (1) *Habanos, S.A.* (as of October 1, 1994; from 1985 to 1994, it was "Cubatabaco" in this position); (2) *Hecho en Cuba* (prior to 1960, it was in English—"Made in Cuba"); (3) *Totalmente a mano* ("Totally by hand," as of 1989).

• *The habanos chevron.* The latest addition, since 1994, is found across the corner of the box.

Note, however, that even the seals can be faked.

There are legions of fake Havanas for sale everywhere, particularly the Cohiba brand as well as the larger sizes of many others. You should check all the criteria and make sure that they coincide. Christie's auction house in London, for example, was recently forced to reject a lot of Havanas that was to be auctioned, including boxes of Montecristo A's and Cohiba Esplendidos, and Double Coronas from Punch and Hoyo de Monterrey. The labels were all cleverly counterfeited, and closer examination revealed that the factory stamps were incorrect: The Hoyos and Punches had FPG stamps for the Francisco Perez German (Partagas) factory, while those cigars are actually made at the Fernando Roig (La Corona) factory.

The tipoffs are often subtle because counterfeiters are becoming much more sophisticated. Check the aroma: If the cigar smells of fresh, unaged tobacco or even ammonia, it is a fake. And then there's the price. If a box sells on the street for fifty dollars, even though the seller claims to have "a friend who works at the factory," the cigars are most likely homemade from scraps and scrapings. Buy only from authorized dealers, make sure they've been properly cared for, and smoke one before you buy twenty-five.

ABOVE: FRAUDULENT HAVANAS HAVE BEEN MARKETED FOR HUNDREDS OF YEARS, AS THIS WARNING FROM THE ARENTS COLLECTION ATTESTS.

CIGAR ETIQUETTE

In the United States, recent laws have made cigar smoking outside of one's own home more difficult. With the growing number of cigar smokers, however, many restaurants are offering cigar nights. Sometimes toward the end of a night, certain restaurants will allow cigar smoking if it isn't offensive to the remaining diners. Restaurants that have outdoor patios often allow smoking in that particular area. Even though bars allow cigarette smoking, many of them are wary of cigar smoking. It's always polite to ask the proprietor as well as the people around you if they mind before you light up. In 1967 Zino Davidoff outlined a protocol for smokers in his noted essay for connoisseurs. It is a charter and code for cigar smokers everywhere, and it remains as valid today as when he first wrote it. Among his directives were the following dos and don'ts.

DON'T Use a penknife to cut or a lance to pierce the end of the cigar. ("Such is the respect that I have for the British royal family—who have been and continue to be with Prince Philip and Lord Snowdon true devotees of the cigar—that I refuse to give them the advice Edward VII proffered to a young lord in his entourage: 'Pierce the cigar with a lance and, after lighting it, wave it in the air.'") Touch the flame directly to the foot of the cigar. Instead simply rotate it around the edge till it starts to burn, then puff lightly. Ask someone else for a light. ("The lighting of a cigar should be a personal affair. To ask for assistance is to create a relationship of dependence.") Light your cigar too quickly or too slowly. Indulge in exhibitionism in lighting or any other aspect of smoking. Relight your cigar if less than one quarter of it is left. Put the cigar in your mouth to relight it. Just scrape off the ash and turn it in the flame for several seconds till it relights. Clench it between your teeth (and definitely not at a slant). Get the end of the cigar wet, chew it, slobber on it. Smoke too quickly. ("In our nervous, agitated world, I have observed many smokers who follow a much faster cadence. They are fools! The faster one smokes, the less pleasure.") Use a cigar holder. ("Who would want to drink good wine with a straw?") Stick a toothpick or matchstick in the end of the cigar to help hold it in your mouth. ("I am not able even to talk about this aberration.") Dunk your cigar in port or brandy, a habit attributed to Winston Churchill. Smoke while working. Hold a cigar between your index and middle finger. (Churchill is pardoned because he is presumed to have been making his trademark V signal.) Smoke when you're walking. Smoke more than half the cigar. Put the cigar out by crushing it in an ashtray. Chain-smoke cigars.

DO Warm the foot of the cigar slightly before starting to puff on it. Remove the band carefully after lighting the cigar. Take your time smoking it; a puff a minute is about right. Hold the cigar between your index finger and thumb. Let the cigar die a dignified death; after it's smoked halfway, it will go out on its own. Dispose of the dead cigar discreetly and quickly. Wait at least fifteen minutes between cigars; anything less indicates obsessive behavior.

The important thing to remember is that we cigar aficionados should present ourselves as considerate and understanding individuals. Changing people's preconceived notions and giving the growing numbers of aficionados a good name is well worth that little extra effort.

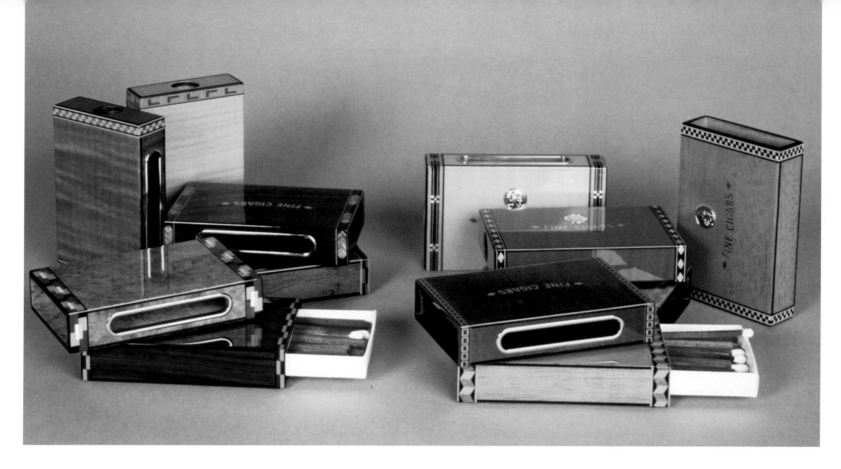

ACCESSORIES AND ACCOUTREMENTS

THERE ARE MANY ELEGANT accoutrements that complement cigar smoking, from sterling silver Dunhill cutters to enameled Dupont lighters costing $500, and $15,000 custom architectural humidors from Viscount Linley.

Cutters. Cutters come in a wide range of prices, from the plastic-encased $9.95 models to luxury gold-plated scissors. The best are the two-bladed "guillotine" types because they exert even pressure on both sides of the cut. A single-bladed guillotine can also work well. Scissors-type cutters are nice but are not as easy to carry around. Occasionally, while hunt-

ing on sugar plantations in Cuba, Hemingway was known to use a machete.

Lighters. Wooden matches work very well, as long as you allow any sulfur to burn off before lighting your cigar. Cedar strips are good but are not so conveniently portable. Butane lighters are often beautifully designed and crafted, very portable, and have the advantage of being windproof. Beware of fluid fuel lighters, however; their fumes can interfere with the taste of the cigar. A candle flame, with its wax parti-

TOP: **A SELECTION OF ELIE BLEU MATCHBOXES.**
LEFT: **SCISSOR-STYLE CIGAR CLIPPER.**

cles, or anything else that may impart an odor, is a bad lighting device for a cigar.

Some of the more spectacular lighters available, used by such prominent connoisseurs as Avo Uvezian and Marvin Shanken, resemble miniature flamethrowers. Among these devices are the Colibri Quantum Premier gas turbo lighter and also one made by Ikari. A number of very smart lighters are made by S.T. Dupont, Davidoff, and Dunhill. The cream of the crop seems to be the Caran D'Ache, which sells for more than $1,000 per lighter and even has a spare gas tank.

Humidors. These handsome items range from a $150 to 200 desktop model for twenty-five to fifty cigars (with a built-in humidification device with a hygrometer to measure humidity and a sponge-type element that needs to be

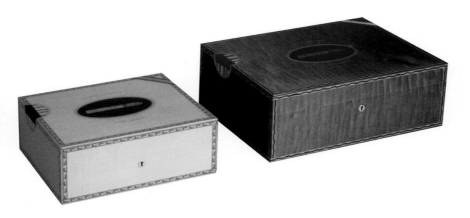

A WORD ABOUT TUBES

THERE ARE THOSE who would counsel you to stay away from tubed cigars altogether. The logic goes something like this. The best wrappers are found on the cigars you can see, so the mismatched, patchier, veinier ones will be hidden by tubes. Furthermore, tubes give the illusion of being airtight, but they are not, and the cigars inside can dry up with time.

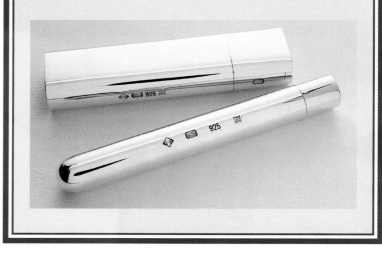

replenished with water when it dries up) to custom humidors that are instant collector's items and may cost $2,000 or more.

There are also large cabinet-sized humidors that can house up to fifteen hundred cigars for the serious connoisseur. Other essential items are a carrying case (make sure it will accommodate your favorite size cigar) and a traveling humidor. All of these items are available from top manufacturers such as Davidoff, Dunhill, Daniel Marshall, Elie Bleu, J. Pendergast, Michel Perrenoud, and Savinelli.

ABOVE: AN ELEGANT CIGAR CUTTER ACCOMMODATES VARIOUS CIGAR SIZES.
LEFT: ELEGANT HANDMADE BURLWOOD HUMIDORS FROM ELIE BLEU.

THE ULTIMATE 1000

GENE WALDER OF Controlled Environments in San Marcos, California, has created the next generation of cigar humidors, one that incorporates both temperature and humidity control. Gene's distinguished career in designing and constructing wine storage systems and commercial walk-in humidors, coupled with his love for cigars, inspired him to develop the Ultimate 1000.

A conventional humidor provides only humidification, which can be affected by temperature. If a conventional humidor is kept in a room at 80 degrees, then its humidity can increase to well over 70 percent, creating an environment that can damage cigars. Excess humidity not only causes wrappers to crack but can allow Lacioderma, or tobacco worm, to hatch. Lower temperatures can decrease the conventional humidor's humidity to well below 70 percent, causing the cigars to age improperly and eventually dry out.

With its adjustable temperature and humidity controls, the Ultimate 1000 eliminates these climate concerns. It can maintain a constant temperature of 67 degrees and 70 percent humidity even in a room that is 80 degrees. The electrically powered Ultimate 1000 is a freestanding, handcrafted cabinet about three feet tall by two feet wide and deep. Its interior is constructed of untreated Spanish cedar, with flow-through drawers for loose cigars and shelves to hold boxes. Constant air circulation inside provides even humidification and eliminates the need for cigar rotation. Efficiency was a major design consideration; among the Ultimate 1000's special features are magnetic door gaskets to ensure a sealed environment, and two inches of insulation between the cedar interior and the hardwood exterior.

As its name implies, the Ultimate 1000 has space for a thousand cigars. It also has a digital temperature and humidity gauge and a humidifying element with a capacity for 12 ounces of distilled water, meaning it can run for more than a month without refilling. Several exotic hardwood exteriors are available, including Honduran mahogany and African rosewood. Incorporating this same technology, Controlled Environments also makes larger humidors as well as units that combine wine and cigar storage.

STORAGE AND CARE

THE ABIDING PRINCIPLE of caring for your premium cigars is to keep the conditions constant, without subjecting them to extreme variations. A properly stored cigar is neither too dry nor too moist. If your cigars are overhumidified, they will become soft and will burn slowly and improperly. And if they are underhumidified, they will be stiff to the touch, burning hard and fast. Dry cigars have less flavor and aroma, are less mild, and flake off in the mouth. Dryness is the major cause of unraveling wrappers—the second most frequent complaint among premium-cigar smokers. The more extreme the climate or its variations, the greater the potential damage. Over time a cigar will become unsmokable if it is kept improperly.

Some experts maintain that the world's finest cigars should either be smoked within three months of their manufacture or be allowed to mature for a year. The reason is that they will continue to ferment in the box, with a few drops of oil coming from the leaf each year around midsummer. (The oil dries to a white dust that can simply be brushed off.) Many aficionados choose to age their cigars in humidors, sometimes from three to five years or more.

If you keep your cigars at 70 percent relative humidity

and 70 degrees Fahrenheit, they'll eventually dry out. Remember that, after rolling them, cigar makers "equilibrate" cigars in their big storage humidors at room temperature and about 72 percent relative humidity. At this level of temperature and humidity, all three parts of a cigar are allowed to equalize in moisture content and slowly, ever so slowly, *dry down*. Room temperature (68 to 72 degrees Fahrenheit) with 72 percent humidity will dry down cigars over time, but 73 percent humidity will keep them perfect forever.

Do not expose the cigars to the sun or strong light or dry heat. Always keep them in an airtight, cedar-lined box. And remember that the lower the temperature, the higher the humidity needs to be. As the temperature falls, a commensurate rise in the humidity can keep the cigars fresh. But never let the temperature get too high. High temperatures coupled with high humidity create an incubator atmosphere in your humidor, and before you know it, there will be little bugs flying around to ruin your entire selection, with white mold developing soon thereafter.

With a little care and patience, dried-out cigars can be salvaged. Gradually reintroduce them to a moist environment by partially replenishing the humidifier in your humidor in the first week and slowly increasing it to the full humidity by the third week. Never freeze a cigar or put it in the refrigerator, as this denies it the opportunity to age

ABOVE: THE DUNHILL HUMIDOR ROOM, ST. JAMES'S, LONDON.
OPPOSITE: THE PRIVATE HUMIDORS AT THE GRAND HAVANA ROOM.

in natural humidity. Any dramatic change in temperature can also cause a cigar to crack or break.

Is a humidor absolutely necessary? We think so, especially if you plan to invest the time and expense to become a connoisseur of the world's finest cigars. If you love your cigars, treat them well. In a pinch, you can make your own humidor by putting a damp sponge or cloth in a small plastic bag and placing it in your cigar box or in a plastic resealable container with the cigars.

To maintain humidity, there are several inexpensive devices, called the Creedo and the Humatic systems, that fit into plastic containers and humidors.

And always be sure to rotate your cigars from bottom to top every few months, for even humidification.

"SMOKEASIES": THE CLUBS

THE GRAND HAVANA ROOM'S TOP TEN

1. Fuente Fuente Opus X Double Corona
2. Ashton Cabinet #8
3. La Gloria Torpedo
4. Padron Anniversary Pyramid
5. Diamond Crown #3
6. Paul Garmirian Belicoso
7. Thomas Hinds Robusto Maduro
8. Leon Jimenes Robusto
9. Macanudo Vintage
10. H. Upmann Columbo

HAVANA STUDIOS' TOP TEN

1. Padron Anniversario
2. Flor de Florez Cabinet Selection
3. Arturo Fuente Short Story
4. Padron 3000 (natural)
5. Butera Vintage Bravo Corte
6. Avo No. 5
7. Savannah Reserve
8. Ashton Magnum
9. Puros Indios Rothschild
10. Cohiba Robusto (when they're authentic)

THROUGH AN AROMATIC haze of blue smoke, cigar clubs are popping up like palm trees from Los Angeles to London. They are no mere mirages but welcome oases in a no-smoking desert. These "speakeasies for smokers" are sanctuaries with elegant surroundings: deep leather chairs; custom humidors; crystal ashtrays; vintage wines, ports, and cognacs; dynamic ventilation; fine food; and great company. They represent, quite simply, a renaissance of the good life, accommodating aficionados in cordial cigar-friendly environments where they can eat, drink, relax, and enjoy a favorite cigar in comfort, and forge friendships.

In Beverly Hills, members enter the gracious Grand Havana Room from a private entrance on North Canon Drive and identify themselves to a hostess, who unlocks a private elevator that glides soundlessly up to a cloudless smoker's heaven. The centerpiece of the club's double-tiered main room is a glassed-in area containing 350 Spanish cedar lockers, stacked floor to ceiling, functionally decorated with brass plates identifying such members as Mel Gibson, Robert DeNiro, Danny DeVito, Arnold Schwarzenegger, Jack Nicholson, and Jim Carrey.

Here one pays for the privilege of puffing in peace. Membership requires a $2,000 initiation fee and $150 a

OPPOSITE: CLUB MACANUDO IN NEW YORK.

month for your private humidor. Managing director Stan Shuster would like to confer membership upon anyone willing to join but, alas, there is a waiting list. With its forest green drapes and deep leather chairs, the Grand Havana Room is grand indeed—not necessarily Havana, but a place to enjoy one's cigars with great pride. Patrons can also enjoy Grand Havana Rooms in New York City and Washington, D.C.

Across Beverly Hills over in Burbank is another exclusive and elegant club, Havana Studios. An upscale private enclave that opened in July 1995, Havana Studios offers a full bar with a comprehensive list of beers, single malts, and cognacs. There are 125 personal humidified lockers, each storing up to thirty boxes of cigars, along with a billiard room. It is a beautiful and comfortable place to entertain friends and socialize with other members. There is also a conference room, telephones, fax machine, copier, and outlets for laptop computers for conducting business. A large percentage of the clientele comes from the entertainment industry, due in part to the club's proximity to several major motion picture, television, and recording studios. In front of the club, there is a Havana Studios retail store, which offers first-class service and one of Los Angeles's better selections of cigars and accessories.

Another popular Havana Studios location is their cigar store and coffeehouse on Sunset Boulevard, where patrons can enjoy a cigar and a cappuccino. Havana Studios has plans to open in San Francisco.

In the tradition of its "patron saints," George Sand and Marlene Dietrich, a club called the George Sand Society, located in Santa Monica, California, is the largest cigar-smoking society for women in the United States. Sand fought for women's rights, wore men's clothing, and smoked several cigars a day. The society chose Sand as its namesake for "her uncompromising individuality and spirit of freedom." The society holds frequent special events and smokers at selected restaurants throughout the country.

With cigars enjoying a spectacular return, the sumptuous Monte's on Sloane Street in London offers a new cigar experience. Its Havana Club retail section is open to the general public during the day, and it offers the finest  selection of cigars in Great Britain. At night the back of the store transforms itself into a walk-in humidor where members and guests of the private club are invited to indulge in a room not unlike the smoking clubs of the Victorian era. Monte's, where clearly no expense was spared, features an atrium with inlaid marble floors; there is plenty of bronze, mahogany, and etched glass throughout. A gourmet menu, created in consultation with the great French chef Alain Ducasse, is served in a ninety-seat restaurant. The club, which also offers original cocktail inventions with cigar themes, has a noteworthy collection of Cuban and non-Cuban cigars. They include rare Montecristo A's and Hoyo de Monterrey Double Coronas, recommended special

ABOVE: THE GRAND HAVANA ROOM IN BEVERLY HILLS.
BELOW: CITY WINE & CIGAR CO. IN NEW YORK.

selections from Hunters & Frankau, the largest distributor in the U.K.

Even with the advent of such sparkling venues as Monte's, few "smok-easies" in London can compete with Alfred Dunhill's smoking room on Duke Street. With leather chairs and cedar storage cabinets, the room, which dates from the reign of Edward VII, has an authentic aura of earthy Havana tobacco—in a country where Cuban cigars are legal.

Club Epicur in Barcelona and Madrid is an ultra-exclusive club offering members extraordinary smokers' dinners and one of the best magazines in Europe.

In New York, the Beekman Bar and Books on First Avenue caters to cigar connoisseurs and wannabe cigar-ophiles. Of particular note is Club Macanudo, which stakes its claim as "New York City's first true cigar bar."

"Club Macanudo isn't a private club—it just looks like one," says its manager, Philip Darrow. With friendly, out-going, and highly efficient service, the club offers the requisite collection of premium cigars along with spirits, wines, and a lively American snack menu with foreign accents. It has three handsome rooms, five hundred humidors, and a capacity of 125 patrons. Humidors with brass nameplates are available for $800 per year. The comfortable Club Room provides an ideal environment for backgammon, chess, and bridge. Club Macanudo also features a full array of business conveniences.

JAMES J. FOX, LTD.

ONE OF THE OLDEST commercial establishments in the tony St. James district of London is the James Fox cigar shop at 19 St. James Street. The shop, with its lovely wood-trimmed storefront, which for 207 years had been operating out of this location under the elegantly simple sign ROBERT LEWIS, CIGAR MERCHANT, was merged with the equally venerable Dublin firm of James J. Fox in 1992 and is now known by that name. Fox and Lewis, as it is sometimes referred to, provides personalized service to its clientele. It features an excellent selection of the world's best cigars, mostly Havanas, and it also has a small museum area displaying a ledger with such distinguished names as Winston Churchill and Oscar Wilde. John Croley, who put in more than fifty years of service at his family business, passed away in 1995; his son Michael, representing the third generation of Croleys at the shop, still works there. The affable Robert Emery is the director.

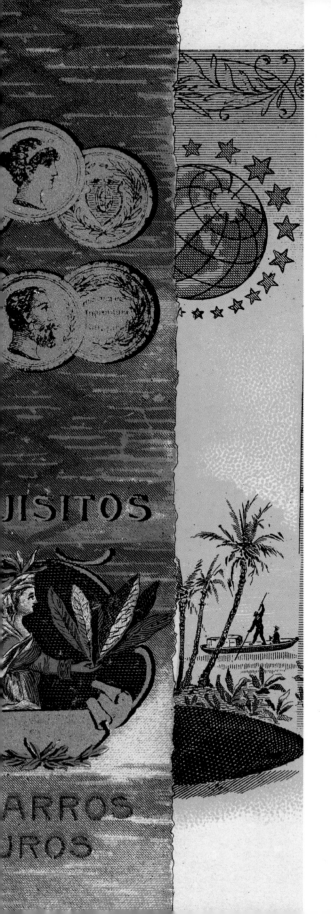

7

COUNTRY BY COUNTRY

DETERMINING THE ORIGIN of a cigar or its components is not always a clear-cut proposition. Premium-cigar tobacco is grown in several regions of the world, but the cigars themselves may be manufactured elsewhere. Some countries do one or the other; a few do both. Cameroon, for example, grows some of the best wrapper leaves but has no manufacturing;

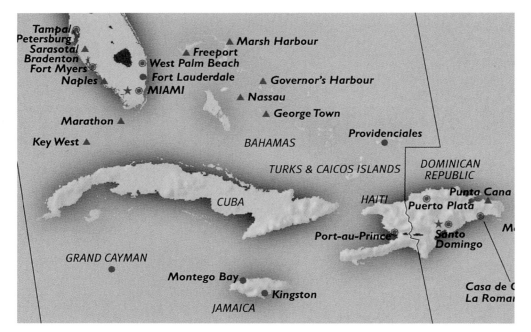

the world's finest cigars is Pinar del Rio, a province that lies between the mountains and the sea at the western end of Cuba. Here the agricultural conditions are ideal for tobacco cultivation: The soil is a reddish sandy loam; the climate is humid; the rainfall is consistent and predictable. In the Vuelta Abajo region of this province, centered around the towns of San Juan y Martinez and San Luis, the tobacco for the Habanos is grown. Temperatures reach average highs of 80 degrees Fahrenheit, with an average relative humidity of 64 percent and about eight hours of sunshine each day. *Vegueros* (planters) farm select plots, most of five to ten acres but none more than 150, out of the 100,000 acres devoted to tobacco in the province.

Cuba and the Dominican Republic both grow great tobacco and manufacture some of the finest cigars.

But cigar production is not limited to Cuba and the Dominican Republic. Jamaica has been at it for over a century, and many other Latin American countries, such as Mexico, Brazil, Honduras, and Ecuador, produce outstanding tobacco and cigars. Here is a brief survey of each nation's contributions to the cigar-making trade.

A second growing area within Pinar del Rio is the Semi Vuelta, which produces thicker, stronger leaves destined for domestic consumption. The Partido region grows quality wrappers, and Remedios and Oriente grow fine tobacco as well. Cuban tobacco is flavorful, strong, and full-bodied.

The vast majority of cigar factories are located in the capital city of Havana, including six venerable cigar

Cuba

THE INSCRIPTION *"Hecho a mano"* ("made by hand") on every box authenticates the construction of the Cuban cigar. Cigar making comes from the Cuban soul, from passion tempered by experience, patience, and perfectionism.

Many connoisseurs and aficionados agree that the cradle of

fábricas that were founded at the beginning of the first golden age of the cigar, in the first half of the nineteenth century, and are still making many of the world's finest cigars. In the modern era they have been renamed for revolutionary heroes (noted in parentheses), but they are still informally called by their original names: H. Upmann (José Martí); Partagas (Francisco Perez German); Romeo y Julieta (Briones Montoto); La Corona (Fernando Roig); El Laguito; El Rey del Mundo (Heroes del Moncada). In addition, each factory's initials (JM, FPG, BM, and so forth) are stamped on the boxes of cigars made there.

Because of the weather-created tobacco shortages in Cuba today, an experimental program is under development to extend the growing season by as much as five months. Cuba is also growing Connecticut seed in a joint venture with the Dutch concern Lippoel.

The Dominican Republic

TOBACCO FOR CIGARS has been grown in the Dominican Republic for many, many years, but the country did not become a producer of fine handmade cigars until the early 1970s.

After the Cuban revolution the firm of Menendez y Garcia set up shop in the Canary Islands, across the Atlantic, to continue its illustrious tradition of making the

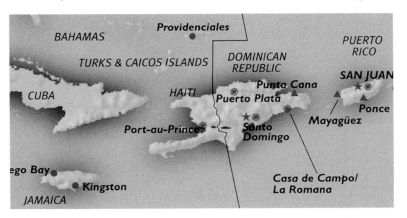

H. Upmann and Montecristo brands. There too it began producing other brands such as Montecruz and Dunhill. When the firm's tax abatement in the Canaries expired, it decided to move its operations elsewhere. Since the firm was owned by Gulf + Western, a conglomerate that had major investments in the sugar and tourism industries in the Dominican Republic, it seemed the logical place to go.

Menéndez and García just became pioneers of fine handmade cigars in that country, establishing outposts both in Santiago and La Romana, near the world-famed resort of Casa de Campo. There the Consolidated Cigar Corporation's state-of-the-art facility now turns out a number of the world's finest cigar brands, such as Santa Damiana, Don Diego, Upmann, Primo del Rey, Montecruz, and Dunhill.

General Cigar, which manufactures the great Partagas under the supervision of Ramón Cifuentes and now Benjamín Menéndez, and the world's best-selling premium-cigar brand, Macanudo, opened up its factory in Santiago, mostly as a hedge during the regime of the leftist prime minister Michael Manley in Jamaica in the 1970s. It turned out to be a fortunate move since the Dominican factory now turns out more cigars than the Jamaican one.

Two other major Dominican operations are MATASA (Manufacturas de Tabacos, S.A.), which is run by the Quesada family, formerly big growers and brokers of tobacco in Cuba who relocated to the Dominican Republic after the revolution; and Tabacos Dominicanos, led by Hendrik Kelner, which now makes and carries on the great tradition of the Davidoff brand, along with Avos and Griffin's.

The Fuente family's manufacturing operation was based in Nicaragua until the Sandinista movement arose. Their

and the sandy loam of the Connecticut valley. But extraordinary wrappers have now been developed by Carlos Fuente and Hendrik Kelner.

There are two types of locally grown tobacco, *piloto cubano* and *olor*. The former is a heavier, Cuban-seed tobacco, while the latter is lighter. The Yaque del Norte River valley, also known as the Cibao valley, is the primary Dominican growing region. It is one of the few east-west-flowing rivers in the hemisphere (another more prominent one being the Amazon), and three growing areas can be found along its banks: La Vega, Moca, and Bonao. Inspired by the U.S. embargo on Cuba and the premium-

fábricas were either burned or confiscated, and they moved to the Dominican Republic in the early 1980s.

Next door to Cuba, the Dominican Republic has a similar climate with rich soil conditions. Over the last twenty years it has produced cigars comparable to the Havana. Traditionally, most Dominican tobacco has been used for filler blends, with other leaves imported from Brazil, Honduras, Ecuador, Connecticut, and Cameroon. The most popular binder tobacco used in the country, for example, has been Mexican Sumatra, while its wrappers have traditionally been imported from the rain forests of Cameroon

cigar boom, the Fuente family took up the challenge of developing a cigar like a Havana at Château de la Fuente. With Cuban experience and ingenuity, they succeeded with a crowning achievement, the Opus X.

Today the Dominican Republic is the largest producer of premium handmade cigars in the world. It is the primary supplier for the U.S. market, producing some of the best-quality cigars in the world. They are lighter in body than the classic Cuban-style cigars, but they have plenty of flavor and complexity and are highly esteemed by connoisseurs everywhere.

Honduras

ALTHOUGH TOBACCO HAS BEEN grown here since long before Christopher Columbus encountered it on his third expedition in 1502 and although there has been a cigar factory in Santa de Lopan since 1785, Honduras had no illustrious history of premium-cigar tobacco cultivation or production until the Cuban exiles arrived.

Honduras has climate conditions remarkably similar to those of Cuba. It lies on roughly the same latitude, and it has a central mountain range, where warm moist air moving with the prevailing westerly winds provides predictable and consistent annual rainfall.

In the early 1960s Angel Oliva, patriarch of the world's greatest tobacco-growing family, went to Honduras and

RIGHT: **A LABEL FOR THE ORIGINAL CUBAN PUNCH CIGAR.**

cultivated Cuban-seed tobacco. With little infrastructure the Olivas were truly the pioneers of the Honduran premium-cigar industry. To this day, the infrastructure in Honduras, as well as in Nicaragua, provides difficult conditions for cigar makers, who must ship their goods by truck over miles of rough, unpaved roads and stamp their cigar boxes with one-hundred-year-old mechanical presses.

The Olivas' farm in La Entrada (only forty miles from the tobacco-growing region of Nicaragua) produces some of the world's finest cigar tobacco, following a Cuban legacy under the direction of manager Ramón Martinez.

Frank Llaneza of Villazon, another Cuban exile, joined the Olivas in Honduras, establishing the first premium-cigar-making facility in the town of Cofridia. He used tobacco grown by the Olivas, acquired the Hoyo de Mon-

terrey and Punch brand names from the Palicio family, and expanded his operation to include another plant in Danlí.

Estello Padron, another distinguished expatriate Cuban cigar maker working in Honduras, now runs the Cofridia facility. Villazon makes Hoyo de Monterrey, Punch, Belinda, El Rey del Mundo, and JR Ultimates, all heavy, full-bodied, "Cuban-style" cigars with delicious, oily wrappers, the closest thing in flavor and aroma to a pre-embargo Cuban cigar available on the U.S. market today. Honduras is now also home to the great Rolando Reyes and his Aliados factory which produces the popular Puros Indios.

Mexico

MEXICO'S LONG HISTORY of cigar making centers in the town of San Andrés Tuxtla and the surrounding San Andrés valley, in the state of Veracruz. In the United States, their biggest export market, Mexican cigars were traditionally very inexpensive. Even though they were excellent

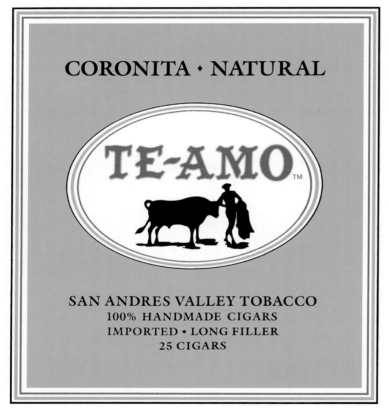

CORONITA · NATURAL

TE-AMO™

SAN ANDRES VALLEY TOBACCO
100% HANDMADE CIGARS
IMPORTED · LONG FILLER
25 CIGARS

and handmade, they were perceived as too harsh and dry and therefore less desirable. That changed in 1968 when a brand called Te-Amo was introduced with an aggressive push by one of its owners, Al Greenwald. Almost overnight Mexico was recognized as a major source of premium cigars.

Mexico had always grown tobacco that was used primarily as binder and sometimes filler for cigars made elsewhere. A superb sun-grown Sumatra-seed Mexican maduro wrapper is renowned for its ability to "take the heat." Until very recently, Mexico did not allow the importation of tobacco for manufacturing purposes, so its native product was always a *puro,* made from local tobacco. Mexican cigars have a taste all their own, leading to an "inelastic demand." In other words, either one prefers their taste or not; there doesn't seem to be much in between. Some call them "dry" cigars, dry not necessarily in moisture content but in taste. Others enjoy them as smooth, easy smokes.

The classic Te-Amo brand and its main competitor, Santa Clara, which is made by Jorge Ortíz, along with a few others, such as Aromas de San Andrés, constitute the Mexican share of the premium-cigar market, estimated at about 5 percent, or 8 million cigars per year.

Nicaragua

THE OLIVAS WERE pioneers in Nicaragua, just as they were in neighboring Honduras. Here they were able to produce superb crops of the oily wrappers for the Cuban-style cigars at the Villazon factory in Honduras.

In the late 1960s Franklin Lewis and Simón Camacho formed a partnership with Nicaraguan strongman Anastasio Somoza to produce several brands, including Count Christopher, Hoyo de Nicaragua, Jericho, and El Caudillo, which was made for JR Tobacco. Not only did these brands gain limited acceptance in the all-important U.S. market, in 1972 they gave rise to another interesting innovation: JR Alternatives. JR began to buy up millions of high-quality, low-cost handmade Nicaraguan cigars, selling them first in bundles, then eventually as substitutes for high-priced premium brands.

Nicaraguan cigars, like those from Honduras, are full-bodied, made in the Cuban style. At times their construction is not as fine as their Honduran neighbors', but most connoisseurs feel that those problems are only temporary. Beginning in the early 1980s, the Sandinista revolution and the subsequent ten-year civil war drove away many makers, but the country is on the rebound, and the cigar-making industry should fully recover.

The Canary Islands

AFTER THE CUBAN REVOLUTION, the Menéndez and García family firm relocated to the Canary Islands, which offered tax incentives. The Canaries are essentially on the same latitude as the Sahara Desert and the climate is quite dry, with little tobacco-growing potential. Although there is only a small growing region on the island of La Palma, the Canaries have a great tradition of tobacco manufacturing. Their status as a duty-free zone has allowed manufacturers to import tobaccos from Cuba, the Dominican Republic, Cameroon, and Sumatra under very favorable

conditions, and they make cigars of a quality and finish at least equal to, if not superior to, the Dominicans, Hondurans, and North Americans. There are also small artisans' workshops turning out cigars that haven't yet reached the international market, with the exception of those sold by CITA, a trading subsidiary of Tabacalera. Cigars made in the Canaries don't generally have the same moisture content as most other cigars; they weigh less than a comparably sized Dominican or Honduran cigar, and therefore they have a tendency to burn faster and harsher. Yet the very mild and fine Dunhill Grande Corona is made in the Canaries.

Jamaica

JAMAICA PRODUCES CIGARS with a mild to medium flavor, like the Macanudo, that aficionados from New York to San Francisco find irresistible. Unlike most current cigar-producing nations (with the notable exception of Cuba), Jamaica has at least a hundred-year history of making fine handmade cigars.

The emigration of cigar makers from Cuba in the early 1960s had been preceded by several earlier migrations, including one that took place a hundred years earlier, during Cuba's 1868–1878 struggle against Spain. Although many Cuban cigar makers settled in Key West and the Tampa area, a significant number went to Jamaica and continued to make cigars there. A second influx of Cuban expertise

ABOVE: CHURCHILL, CEDROS, ROYAL, AND SOLERA SIZES FROM LA FAMA, MANUFACTURED IN THE CANARY ISLANDS.
RIGHT: MACANUDO'S DISTINCTIVE *FILETE* AND *VISTA*.

SPAIN: THE VIEW FROM HERE
BY DAVID ILARIO,
EPICUR

That Columbus and his men brought tales of tobacco back to Spain and that the Spanish court in Madrid, the most powerful in Europe in those times, introduced the custom of smoking tobacco to all of Europe is a well-known chapter of history.

Tobacco was originally smoked in a very different manner from that to which we cigar smokers are accustomed. Following the mariners' example, it was smoked in pipes. Tobacco in the familiar form of a *puro,* or cigar, was first made in the oldest tobacco factories in the world, in Seville, under the control of the royal Spanish *compania,* known today as Tabacalera, S.A.

At the beginning of the nineteenth century, planters in Cuba, who until that time were limited to sending bunches of tobacco to Europe for manufacturing, began developing a local industry, first following the model of Seville's factories and subsequently developing their own innovations. The first Cuban *puros* resembled Spanish *farias,* which were large and round in the middle and tapering at the ends.

Seville is the birthplace not only of the cigar as we know it but also of the legend that the *puros* were rolled on the thighs of the beautiful women workers in the *fábricas,* which I suspect is only a legend. But maybe not.

It was men of Spanish heritage living in Cuba who launched the Cuban tobacco industry: José Gener of Hoyo de Monterrey, Jaime Partagas of Partagas, José Rodríguez of Romeo y Julieta, and José Gispert of Gispert. Other great Cuban brands such as Fonseca, Quintero, Sancho Panza, and Montecristo originated with families from Spain.

My country is the top importer of Cuban cigars in the world, and Barcelona and Havana share the distinction of being the cigar-smoking capitals of the world.

Tabacalera imports all tobacco to Spain and is jointly owned by the public and private sectors. It controls all distribution through the *estancos,* licensed tobacconists who are the only authorized vendors of cigars and cigarettes.

Cuban tobacco in the form of *puros,* or cigars, represents a mere five to ten percent of the total sales of Tabacalera. Last year 28 million cigars were imported from Cuba. That figure could easily have been 40 percent higher if Cuba had been able to supply the demand. With its own factories in Spain where it manufactures dark and light cigarettes, *brevas,* small *puros,* and the above-mentioned *farias,* Tabacalera sold more than 200 million units last year.

Tabacalera also sells cigars manufactured in the Canary Islands as well as imports from the Dominican Republic, Honduras, and the Netherlands, along with cigars from the only factory in Asia, Tabacos de Filipinas, formerly a competitor of Tabacalera de España. Since the nineteenth century, it has made recognized brands such as La Flor de Isabela.

Spain is a nation of tobacco, and soccer is the national sport. Barcelona's Nou Camp Stadium draws 100,000 spectators, who will smoke 10,000 *puros* during one afternoon match. At the Feria de San Isidro bullfights in Madrid, with thirty-five *corridas,* more than 100,000 easily go up in smoke.

We have an antismoking movement, although not as powerful as the one in the United States. Yet there is still a genuine fever for the quality of *puros*. For the Spanish, it's a matter of course that Cuban cigars are the best in the world and that cigars from anywhere else in the world are not as good.

Until now, the exclusive Epicur cigar-smoking club has been strictly devoted to Havanas, with the notable exceptions of Davidoff cigars and a few of the Canarian artisans' brands. The club is based in Barcelona with satellites all over Spain, especially in Madrid and Bilbao. The Barcelona chapter has two hundred members and a long waiting list. At first dinners were organized monthly in Barcelona and Madrid. Recently there were two inaugural dinners in Lisbon. Now as many as twenty dinners are held every few months all over Spain: in S. Agaro, Marbella, Palma de Mallorca, Oporto, and of course Barcelona and Madrid.

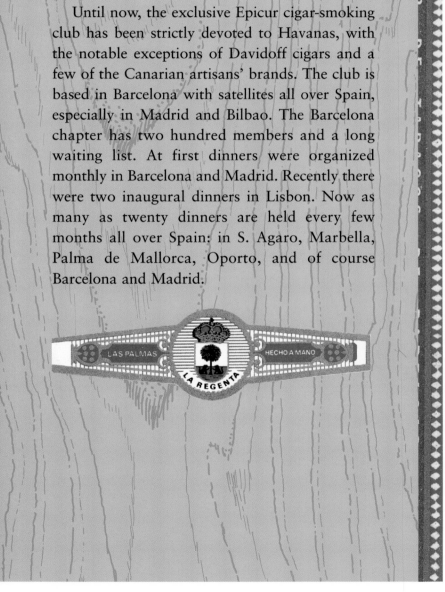

came to Jamaica at the end of the nineteenth century.

Part of the British Commonwealth, Jamaica enjoys excellent tax and tariff advantages for export to Britain and other Commonwealth nations. A significant portion of the great Macanudos are made there. Another fine brand, Temple Hall Estates, also originates in Jamaica, but recently it is no longer available in the U.S. market because its maker, General, can sell every single cigar it makes under the name Macanudo. As everywhere, the demand for premium cigars is high, resulting in a shortage on the market. No doubt a brand like Temple Hall Estates will become available again if market conditions warrant it.

Brazil

MADE MAINLY FROM TOBACCO grown in Cruz des Almos, Brazilian cigars are immensely respected and have a dedicated following. Full-bodied, they are popular with many German smokers. Some cigars, made by Danneman and Suerdieck, are extremely dark in color and rich in flavor, yet surprisingly mild.

IMPORTED hand made since 1868

The United States

Tampa. At one time Tampa produced more cigars than any place in the world. Between 1900 and 1960 Ybor City, home of the Clear Havana, was credited with 80 percent of the production of Cuban cigars. After the U.S. embargo was imposed in 1961, manufacturers looked to Honduras and the Dominican Republic for tobacco. Today many machine-made cigars come from old Tampa factories. Bering makes cigars there, in the intriguing and well-regarded Spanish Colonial style.

The Connecticut Valley. Some of the world's best and most expensive wrapper leaves, called Connecticut shade, are grown in the Connecticut River valley north of Hartford, under large ten-foot-high tents. Connecticut broadleaf is a very dark sun-grown variety used for maduro wrappers. The growing season lasts from March until August, and the wrappers are used for such superior brands as Davidoff and Macanudo. Years ago, Connecticut seeds were exported to Cuba, and they are used for some Cuban leaves grown today. And Connecticut wrapper seeds come from a strain of Cuban tobacco called Hazelwood. So over the years the interchange has been reciprocal.

The Connecticut wrapper crop is essentially controlled by two growers: Culbro, which is the parent company of General Cigar, with about 65 percent, and Windsor Shade, with the other 35 percent. This division gives General's longtime customers, along with Windsor Shade's, the pick of the best Connecticut leaf. It also creates an incentive for other producers to develop fine wrapper leaves elsewhere.

Europe

France. The French national tobacco company, SEITA, produces more than 2 billion cigars a year for the domestic market. Most are very small, thin cigars. The Picaduro is made entirely from French tobacco. Other cigars, such as the Voltigeur, use Brazilian blends.

Italy. Italy is famous for its very strong Toscani—cigars with an unusual, uneven shape.

Denmark. This Scandinavian country has the highest per capita consumption of cigars in Europe and produces the famous E. Nobel, made from Sumatran leaves.

Germany. Germany's very popular cigar is the Handelsgold, made from Brazilian and Sumatran tobacco.

Spain. More than any other country, Spain typifies a cigar culture. Spaniards adore their Havanas with a passion, smoking 30 million cigars a year. Recently, Spain has financed a partnership giving much-needed financing to Cubatabaco, now called Habanos, S.A. After Havana, Barcelona is considered the top cigar-smoking city in the world. Spain is also thought to produce the best-quality cigars in Europe. The Penamil is a cigar of impeccable quality.

Asia

MANILA'S TABACALERA PRODUCES handmade cigars in twelve sizes, with coronas being very popular in the Philippines. Philippine tobacco, mild and very aromatic, is used mostly for small cigars. Sumatra, Borneo, and Burma also manufacture cigars with a collective "Dutch flavor." The Indonesian islands of Java and Sumatra produce dark brown wrappers, mostly for small cigars.

Africa

CAMEROON WRAPPERS, rich and dark, grown from Sumatra seed in the open areas of the rain forests of West Africa, are simply among the finest and most sought-after leaves exported all over the world. They are greenish brown to dark brown in color, with a distinctive grain on the leaf.

Havanas: The Struggle for Excellence

by Simon Chase

As marketing director of Hunters & Frankau, cigar importers in London since 1790, Simon Chase has long been regarded as a leading expert on the Havana cigar. Acknowledged by Cigar Aficionado *as a man of extensive knowledge in all things cigar related, his experience makes him uniquely qualified to contribute these words on the Havana cigar. He is also co-author of* The Cigar Companion.

"The Cuban cigar is a luxury article. As such, it goes to market without any intention of competing with any other cigar. Rather, it is designed for the minority who can afford such luxuries."

I found these words in a pamphlet published by no less an authority than the United States Department of Agriculture and written by one May Coult in 1952. They embody an assertiveness, an arrogance even, that is hard to comprehend.

It has been my privilege for the last twenty years to work with Cuban cigars, to sell them, to smoke them, to study their history and manufacture, and ultimately to become deeply fascinated by them. I am beginning to understand what she was getting at.

There may be those who would challenge the notion that the cigars referred to in the 1952 article could be compared to Cuba's present-day output. Surely the island's recent history and current predicament could not sustain such aspirations. One of the characteristics of a planned economy, however, is a resistance to change. The same forces that retain 1950s Plymouths and Chevy as popular modes of transport on the streets of Havana also protect the traditional methods of making cigars in the city.

The only issue on which I would challenge Ms. Coult is the definition of the article. She says "Cuban" cigars. I would say "Havanas," or "*Habanos*" if I am to satisfy my Spanish-speaking colleagues. It was as true in her day as it is now that all Havanas are Cuban, but not all Cuban cigars are Havanas.

The quality of a cigar is dictated by a process of selection. From the tiniest seedling to the final choice of each cigar placed in a box, it is the amount of material that the farmer, the tobacco processor, and the cigar maker are prepared to discard as second rate that ultimately creates quality.

The term *Havana* is reserved for cigars of "export quality." These days they are as likely to be sold in any

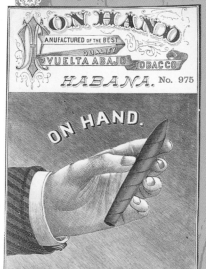

of the booming stores on the island as at one of London's revered cigar merchants, but by definition they are the direct descendants of the cigars that first enthralled the smoking world during the second half of the nineteenth century.

Their history has been one of constant struggle; against the forces of imperial Spain, against commercial tariff barriers, against war and revolution.

Sometimes I find it hard to imagine why such a comparatively small country should have endured so turbulent a past. The answer must lie in the beauty of her landscape, the appeal of her climate to generations of settlers, and to her strategic location. Certainly "The Pearl of the Antilles," as the Spanish named her, has offered many challenges to those who sought to nurture the article for which the world knows her best—the cigar.

Recent times are no exception. Fidel Castro's overthrow of Fulgencia Batista's cruel regime in January 1959 caused enormous upheaval to the industry. At first little changed. Several of the independent Cuban

factory owners had supported the revolution which, although there was a strong socialist element within it, was just as much about pure patriotism.

Within two years the direction Cuba would take became clear. First the foreign-owned interests departed followed closely by the owners and managers of Cuban companies, which were nationalized in a process known as "intervention."

In Havana the industry was reorganized under one controlling state-owned company called Cubatabaco. In 1966 it was given total responsibility for all aspects of tobacco growing, processing, and cigar making, although in the early 1970s the agricultural and industrial functions were hired off to two domestic ministries, leaving Cubatabaco responsible for exports only under the Ministry of Foreign Trade. This setup persists more or less unchanged today, although most of Cubatabaco's role was taken over by a new company called Habanos, S.A., in October 1994.

Organization under one roof, so to speak, meant that there was no longer any need to compete for the pick of the crop; it was all there for the taking. The pitfalls were legion, but so were the opportunities.

Cubans had always regarded the creation of Havanas as a national heritage, something they could do better than anyone else in the world. The rewards for growing the greatest tobaccos, selecting the finest leaves, and making the best cigars had never been measured simply in terms of a pay packet but more as an art. As a result, those who remained just closed ranks and got on with the jobs they loved.

The manufacture of brands owned by foreign interests such as Calixto Lopez, Bock, Henry Clay, and Villar y Villar ceased. Production concentrated on the

Cuban marques such as Partagas, Bolivar, H. Upmann, Montecristo, Hoyo de Monterrey, and Romeo y Julieta.

The level of exports during the four decades since the revolution has oscillated, in much the same way as it did in the preceding century and a half at the whim of various pressures both internal and external. Generally, the shipments of finished cigars have exceeded the levels of the 1950s, although a curious ten-year cycle of setbacks is evident.

By the late 1960s Cuba's emphasis was on new industries, the idea being to reduce her dependency on tobacco and sugar. As investment in tobacco fell, so did cigar production, and by 1970 exports stood at just 55 million. The error was recognized, corrected and in 1976 a total of 120 million were shipped. The outbreak of blue mold disease in 1980 destroyed 95 percent of the crop and decimated production. Huge efforts were made to combat the disaster, and with the help of a good harvest in 1981, exports soon rose to 75 million. In 1990 they topped the 80 million mark; then the Soviet Union collapsed and the present problems began.

Cuba lost around half of her economy in a two-year period. Whole industries were mothballed for want of raw materials. Cigars suffered lightly by comparison because their essential raw material grows naturally on the island. Nevertheless, shortages of fertilizers, cheesecloth for the *tapado* fields, and even such basic items as string, hampered production.

Weather, the old enemy, also took its toll, with unseasonal storms during 1991, 1992, and worst of all, 1993. Exports fell to 50 million.

Somehow, under these crippling circumstances, the industry's decline was halted and steady increases were recorded in 1994, 1995, and 1996.

Coincidental to this difficult era, known in Cuba as "the special period in a time of peace," was the launch in September 1992 of Marvin Shanken's *Cigar Aficionado* magazine. Demand for premium cigars in the United States took off.

The embargo has prevented Havanas from playing a major role in the U.S. boom, although Shanken took the view from the start that, without covering them, his magazine could not be considered credible. The boom then spread internationally, which combined with the fact that nothing stimulates demand amongst Americans like prohibition, meant that the Cuban industry could have sold around twice the number of cigars it was capable of exporting at the time.

Talk in Havana has turned to "a great leap forward" by the end of the century. The powers that be, conscious of the dangers of missing the wave, have decided to shoot at a target of 200 million compared to 70 million in 1996. New brands such as Cuaba, in its figurado shapes, and Vegas Robaina have been launched to stimulate demand but the goal remains a tough one.

More acres of tobacco can be planted, more rollers trained, more factories opened but, in the end, forces beyond the power of man will have to cooperate. Man must, however, make the final decision as to whether a cigar made in Cuba meets the time-honored criteria to be called a Havana.

SIMON CHASE'S TOP TEN

Over twenty years of privileged access to most of the leading brands and sizes of Havanas, I have learned just how difficult it is to make a selection. My top ten, therefore, should be taken as a stab at the time of writing rather than as a definitive list. All these cigars have given me particular pleasure at one time or another. It is probably true to say that they have proved reliable over time in delivering an experience suitable to my palate. Whether they appeal to you is for you to decide.

1. Ramon Allones Specially Selected (4⅞ × 50)

When asked which cigar I'd choose before facing the firing squad, this is my selection. Most people say I would do better to choose something longer. It's a traditional robusto, full of rich, earthy flavors for those exceptional moments, not every day.

2. Partagas Short (4½ × 42)

I like small cigars. This one has the girth of a corona, packed with the rich taste associated with a Cuban Partagas. Best when taken from a cabinet selection bundle of fifty.

3. Rafael Gonzalez Corona Extra (5½ × 46)

And now for something completely different. Light—grassy even, if it wasn't a term of abuse. It is a cigar I can share with my wife, who smokes a lot less than I do but finds this a joy.

4. Partagas Lusitania (7⅝ × 49)

Maybe this is a better choice for the firing squad. Another rich cigar. Its length means that you experience a remarkable range of flavors when you smoke it, from a delicate start through to a powerful finish. Again, bundles of fifty are preferred.

5. Cohiba Siglo III (6⅛ × 42)

This proved to be my favorite when we launched the Siglos in London in November 1993, and it still is. Be warned, however: Few people agree with me.

6. Montecristo No. 2 (6⅛ × 52)

The definitive *piramide*. Instantly recognizable. Burns beautifully. Let's face it, we all love it.

7. Romeo y Julieta Cedros No. 1 (6½ × 42)

Romeo's only true Lonsdale, wrapped in cedar. I find this size has a particular delicacy. Whether it's the cedar wrap that does it, goodness knows.

8. Cohiba Exquisito (5 × 36)

A unique size for a Cuban. The ring gauge is smaller than I usually like, but it's a wonderfully elegant, smooth cigar. Cohiba's director, Emilia Tamayo, tells me it's her favorite.

9. Hoyo de Monterrey Epicure No. 2 (4⅞ × 50)

My second robusto, but this is a comparatively light one.

10. Punch Petit Corona del Punch (5 × 42)

There are so many petit coronas to choose from, it's tough to settle on one. It is an essential size, and Punch wins by a hairsbreadth.

EXCLUSIVE
DISTRIBUTOR
IN HABANA

FABRICA DE TABACOS
"LA DIANA"

KING SALOMON'S
STORE

E PLURIBUS UNUM

PAX ET

JUSTITIA

CLARO HABANA

MADE BY HAND

PRADO 515 - HABANA - CUBA

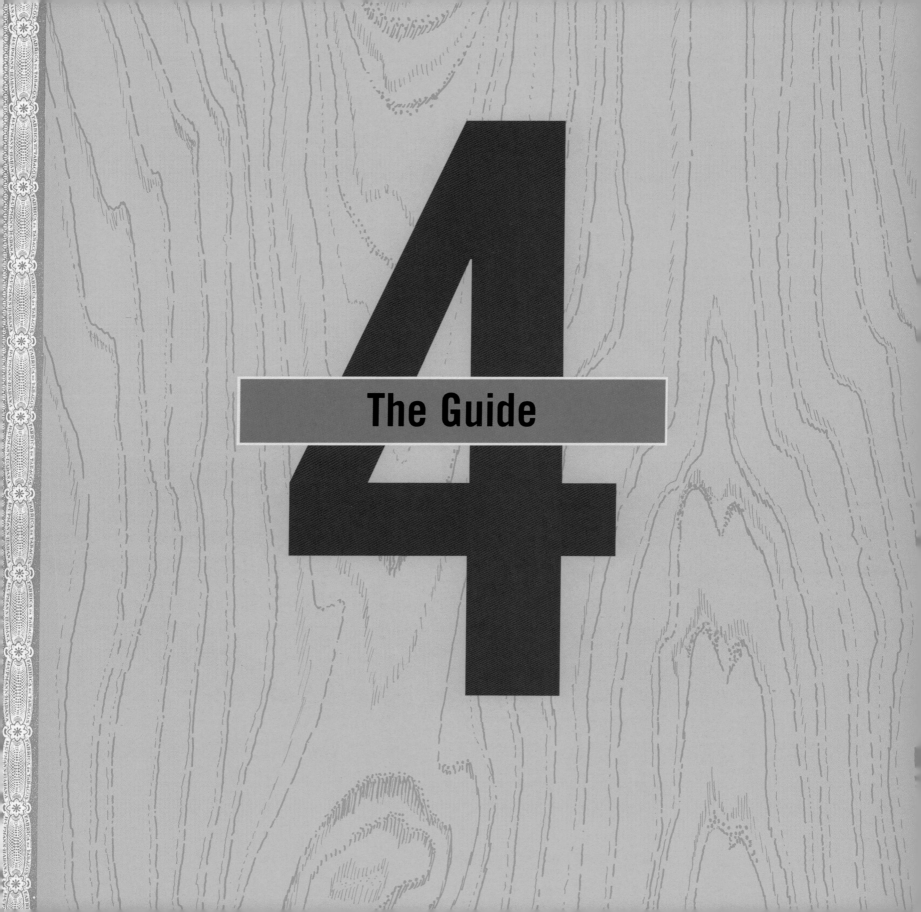

4

The Guide

PREMIER CIGARS BY SIZE

CIGARS ARE MADE in forty-two different sizes, varying in length from four to nine inches. The ring gauge, or diameter, runs from 26 to 52 points, counted in sixty-fourths of an inch. Cigar dimensions (ring gauge and length) are more precise than names or nicknames, which may vary from brand to brand. A panatela, for example, may have a different length and ring gauge, depending on whether it is a Romeo y Julieta or a Cohiba.

The Cuban *vitolas de galera* Cervante ($6\frac{1}{2} \times 42$) and Corona Grande ($6\frac{1}{8} \times 42$) are both often referred to as Lonsdales, after the Earl of Lonsdale, the great English aristocrat and sportsman. At $6\frac{1}{2}$ inches with a 42 ring gauge, the Lonsdale is a longer version of the classic and ever-popular midsize Havana, the Corona, which is $5\frac{1}{2} \times 42$. The Petit Corona (or *Mareva*, if you're going by the Cuban factory name) is a 5-inch cigar, still with the 42 ring gauge. Virtually all of the top Cuban brands offer cigars in both of these sizes. Rafael Gonzalez, however, has a Petit Corona or Mareva *and* what is called a Petit Lonsdale in the 5×42 size, while Flor de Cano's Petit Corona comes in a smaller $4\frac{3}{4} \times 40$ size. The Cuban Ramon Allones brand offers a Petit Corona, and so does the Dominican Ramon Allones, although that one's called a D.

This guide will help sort out the differences.

Key

Vitola	=	*vitola de galera* (Cuban factory name)
CW	=	cedar-wrapped
PB	=	polished box
T	=	tubed
UB	=	unvarnished box
VB	=	varnished box

VITOLAS DE GALERA (CUBAN FACTORY NAMES) IN DESCENDING ORDER BY SIZE

$9\frac{1}{4} \times 47$—Gran Corona

$7\frac{5}{8} \times 49$—Prominente
$7\frac{1}{2} \times 38$—Laguito No. 1
$7\frac{1}{16} \times 36$—Delicados extras
7×47—Julieta No. 2
7×33—Ninfa

$6\frac{7}{8} \times 28$—Panetela Larga
$6\frac{3}{4} \times 43$—Dalia
$6\frac{3}{4} \times 33$—Palma
$6\frac{9}{16} \times 38$—Parejo
$6\frac{1}{2} \times 42$—Cervante
$6\frac{1}{8} \times 52$—Piramide
$6\frac{3}{8} \times 44$—Cazadore
$6\frac{5}{16} \times 39$—Topper
$6\frac{1}{4} \times 35$—Delicioso
$6\frac{1}{8} \times 47$—Tacos
$6\frac{1}{8} \times 42$—Corona Grande
$6\frac{1}{16} \times 37$—Nacionale
6×38—Laguito No. 2
6×32—Palmitos

$5\frac{7}{8} \times 41$—Cristale
$5\frac{3}{4} \times 40$—Superiore
$5\frac{3}{4} \times 39$—Culebras
$5\frac{11}{16} \times 44$—Conserva
$5\frac{5}{8} \times 46$—Corona Gorda
$5\frac{5}{8} \times 44$—Franciscos
$5\frac{5}{8} \times 35$—Carlota
$5\frac{9}{16} \times 40$—Las Tres Coronas
$5\frac{1}{2} \times 52$—Campana
$5\frac{1}{2} \times 42$—Corona
$5\frac{1}{2} \times 40$—Crema/Nacionale
$5\frac{3}{8} \times 46$—Britanica
$5\frac{5}{16} \times 40$—Cosaco
$5\frac{1}{4} \times 45$—Especiale
$5\frac{1}{4} \times 38$—Universales
$5\frac{3}{16} \times 44$—Eminente
$5\frac{1}{8} \times 40$—Almuerzo
$5\frac{1}{16} \times 42$—Mareva
$5\frac{1}{16} \times 40$—Petit Cetro

5×48—Hermosa No. 4
5×44—Perfecto
5×40—Londres

5×38—Preferido
5×37—Veguerito
5×36—Seoane
5×35—Conchita
5×29—Demi Tip

$4\frac{15}{16} \times 34$—Placera
$4\frac{7}{8} \times 50$—Robusto
$4\frac{3}{4} \times 40$—Standard
$4\frac{3}{4} \times 26$—Carolina
$4\frac{5}{8} \times 40$—Coronita
$4\frac{9}{16} \times 35$—Sport
$4\frac{9}{16} \times 34$—Panetela
$4\frac{1}{2} \times 40$—Franciscano
$4\frac{9}{16} \times 36$—Cadete
$4\frac{1}{2} \times 26$—Laguito No. 3
$4\frac{3}{8} \times 42$—Minuto
$4\frac{5}{16} \times 38$—Trabuco
$4\frac{5}{16} \times 35$—Epicure
$4\frac{1}{4} \times 31$—Petit
$4\frac{1}{8} \times 29$—Chico
4×40—Perla

$3\frac{15}{16} \times 32$—Demi Tasse
$3\frac{7}{8} \times 37$—Infante
$3\frac{7}{8} \times 30$—Entreacto

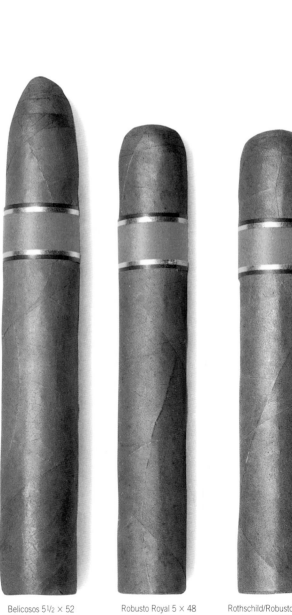

Belicosos 5½ × 52
(140mm × 20.64mm)

Robusto Royal 5 × 48
(127mm × 19.05mm)

Rothschild/Robusto 4⅞ × 50
(124mm × 19.84mm)

Corona Grande 6¾ × 43
(170mm × 17.07mm)

Lonsdale 6½ × 42
(165mm × 16.67mm)

Lonsdale 6⅛ × 42
(155mm × 16.67mm)

Corona 5½ × 42
(142mm × 16.67mm)

Petit Corona 5½ × 4
(140mm × 15.87mm)

CM

52 / 20.64

50 / 19.84   49 / 19.45

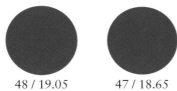

48 / 19.05   47 / 18.65

46 / 18.26   43 / 17.07

42 / 16.67   40 / 15.87

38 / 15.08   36 / 14.29

34 / 13.49   33 / 13.10

30 / 11.91   26 / 10.32

ABOVE ARE FIFTEEN OF THE
MOST COMMON CIGAR RING
SIZES IN SIXTY-FOURTHS OF AN
INCH AND MILLIMETERS. USE
THESE GUIDES AND THE RULERS
TO DETERMINE THE SIZE OF
YOUR OWN FAVORITES.

LARGE RING GAUGE

Gigante 9¼ × 47
(235mm × 18.65mm)

Double Corona 7⅝ × 49
(194mm × 19.45mm)

Churchill 7 × 47
(178mm × 18.65mm)

Torpedo 6⅛ × 52
(156mm × 20.64mm)

Corona Extra 5⅝
(143mm × 18.26

1. LARGE RING GAUGE 47–52

Popular name: **Gigante**
Vitola: **Gran Corona**
Size: **9¼ × 47**

Cuban
Montecristo A (PB)
Punch Diademas Extra
Romeo y Julieta Fabulosos
Sancho Panza Sanchos
Hoyo de Monterrey Particulares

Dominican
Opus X Reserva A

Popular name: **Double Corona**
Vitola: **Prominente**
Size: **7⅝ × 49**

Cuban
Hoyo de Monterrey Double Corona
Punch Double Corona
Partagas Lusitanias

Dominican
Arturo Fuente Royal Salute
Opus X Double Corona

Popular name: **Churchill**
Vitola: **Julieta**
Size: **7 × 47**

Cuban
Bolivar Corona Gigantes
Cohiba Esplendidos
El Rey del Mundo Tainos
La Flor de Cano Diademas
H. Upmann Monarchs (T)
H. Upmann Sir Winston (PB)
Hoyo de Monterrey Churchills
La Gloria Cubana Tainos
Partagas Churchills De Luxe
Punch Churchills
Romeo y Julieta Churchills (T)
Romeo y Julieta Prince of Wales
Saint Luis Rey Churchills
Sancho Panza Corona Gigantes

Dominican
Arturo Fuente Hemingway Classic

Popular name: **Torpedo (shaped)**
Vitola: **Piramide**
Size: **6⅛ × 52**

Cuban
H. Upmann No. 2
Montecristo No. 2
Diplomaticos No. 2

Popular name: **Corona Extra**
Vitola: **Corona Gorda**
Size: **5⅝ × 46**

Cuban
Cohiba Siglo IV
H. Upmann Magnum 46
Hoyo de Monterrey Epicure No. 1
Punch Punch Punch
Rafael Gonzalez Corona Extras
Saint Luis Rey Serie A

Dominican
Davidoff 5000
Fuente Fuente
H. Upmann Churchills

Honduran
Hoyo de Monterrey Coronas
JR Ultimate Corona
Punch Grand Cru Superior

Popular name: **Belicosos (*figurado*/shaped)**
Vitola: **Campana**
Size: **5½ × 52**

Cuban
Bolivar Belicosos Finos
Belicosos: Romeo y Julieta, Sancho Panza

Popular name: **Robusto Royal**
Vitola: **Hermoso No. 4**
Size: **5 × 48**

Cuban
El Rey del Mundo Choix Supreme
H. Upmann Connoisseur No. 1
Romeo y Julieta Exhibicion No. 4
Saint Luis Rey Regios

Dominican
Dunhill Altamiras

Popular name: **Rothschild/Robusto**
Vitola: **Robusto**
Size: **4⅞ × 50**

Cuban
Bolivar Royal Corona
Cohiba Robustos
Flor de Cano Short Churchill
Hoyo de Monterrey Epicure No. 2
Partagas Serie D, No. 4

2. MEDIUM RING GAUGE 40–46

Popular name: **Corona Grande**
Vitola: **Dalia**
Size: 6¾ × **43**

Cuban
Cohiba Siglo V
Partagas 8-9-8 (VB)

Dominican
Cubita 8-9-8
Jose Benito Corona
Licenciados Excelente
Licenciados 300
Nat Sherman Algonquin
Partagas No. 1
Partagas Limited Reserve Royale
Ramon Allones Trumps

Popular name: **Lonsdale**
Vitola: **Cervante**
Size: 6½ × **42**

Cuban
Diplomaticos No. 1
La Gloria Cubana Cetros
Montecristo No. 1
Quintero Churchills
Romeo y Julieta Cedros De Luxe No. 1 (CW)
Sancho Panza Molino
Lonsdales: El Rey del Mundo, H. Upmann (aka No. 1), Partagas, Por Larranaga, Rafael Gonzalez, Saint Luis Rey

Dominican
Arturo Fuente Spanish Lonsdale
Casa Blanca Lonsdale
Cuesta-Rey Dominican No. 4
Montecruz No. 210
Nat Sherman Butterfield 8
Ramon Allones B
Santa Damiana Seleccion No. 700

Honduran
Cuba Aliados Lonsdale
Hoyo de Monterrey No. 1
Punch Lonsdale

Jamaican
Macanudo Baron de Rothschild

Popular name: **Lonsdale**
Vitola: **Corona Grande**
Size: 6⅛ × **42**

Cuban
Cohiba Siglo III
Hoyo de Monterrey Le Hoyo des Dieux
La Gloria Cubana Sabrosos

Dominican
Davidoff 4000
Davidoff Grand Cru No. 1

Popular name: **Corona**
Vitola: **Corona**
Size: 5½ × **42**

Cuban
Diplomaticos No. 3
El Rey del Mundo Corona de Luxe
H. Upmann Royal Corona (T)
Montecristo No. 3
Romeo y Julieta Cedros De Luxe No. 2 (CW)
Hoyo de Monterrey Le Hoyo du Roi
Punch Royal Coronation
Coronas: Bolivar, H. Upmann, Hoyo de Monterrey, Partagas, Por Larranaga, Punch, Quintero, Romeo y Julieta

Dominican
Montecruz No. 220
Montesino Diplomatico
Nat Sherman Hampshire
Primo del Rey Seleccion No. 4
Coronas: Casa Blanca, Jose Marti, Santa Damiana

Honduran
El Rey del Mundo Habana Club

Jamaican and Dominican
Macanudo Duke of Devon

Popular name: **Petit Corona**
Vitola: **Nacionales/Crema**
Size: 5½ × **40**

Cuban
Quintero Media Corona

Dominican
Avo No. 8
Pleiades Antares

Popular name: **Petit Corona**
Vitola: **Mareva (or Petit Corona)**
Size: 5 × **42**

Cuban
Cohiba Siglo II
Diplomaticos No. 4
Gispert Petit Corona De Luxe
Montecristo No. 4
Montecristo Petit Tubos (T)
Punch Coronation (T)
Punch Royal Selection No. 12
Rafael Gonzalez Petit Lonsdale
Romeo y Julieta Cedros De Luxe No. 3 (CW)
Petit Coronas: Bolivar, El Rey del Mundo, H. Upmann, Partagas, Por Larranaga, Punch, Rafael Gonzalez, Ramon Allones, Romeo y Julieta, Saint Luis Rey

Dominican
Davidoff 2000
Davidoff Grand Cru No. 3
Montecruz Cedar-aged
Ramon Allones D
Santa Damiana Petit Corona
Santa Damiana Tubulares No. 400 (T)

Mexican
Te-Amo No. 4

Popular name: **Petit Corona**
Vitola: **Petit Cetro (Exquisitos)**
Size: 5 × **40**

Cuban
Bolivar Bonitas
Hoyo de Monterrey Le Hoyo du Prince

Popular name: **Petit Corona**
Vitola: **Standard**
Size: 4¾ × **40**

Popular name: **Half Corona**
Vitola: **Minuto**
Size: 4⅜ × **42**

Popular name: **Half Corona**
Vitola: **Franciscano (Tres Petit Corona)**
Size: 4½ × **40**

GAUGE

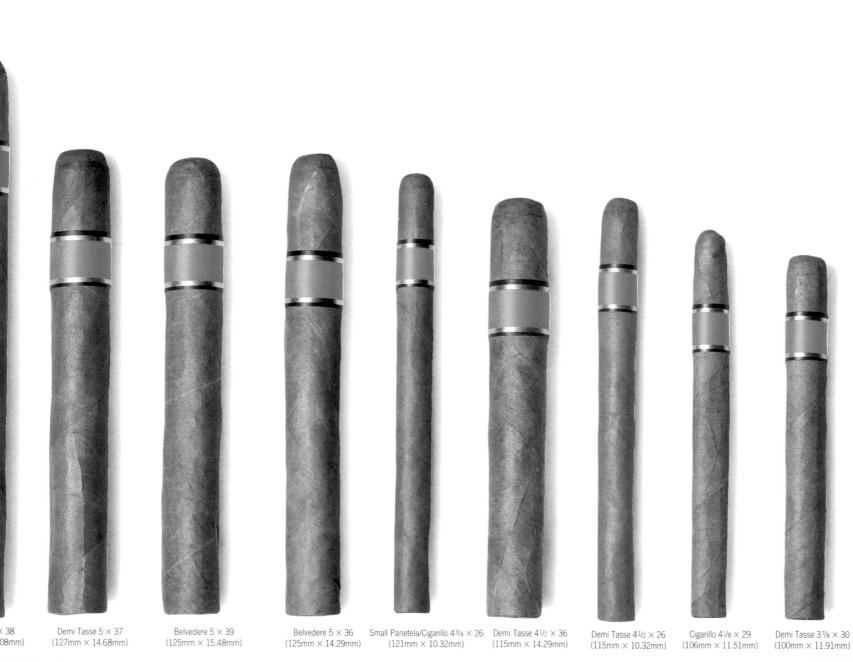

× 38
5.08mm)

Demi Tasse 5 × 37
(127mm × 14.68mm)

Belvedere 5 × 39
(125mm × 15.48mm)

Belvedere 5 × 36
(125mm × 14.29mm)

Small Panetela/Cigarillo 4³/₄ × 26
(121mm × 10.32mm)

Demi Tasse 4¹/₂ × 36
(115mm × 14.29mm)

Demi Tasse 4¹/₂ × 26
(115mm × 10.32mm)

Cigarillo 4¹/₈ × 29
(106mm × 11.51mm)

Demi Tasse 3⁷/₈ × 30
(100mm × 11.91mm)

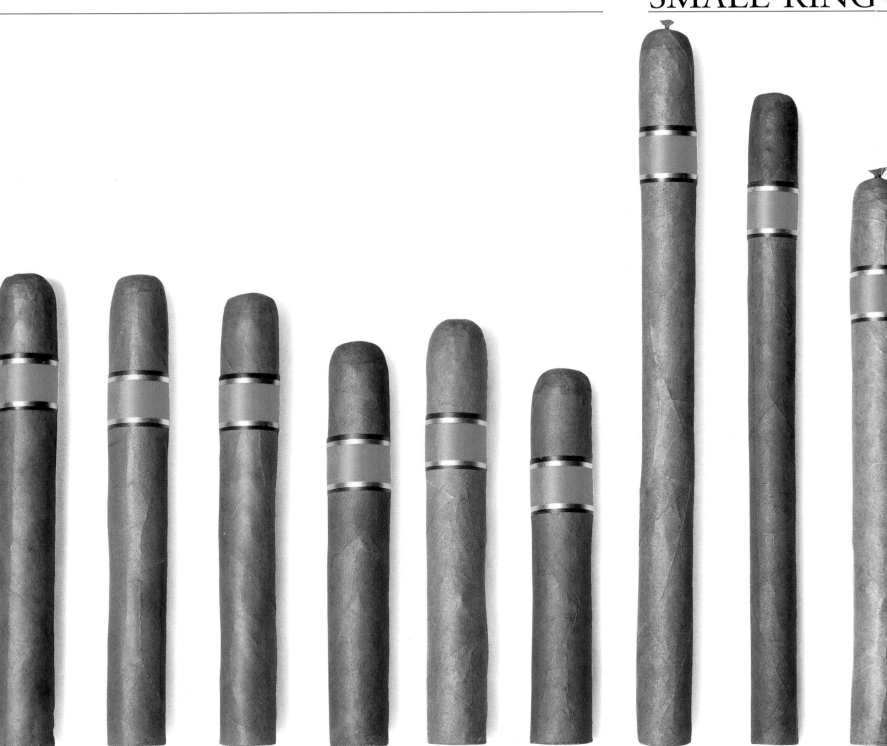

Petit Corona 5 × 42
(129mm × 16.67mm)

Petit Corona 5 × 40
(129mm × 15.87mm)

Petit Corona 4³/₄ × 40
(123mm × 15.87mm)

Half Corona 4³/₈ × 42
(110mm × 16.67mm)

Half Corona 4¹/₂ × 40
(116mm × 15.87mm)

Half Corona 4 × 40
(102mm × 15.87mm)

Gran Panetela 7¹/₂ × 38
(192mm × 15.08mm)

Long Panetela 7 × 33
(178mm × 13.10mm)

Panetela
(152mm ×

Cuban
La Gloria Cubana Minutos
Por Larranaga Small Corona
Punch Coronets
Rafael Gonzalez Tres Petit Lonsdales
Tres Petit Corona: Partagas, Romeo y Julieta

Dominican
Davidoff Grand Cru No. 4

Popular name: **Half Corona**
Vitola: **Perla**
Size: **4 × 40**

Cuban
Cohiba Siglo I
Diplomaticos No. 5
Montecristo No. 5
Punch Petit Punch
Romeo y Julieta Petit Prince

3. SMALL RING GAUGE 26–39

Popular name: **Gran (long) Panetela**
Vitola: **Laguito No. 1/Delicado**
Size: **7½ × 38**

Cuban
Cohiba Lanceros
Diplomaticos No. 6
Montecristo Especial
Trinidad

Dominican
Davidoff Tubo No. 1 (T)
H. Upmann Chairman's Reserve
Macanudo Vintage No. 7

Popular name: **Long Panetela**
Vitola: **Ninfas**
Size: **7 × 33**

Cuban
Bolivar Palmas
Partagas Palmes Grandes

Dominican
Davidoff 3000

Popular name: **Panetela**
Vitola: **Laguito No. 2**
Size: **6 × 38**

Cuban
Cohiba Coronas Especiales
Diplomaticos No. 7
Hoyo de Monterrey Le Hoyo du Dauphin
Montecristo Especial No. 2

Dominican
Davidoff Tubo No. 2 (T)
Griffin's No. 400
Nat Sherman Murray 7

Popular name: **Demi Tasse**
Vitola: **Veguerito**
Size: **5 × 37**

Cuban
Rafael Gonzalez Panetelas Extra

Popular name: **Belvedere**
Vitola: **Belvedere**
Size: **5 × 39**

Popular name: **Belvedere**
Vitola: **Seoane**
Size: **5 × 36**

Cuban
Cohiba Exquisitos

Honduran
Cuba Aliados Petit Cetro

Popular name: **Small Panetela/Cigarillo**
Vitola: **Carolina**
Size: **4¾ × 26**

Cuban
Margaritas: Hoyo de Monterrey, Punch

Popular name: **Demi Tasse**
Vitola: **Cadete**
Size: **4½ × 36**

Cuban
Fonseca K.D.T. Cadete
H. Upmann Corona Junior (T)
H. Upmann Petit Upmann

Popular name: **Demi Tasse**
Vitola: **Laguito No. 3**
Size: **4½ × 26**

Cuban
Cohiba Panetelas
Montecristo Joyitas
Rafael Gonzalez

Popular name: **Cigarillo**
Vitola: **Chicos**
Size: **4⅛ × 29**

Popular name: **Demi Tasse**
Vitola: **Entreacto**
Size: **3⅛ × 30**

Cuban
Romeo y Julieta Petit Julietas
Demi Tasse: Bolivar, El Rey del Mundo,
Rafael Gonzalez

THE CIGAR CONNOISSEUR'S CHOICE

Following is a list of The Cigar Connoisseur's *top ten favorite cigars. They are all highly recommended and are therefore presented in alphabetical order.*

Arturo Fuente Flor Fina 8-5-8: "Mild and easy."

Avo: "Smokes like silk."

Cohiba Robusto: "A rich, smooth-drawing cigar."

Davidoff Special Blends: "Smooth and gracious."

Hoyo de Monterrey Epicure No. 2: "Full and elegant."

Macanudo Vintage No. 3: "Well made with sweet spice flavors."

Montecristo No. 4 (Cuban): "Rich and relaxed."

Opus X No. 2 (pyramid): "A beautiful draw with cedar and nut flavors."

Partagas Churchill De Luxe (Cuban): "The quintessential Havana, flavorful, full-bodied, worthy of its name."

Partagas Limited Reserve Regale (Dominican): "A short Churchill, well-rounded sweetish flavor, in a superior Cameroon wrapper."

BRAND BY BRAND LISTING

The following is a selection of the world's finest hand-rolled premium cigars—it is not meant to be encyclopedic. It was prepared in consultation with two of the foremost experts in the field, Simon Chase and Lew Rothman. All lengths are noted in inches; ring gauges are measured by ¹/₆₄ inch.

THE WORLD'S FINEST CIGARS BY COUNTRY

CUBA

Bolivar, Cohiba, Cuaba, Diplomaticos, El Rey del Mundo, Fonseca, Gispert, H. Upmann, Hoyo de Monterrey, La Flor de Cano, La Gloria Cubana, Montecristo, Partagas, Por Larranaga, Punch, Quintero, Rafael Gonzalez, Ramon Allones, Romeo y Julieta, Saint Luis Rey, Sancho Panza, Trinidad

DOMINICAN REPUBLIC

Arturo Fuente, Ashton, Avo, Bauza, Canaria d'Oro, Casa Blanca, Cifuentes, Cubita, Cuesta-Rey, Davidoff, Don Diego, Dunhill, Griffin's, H. Upmann, Jose Benito, Jose Marti, JR Cigars Special Jamaicans, Las Cabrillas, Licenciados, Macanudo (also made in Jamaica), Montecristo, Montecruz, Montesino, Nat Sherman, Partagas, Pleiades, Por Larranaga, Primo del Rey, Ramon Allones, Romeo y Julieta Vintage, Royal Jamaica, Santa Damiana

HONDURAS

Cuba Aliados, El Rey del Mundo, Hoyo de Monterrey, Hoyo de Monterrey Excalibur, JR Cigars Special Coronas, JR Cigars Ultimates, Punch, Puros Indios, Jose Marti, Zino

ITALY

Toscani

JAMAICA

Macanudo (also made in the Dominican Republic), Temple Hall

MEXICO

Santa Clara, Te-Amo

NICARAGUA

Flor de Farach, Jose Marti, Villar y Villar

SPAIN

Casa Buena, Penamil

UNITED STATES

La Gloria Cubana

ARTURO FUENTE (DOMINICAN REPUBLIC)

The Fuente family, with roots in Spain and Cuba, has been in the cigar manufacturing business for three generations. The patriarch, Don Arturo, set up operations in Tampa in 1912, after working for a number of American cigar makers around the turn of the century. Don Arturo's son Carlos and his grandchildren, Carlos Jr. and Cynthia, work in the family business, which is now based primarily in Santiago, the Dominican Republic (550 employees; 70,000-square-foot factory, originally established in 1980). There is another factory in Moca (150 employees, established in 1990). The largest producers of premium cigars in the Dominican Republic, the Fuentes also use many types of fine tobaccos from Connecticut, Mexico, Brazil, Cameroon, and Nicaragua for their wrappers, binders, and fillers.

They produce a wide range of excellent cigars under Don Arturo's name, including the Flor Fina 8-5-8; they also make other distinguished brands such as Ashton and Cuesta-Rey. In the early 1990s the Fuentes bought a farm in El Caribe from the Olivas and renamed it Château de la Fuente. Many were skeptical about their plan to grow fine wrapper leaves, but now that these wrappers are on the market with the Opus X, the experiment is considered to have been a great success. *Cigar Aficionado* gave the cigar highest ratings.

The Arturo Fuente is a "Cuban-style" cigar featuring a colorado Cameroon wrapper, with light-to-medium body and fine flavor. There is a standard range, a Hemingway series of larger *figurado* cigars, and of course the superb Opus X. Most of the standard sizes are available in a choice of EMS or maduro wrapper. Some of the sizes, such as the Rothschild and Double Corona, have individual cedar encasements. The Hemingway series brings back the old torpedo or perfecto shape, also known as an *obsequio*, which is like the plumb bulb on a surveyor's instrument.

Model	Length	Ring Gauge
Canones	8½	52
Chateau Fuente Royal Salute**	7⅝	54
Churchill	7¼	48
Panetela Fina	7	38
Chateau Fuente Double**	6¾	50
Seleccion Privada No. 1	6¾	44
Spanish Lonsdale	6½	42
Corona Imperial	6½	46
Flor Fina 8-5-8	6	47
1912	6	42
Cuban Corona	5¼	45
Petit Corona	5	38
Chateau Fuente**	4½	50

Opus X Series

Model	Length	Ring Gauge
Double Corona	7⅝	46
Reserve Chateau	7	58
Perfection No. 2	6⅜	52
Petit Lancero	6¼	38
Fuente Fuente	5⅝	46
Robusto	5¼	50
Perfection No. 5	4⅛	40

Hemingway Series (torpedo or perfecto shaped)

Model	Length	Ring Gauge
Masterpiece	9	52
Classic	7	47
Signature	6	47

**cedar-encased

ASHTON (DOMINICAN REPUBLIC)

The brand was established in the mid-1980s by Philadelphia tobacco retailer Robert Levin of Holt's Tobacco. It's made at the Fuentes' Santiago factory and consequently, like other Fuente products, "packs a lot more wallop" than most Dominican cigars. There are three lines: standard, Cabinet Selection, and Aged Maduro. All three feature fine Connecticut wrappers—the maduro a broadleaf, the others shade—and Dominican filler blends. The new Ashton Crown series has a Chateau de la Fuente wrapper. The Cabinet Selection is the mildest; the standards are mild-to medium-bodied; the Maduro No. 10, for example, has a sweeter flavor.

Model	Length	Ring Gauge
Churchill	7½	52
Prime Minister	6⅞	48
8-9-8	6½	44
Elegante	6½	35
Double "R"	6	50
Panetela	6	36
Corona	5½	44
Magnum	5	50

Cabinet Selection		
No. 1	9	52
No. 10	7½	52
No. 2	7	46
No. 8	7	50
No. 7	6¼	52
No. 3	6	46
No. 6	5½	50

Aged Maduro		
No. 60	7½	52
No. 50	7	48
No. 30	6¾	44
No. 40	6	50
No. 20	5½	44
No. 10	5	50

AVO (DOMINICAN REPUBLIC)

The Avo was introduced in 1986 by the composer and entrepreneur Avo Uvezian, who inspired the song "Strangers in the Night." Avos are made by the Tabacos Dominicanos (Tabadom) factory, which also makes Davidoffs, under the expert supervision of Hendrik Kelner. (In 1996 Tabadom made more than 6 million Davidoffs, more than 2 million Avos, and about 700,000 Griffin's.) The XO Series and the regular Avo line have a subtle balance of flavor between their Connecticut wrappers and Dominican fillers and binders and offer a mild-to-medium-strength smoke. These are very well-constructed cigars with several interesting pyramid and belicoso sizes, although they're different from the classic Cuban sizes of the same name.

Model	Length	Ring Gauge
Especiales	8	48
No. 3	7½	52
Pyramid	7	54
No. 4	7	38
No. 5	6¾	46
No. 1	6¾	42
No. 6	6½	36
No. 2	6	50
Belicosos	6	50
No. 7	6	44
Petit Belicosos	4¾	50
No. 8	5½	40
No. 9	4¾	48

XO Series		
Maestoso	7	48
Preludo	6	40
Intermezzo	5½	50

BAUZA (DOMINICAN REPUBLIC)

This brand, created by Cuban exile Oscar Boruchin and his team at Mike's Cigars in Miami, is manufactured by the Fuentes in the Dominican Republic to their usual excellent quality standards. The packaging and presentation recall the great Cuban prerevolution tradition, but the cigars themselves are in the style of premium Dominicans. They offer a mild-to-medium-bodied smoke with very fine colorado Cameroon wrappers and a blend of Dominican and Nicaraguan fillers. They are reasonably priced given their quality. Mike's is hands down one of the top cigar emporiums in the world, well worth a visit. They also do a very healthy mail-order business, so you can order a box of Bauzas over the phone.

Model	Length	Ring Gauge
Fabulosos	7½	50
Medalla de Oro		
No. 1	6⅞	44
Florete	6⅞	35
Casa Grande	6¾	48
Jaguar	6½	42
Robusto	5½	50
Grecos	5½	42
Petit Corona	5	38

BOLIVAR (CUBA)

"El Libertador," Simón Bolívar, freed much of South America from Spanish rule. Bolívar died in 1830, and his great deeds were commemorated with many monuments, including this brand of cigars, which was introduced in 1901 by the Rocha company of Havana and features his distinctive portrait on its bands and boxes. Bolivars achieved their current status as among the best Havanas in the 1950s, when Ramón and Rafael Cifuentes took over the operation. It is a full-bodied line of hand-made cigars that offer good value among Havanas. Definitely not recommended for beginning smokers, their wrappers are quite dark and their flavor strong due to the fact that the blend has more *seco* than *volado*. The machine-made Bolivars are of poor quality; choose only the large handmade ones. Five sizes are made in the Dominican Republic, but aficionados feel that they don't really measure up to the Cubans.

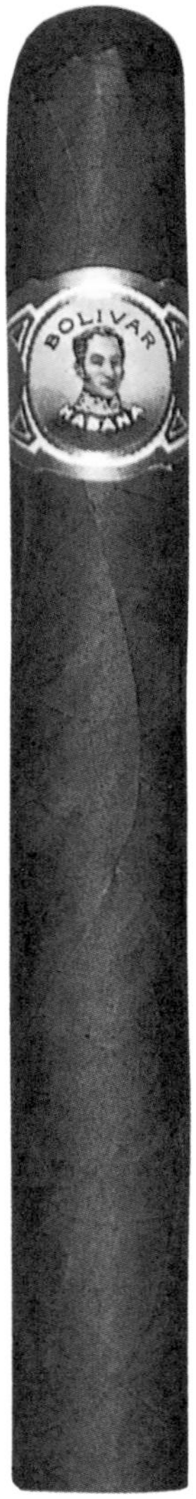

Model	Length	Ring Gauge
Corona Gigantes	7	47
Palmas	7	33
Inmensas	6⅝	43
Gold Medal	6⅜	42
Corona Extra	5⅝	44
Belicosos Finos	5½	52
Corona	5½	42
Petit Corona	5	42
Bonitas	5	40
Royal Corona	4⅞	50
Corona Junior	4¼	42

CANARIA D'ORO (DOMINICAN REPUBLIC)

With its striking red bands featuring a white dove and its classic packaging, this well-made, consistent brand from Consolidated offers a sweetish mild to medium smoke with a medium brown EMS-style Cameroon wrapper. The excellent Rothschild robusto size comes with a maduro wrapper and is highly recommended.

Model	Length	Ring Gauge
Supremo	7	45
Lonsdale	6½	42
Vista	6¼	32
Fino	6	31
Inmenso	5½	49
Corona	5½	42
Rothschild	4½	50

CASA BLANCA (DOMINICAN REPUBLIC)

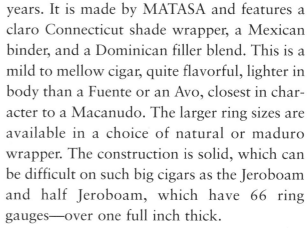

Casa Blanca, which means "White House" in Spanish, was originally created to be smoked there during the Reagan years. It is made by MATASA and features a claro Connecticut shade wrapper, a Mexican binder, and a Dominican filler blend. This is a mild to mellow cigar, quite flavorful, lighter in body than a Fuente or an Avo, closest in character to a Macanudo. The larger ring sizes are available in a choice of natural or maduro wrapper. The construction is solid, which can be difficult on such big cigars as the Jeroboam and half Jeroboam, which have 66 ring gauges—over one full inch thick.

Model	Length	Ring Gauge
Jeroboam	10	66
Presidente	7½	50
Magnum	7	60
Lonsdale	6½	42
De Luxe	6	50
Panetela	6	35
Corona	5½	42
Half Jeroboam	5	66
Bonitas	4	36

Casa Buena (Spain)

This brand, which recently replaced the Penamils that were being sold in the United States, is made in the Canary Islands from a blend of Brazilian, Dominican, and Mexican fillers, a Mexican binder, and a Connecticut shade wrapper. It's a mild to medium smoke with plenty of flavor, likely due to the inclusion of Brazilian tobacco, which is not found in many superpremium brands.

Model	Length	Ring Gauge
Especiales Range		
No. 1	7½	50
No. 3	6½	43
No. 2	6	50
No. 4	4¾	50

Cifuentes (Dominican Republic)

The original Cifuentes cigars were created in Cuba by the legendary Partagas master cigar maker Don Ramón Cifuentes and introduced by Jaime Partagas in 1876.

A year short of a century later, Don Ramón's son Ramón sold the brand names Cifuentes, Partagas, and Ramon Allones to General Cigar Company after he realized that he would never be able to make his cigars again in Cuba.

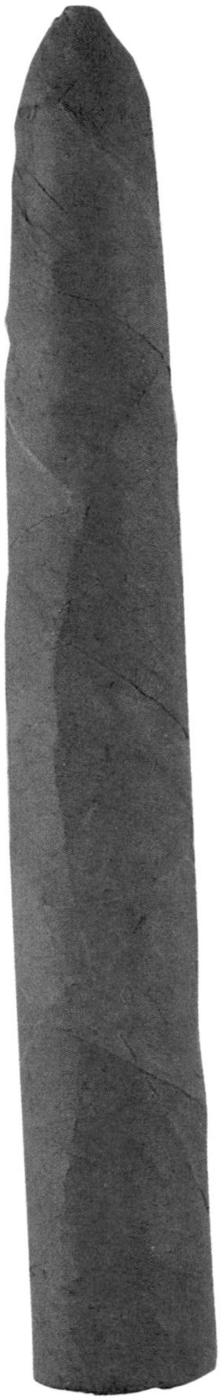

In May 1996, General Cigar released a limited edition of 150,000 Cifuentes by Partagas cigars for distribution in Dunhill stores. The cigars, which had been aged for two years after having been rolled in General Cigar's Jamaica factory, were made with a Connecticut shade wrapper and a rich blend of Dominican and Mexican filler as well as a Cameroon binder, an unprecedented departure for an entire General Cigar brand.

The five sizes in the Cifuentes by Partagas edition included a Petit Corona, a Lonsdale, a Pyramid, a Corona Gorda, and a Churchill. The Pyramid, which is shown here, was available only in boxes of twenty priced at $360 each.

General Cigar plans to release a new, ongoing version of the Cifuentes brand in limited quantities.

COHIBA (CUBA)

Indisputably among the best cigars available, this brand was originally reserved exclusively for Fidel Castro to hand out as gifts of diplomacy. *Cohiba* meant "cigar" to the native Taino Indians of Cuba. Legend has it that one of Castro's bodyguards introduced the president to the cigar maker Eduardo Ribera, who created three sizes: the Lancero, the Corona Especial, and the Panetela. From 1968 until 1994 the factory was run by Avelino Lara, one of four brothers who were expert rollers, but in 1994 Emilia Tamayo became managing director, presiding over the famous Cohiba factory El Laguito, an estate in Havana near Miramar. The majority of the rollers at El Laguito are female, and some Cohibas are now also made at the H. Upmann and Partagas factories.

The secret to their superb, rich smooth flavor is in the leaves, selected from among the top few farms in the Vuelta Abajo growing region, and in the unique third fermentation for the *ligero* and *seco* leaves. In 1992 Cohiba introduced five new sizes in its Siglo series to commemorate the five hundredth anniversary of Columbus's discovery of the Americas.

The original Cohiba is classified as a medium-to-full-flavored cigar among Havanas, while the new line, with its new blend, is a medium. General Cigar registered the trademark in the United States in 1980 and offers a line of non-Cuban Cohibas that don't compare with the Cubans. The genuine Cohiba is among the most expensive and sought-after cigars in the world.

Model	Length	Ring Gauge
Lancero	7½	38
Esplendido	7	47
Coronas Especiales	6	38
Exquisito	5	36
Robusto	4⅞	50
Panetela	4½	26

Siglo Series		
Siglo V	6⅝	43
Siglo III	6⅛	42
Siglo IV	5⅝	46
Siglo II	5	42
Siglo I	4	40

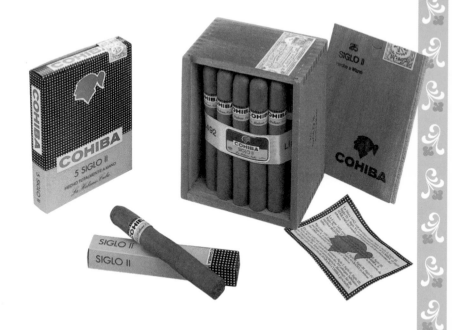

CUABA (CUBA)

Habanos, S.A., launched this new brand in fall 1996 with a lavish charity dinner in London to rival the one given to launch the Cohiba Siglo line back in 1993. The name, like Cohiba, comes from the original natives of Cuba, the Taino Indians, and refers to a bush grown on the island that burns exceedingly well and was used to light the cohibas in past times. Cuabas are manufactured at the Romeo y Julieta (FPG) factory and come in four *figurado* sizes; they are perfectos, that is, pointed at each end, recalling the type of cigars that were popular toward the end of the nineteenth century when Havanas first became world famous. Worldwide distribution of this new brand began mid-1997.

Model	Length	Ring Gauge
Exclusivos	5⅜	46
Generosos	5⅛	41
Tradicionales	4¾	41
Divinos	4	42

CUBA ALIADOS (HONDURAS)

Rolando Reyes, who makes the Cuba Aliados in his Danlí factory, is in the opinion of many experts the greatest cigar maker in the world today. Its rock-solid construction is on a par with that of the Macanudo or any other of the world's finest brands. Cuba Aliados stands out because it maintains such a high standard in rare sizes such as the bulbous 7½ × 60 Diademas or the conical Piramide, also 7½ × 60. With its Ecuadoran Sumatra-seed wrapper, Cuban-seed Honduran binder, and Dominican and Brazilian filler blend, the Aliados is a full-bodied Cuban-style cigar that many believe measures up to the best of the Havanas. Most sizes are available in claro, colorado claro, or colorado wrappers; the latter has an especially rich flavor. The company also recently introduced the excellent Puros Indios.

Model	Length	Ring Gauge
General	18	66
Figurin	10	66
Diademas (torpedo)	7½	66
Piramides No. 1	7½	60
Churchill	7¼	54
Valentino	7	48
Palma	7	36
Corona Deluxe	6½	46
Lonsdale	6½	42
Pyramid No. 2	6	56
Toro	6	54
No. 4	5½	45
Remedio	5½	43
Rothschild	5	51
Petit Cetro	5	36

CUBITA (DOMINICAN REPUBLIC)

Cubita, like its sister brands Fonseca, Casa Blanca, and Romeo y Julieta Vintage, is a fine mild-to-medium-bodied cigar made by MATASA. It is well made with Connecticut shade wrappers, Mexican binders, and a blend of Caribbean-basin fillers.

Model	Length	Ring Gauge
No. 2	6¼	38
No. 2000	7	50
No. 500	5½	43
No. 700	6	50
8-9-8	6¾	43

CUESTA-REY (DOMINICAN REPUBLIC)

This brand, founded in 1884 by Angel LaMadrid Cuesta and his eventual partner Peregrino Rey, moved to Ybor City, Tampa, in 1893. It was made there until the early 1990s, when production was shifted to the Fuente factory in Santiago. Cuesta's son Carl sold out to M&N Cigar of Tampa in 1958. The brand is still the flagship of M&N, owned by the Newman family, which has its own one-hundred-year history in the industry. Stanford Newman, 78, and his sons Eric, 47, and Bobby, 44, run the business today.

This is a medium-bodied, "Fuente-style" smoke available in a large variety of shapes, sizes, and packaging. There are four lines, including standard Cuesta-Reys, Centennial Collection (celebrating the brand's hundredth anniversary in 1984); No. 95 (commemorating the Newman family business's centennial in 1995), Cabinet Selection; and standard. Most sizes are available with EMS or maduro wrappers; the chart shows a selection of the best.

Model	Length	Ring Gauge
No. 1	8½	52
No. 2	7¼	48
Aristocrat	7	46
No. 3	7	36
No. 4	6½	42
No. 5	5½	43
Captiva	6³⁄₁₆	42
Cameo	4¼	32

DAVIDOFF (DOMINICAN REPUBLIC)

An exceptional handmade premium cigar, the Davidoff was created by the legendary Zino Davidoff in 1990 after his 1989 break with Cubatabaco. He had been associated with Cuban cigars since the late 1960s. Along with his friend and successor Ernst Schneider, he built an empire on tobacco products, starting with their house-brand Havanas. They came in three series: The fullest-flavored was the Chateau range; the Thousands series was somewhat milder; and the Dom Perignon Nos. 1 and 2 even milder.

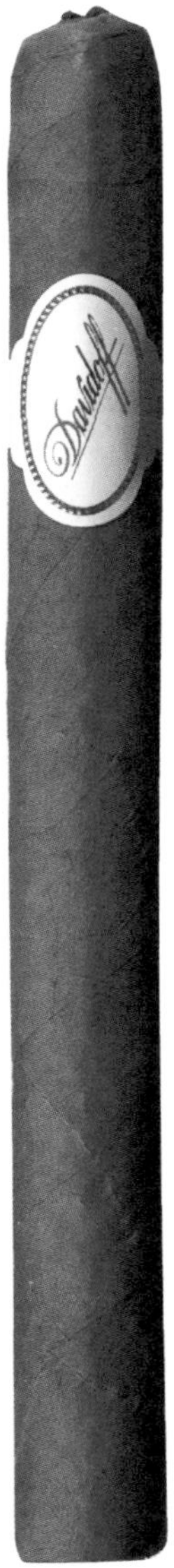

Wrapped in claro Connecticut leaf, the new Dominican cigars are lighter but still maintain the highest standards. The Grand Cru is the richest in flavor; the Thousands series is milder; and the Ambassadrice and Nos. 1, 2, and 3 are very delicate and mild. Davidoff has introduced wider-gauge cigars, like the Special R (a robusto), Special T (a pyramid), and the Double R (a double corona), all of which offer a surprisingly light, mild smoke for their size.

Under the careful and expert eyes of Ernst Schneider, Hendrik Kelner, Rene Hollenstein, and Raymond Scheurer, the cigars are now made with rigid quality controls in the Dominican Republic, starting with some of the best tobacco grown in the world. Davidoffs are rich and robust, milder and mellow, smooth and silky without the hard knockout punch of the classic Cuban, in keeping with today's taste. Each crafted cigar is inspected three times. At any point during the making, a cigar can be pulled from the process for any irregularity. After they're inspected in the Dominican Republic, they are shipped to distribution centers in Basel, Amsterdam, and Stamford, Connecticut. At these centers, they are tested and each cigar inspected for perfect quality, size, and structure before they can be banded and boxed "Davidoff." Rejects are returned to the Dominican Republic.

Model	Length	Ring Gauge
Anniversario No. 1 (wooden tube)	8⅔	48
Tubo No. 1	7½	38
Anniversario No. 2 (wooden tube)	7	48
Special T	6	52
Double R	6	50
Tubo No. 2	6	38
Tubo No. 3	5⅛	30
Special R	5	50
Ambassadrice	4⅝	26
Thousands Series		
3000	7	33
4000	6⅛	42
5000	5⅝	46
2000	5	42
1000	4⅝	34
Grand Cru Series		
Grand Cru No. 1	6⅛	42
Grand Cru No. 2	5⅝	42
Grand Cru No. 3	5	42
Grand Cru No. 4	4½	40

DIPLOMATICOS (CUBA)

The sizes and shapes of these Havanas are similar to the Montecristo; the logo on the band is an old-fashioned livery carriage, which has been copied by the Dominican brand Licenciados. Diplomaticos were introduced in 1966 primarily for export to France. They have darker wrappers and a medium-to-full-bodied flavor. The Nos. 1, 2, and 3 are especially recommended.

Model	Length	Ring Gauge
No. 6	7½	38
No. 1	6½	42
No. 2	6⅛	52
No. 7	6	38
No. 3	5½	42
No. 4	5	42
No. 5	4	40

DON DIEGO (DOMINICAN REPUBLIC)

Cuban exile Pepe García created this brand in the mid-1960s, and it was acquired by the Consolidated Cigar Company several years later, when they formed Cuban Cigar Brands under García in the Canary Islands. The brand is now made at Consolidated's La Romana facility in the Dominican Republic, with a Dominican binder and assorted long fillers, with first-rate claro and colorado claro Connecticut shade wrappers.

A very light, aromatic, and flavorful smoke, similar to the Macanudo or the Casa Blanca, the Don Diego comes in a fairly wide variety of sizes and is a good "beginner's cigar"—that is, a good introduction to the world of premium cigars. The cedar-wrapped variety, Privada Nos. 1 through 4, are recommended. The Corona sizes and the Lonsdales are available in choice of EMS or AMS wrapper; other sizes are EMS.

Model	Length	Ring Gauge
Imperial	7⁵⁄₁₆	46
Monarch Tubes	7¼	46
Lonsdales	6⅝	42
Corona Bravas	6½	48
Grecos	6½	38
Royal Palmas Tubes	6⅛	36
Grandes	6	50
Corona	5⅝	42
Petit Corona	5⅛	42
Corona Major Tubes	5¹⁄₁₆	42

DUNHILL (DOMINICAN REPUBLIC)

A name that has a long and storied association with the finest cigars in the world, Dunhill, like Davidoff, ended its relationship with Cuba in 1989 and moved its handmade cigar operations to the Dominican Republic. Dunhill created its own brand of Havanas in the 1980s with a red band, but the Dominican Dunhills come with a blue band. (The black-banded Canary Islands versions are not of the same quality and offer a harsher smoke.)

Traditionally, Dunhills are cedar-aged for three months, and their "vintages" are listed on the boxes. Like Don Diegos and other fine sister brands such as Upmann, Santa Damiana, and Primo del Rey, they are made by the Consolidated Cigar Company in La Romana. They are light cigars with handsome Connecticut shade wrappers and a Dominican filler blend, offering a medium-to-full-bodied smoke with a delicate aroma.

Model	Length	Ring Gauge
Peravias	7	50
Cabreras (tube)	7	48
Fantinos	7	28
Diamantes	6⅝	42
Samanas	6½	38
Condados	6	48
Tabaras	5⁹/₁₆	42
Valverdes	5⅗	42
Altamiras (tube)	5	48
Romanas	4½	50

EL REY DEL MUNDO (CUBA)

This brand, which was founded in 1882 by the Antonio Allones factory and immodestly named "King of the World," features light-to-medium-flavored tobaccos and is now made in the Romeo y Julieta factory (revolutionary name: Briones Montoto). The brand was a favorite of Hollywood mogul Darryl F. Zanuck, who owned his own tobacco plantation in Cuba during the Batista years, and also of British tycoon Sir Terence Conran.

Made with an oily, smooth wrapper and well constructed, the Cubans come in a large selection of sizes. Even the larger ones are quite mild by Havana standards, possibly disappointing for anyone expecting a classic full-bodied Havana flavor, and they are good for smoking during the morning or after lunch. There is also a very complete line of Hondurans. (See page 188.)

Model	Length	Ring Gauge
Tainos	7	47
Lonsdale	6½	42
Gran Corona	5½	46
Isabel	5½	43
Corona de Luxe	5½	42
Choix Supreme	5	49
Petit Corona	5	42
Demi Tasse	4	30

EL REY DEL MUNDO (HONDURAS)

This heavy-bodied Cuban-style cigar is made by Frank Llaneza of Villazon from all-Honduran tobacco. It comes in a number of superb sizes. There are three robustos, available only in maduro, that some experts consider absolutely the best of their kind: the Robusto, the Robusto Larga, and the Robusto Suprema, all of which come individually wrapped in tissue paper. There's an angular-shaped cigar called a Flor de Llaneza, which some argue is among the best cigars ever made. Frank Llaneza stakes his name and reputation on it, and on an enormous scale. As a point of comparison, craftsmen like Rolando Reyes of Cuba Aliados turn out 750,000 cigars per year, each one excellent; Frank Llaneza makes 60 *million*. Some sizes are available in a choice of EMS and maduro wrapper.

Model	Length	Ring Gauge
Coronation	8½	52
Principale	8	47
Flor del Mundo	7¼	54
Robusto Suprema	7¼	54
Imperiale	7¼	54
Corona Inmensa	7¼	47
Double Corona	7	49
Cedar	7	43
Flor de Llaneza (torpedo)	6½	54
Choix Supreme	6⅛	49
Montecarlo	6⅛	48
Robusto Larga	6	54
Originale	5⅝	45
Classic Corona	5⅝	45
Corona	5⅝	45
Rectangulare	5⅝	45
Habana Club	5½	42
Robusto	5	54
Robusto Zavalla	5	54
Rothschild	5	50
Petit Lonsdale	4⅝	43

FLOR DE FARACH (NICARAGUA)

Lew Rothman bought this distinguished old Cuban trademark, then teamed with Juan Bermejo of NATSA to create this brand, which was introduced in fall 1996. Like its Nicaraguan sister brands, it is a full-bodied Cuban-style cigar. It comes in two large conical-shaped *figurado* sizes, both named after the largest volcano in Nicaragua—Momotombo.

Model	Length	Ring Gauge
Momotombo (torpedo)	6¾	54
Momotombito (torpedo)	7	48

FONSECA (CUBA)

Founded in 1891 by F. E. Fonseca, this small, well-made range of Cuban cigars, like the Honduran El Rey del Mundos, come wrapped in tissue paper. Fonsecas are very popular with cigar aficionados in Spain, particularly in that country's cigar capital, Barcelona. The Fonseca box, with its pictures of Havana's Morro Castle and the Statue of Liberty in New York harbor, recalls a time when relations between Cuba and the United States were better. They are a mild to medium smoke, with a somewhat salty flavor.

Model	Length	Ring Gauge
No. 1	6⅜	44
Cosacos	5¼	40
Invictos	5¼	45
Delicias	4⅞	40
K.D.T. Cadetes	4½	36

GISPERT (CUBA)

This classic old Havana brand originally came from Pinar del Rio and is available in only three handmade sizes. It's a very mild smoke for a Cuban cigar—good for beginners or daytime smoking. It is also rapidly becoming a collector's item.

Model	Length	Ring Gauge
Corona	5⅝	42
Petit Corona De Luxe	5	42
Habaneros No. 2	4⅝	35

GRIFFIN'S (DOMINICAN REPUBLIC)

Named after a famous nightclub in Zino Davidoff's home city, Geneva, and created by the club's owner, Bernard Grobet, a Davidoff friend and protégé, this mild-to-medium-bodied cigar is made by the great Hendrik Kelner at Tabacos Dominicanos with a Dominican binder and filler and a light Connecticut shade wrapper. It is the sister brand to Avo and Davidoff.

Model	Length	Ring Gauge
Don Bernardo	9	46
Prestige	8	48
No. 200	7	44
No. 100	7	38
No. 300	6¼	44
No. 400	6	38
No. 500	5¹/₁₆	43
Robusto	5	50
Privilege	5	32

HECHO A MANO

H. UPMANN (CUBA)

Herman Upmann was one of the first non-Cubans to make a name for himself in the Havana cigar industry. A German banker who immigrated to Havana to open a bank branch in the early 1840s, Upmann loved Havanas so much that he went into the business. The bank lasted until 1922; the cigar business was reinforced by the British firm J. Frankau & Co. It was bought by the Menéndez and García families in 1935, who operated it until nationalization just after the revolution.

In 1944, at the centennial of the brand's founding, a new Upmann factory was opened on Calle Amistad in Old Havana. The factory is now officially named after José Martí, the great revolutionary who was instrumental in gaining his country's independence from Spain (and was a reader in a cigar factory during the 1860s).

Upmann's signature still graces the boxes today. The Dominican version has the founding year printed on the ring, whereas the Cuban band simply reads "H. Upmann Habana." The Havanas are classified as mild to medium flavored for a Cuban cigar and very smooth. Be sure to distinguish between the handmade and machine-made, among the large number of size variations (about thirty total), many of which come in tubes.

Model	Length	Ring Gauge
Monarchs (tube)	7	47
Monarcas (aka Sir Winston)	7	47
Lonsdale (also No. 1)	6½	42
Upmann No. 2	6⅛	52
Grand Corona	5¾	40
Magnum	5½	46
Corona	5½	42
Royal Corona (tube)	5½	42
Corona Major (tube)	5⅛	42
Connoisseur No. 1	5	48
Petit Corona (also No. 4)	5	42
Corona Junior (tube)	4½	36
Petit Upmann	4½	36

H. UPMANN (DOMINICAN REPUBLIC)

Manufactured in the great Menendez y Garcia tradition at Consolidated's La Romana factory, the Dominican Upmanns are wrapped in a brown, sandy, delicate Indonesian shade leaf, with a Santo Domingo binder and a filler blend of Dominican and Brazilian varieties. These are superior-quality mild-to-medium-strength cigars, featuring oily colorado wrappers, available in many different sizes. Often the same cigar will be presented at different times or for different markets in gold tubes and silver tubes with different names, but they're all basically the same quality merchandise. Their band documents "H. Upmann 1844," and there are at least twelve boxed sizes along with six tubed sizes.

The Chairman's Reserve line, originally created for Ron Perelman, whose companies have owned Consolidated twice since 1983, was first offered to the general public in the spring of 1996.

Model	Length	Ring Gauge
Emperadores	7¾	46
Corona Imperiales	7	46
Monarch Tubes	7	46
No. 2000 (boîte nature)	7	42
El Prado	7	36
Extra Finos Gold Tube	6¾	38
Panetela Cristal	6¾	38
Director Royales	6⅝	42
Lonsdales	6⅝	42
Coronas Bravas	6½	48
Finos Gold Tube	6⅛	36
Naturales Tubes	6⅛	36
Amatista	5⅞	42
Churchills	5⅝	46
Coronas	5⁹⁄₁₆	42
Corona Cristals	5⁹⁄₁₆	52
Topacios (semi-boîte nature)	5¼	43
Corona Major Tubes	5¹⁄₁₆	42
Petit Corona	5¹⁄₁₆	42
Tubos Gold Tube	5¹⁄₁₆	42

Cabinet Selection

Model	Length	Ring Gauge
Columbo	8	50
Corsario	5½	50
Robusto	4¾	50

Chairman's Reserve

Model	Length	Ring Gauge
Chairman's Reserve	7½	38
Double Corona	7	50
Churchill	6¾	48
Robusto	4¾	50
Torpedo	6	50

HOYO DE MONTERREY (CUBA)

This classic brand of Havanas was introduced in 1865 by the Vuelta Abajo grower José Gener. A gate still stands in the Vuelta Abajo village of San Juan y Martinez with "Hoyo de Monterrey. Jose Gener. 1860" inscribed above it to mark one of the great old plantations for Cuban sub-grown binder and filler tobacco. (*Hoyo* is a depression in the land that provides drainage.)

The flagship of this medium-bodied brand with delicate flavor and rich taste is the Double Corona. They are made at the La Corona factory (official revolutionary name: Fernando Roig). Zino Davidoff's Chateau range came from cabinet-selection Hoyos. In the 1970s the Le Hoyo series, classified medium to full bodied with more spice, was introduced.

Model	Length	Ring Gauge
Particulares	9¼	47
Double Corona	7½	49
Churchill	7	47
Epicure No. 1	5⅝	46
Jeanne D'Arc	5⅝	35
Corona	5½	42
Epicure No. 2	4⅞	50
Margarita	4¾	26

Le Hoyo Series

Model	Length	Ring Gauge
Le Hoyo des Dieux	6⅛	42
Le Hoyo du Dauphin	6	38
Le Hoyo du Roi	5½	42
Le Hoyo du Prince	5	40

HOYO DE MONTERREY (HONDURAS)

Ironically, the Honduran Hoyos are a stronger smoke than the Cubans of the same name. Made by Frank Llaneza of Villazon with a Cuban-seed Honduran blend, they are to cigars what fine espresso is to coffee—a full-bodied Cuban-style cigar, particularly in the wider-gauge sizes such as the Rothschild, Governor, and Presidents. The larger ring gauge cigars (48 and above) are available in a choice of four wrappers: claro (natural), EMS, maduro, or maduro-maduro.

Model	Length	Ring Gauge
Presidents	8½	52
Sultans	7¼	54
Cetros	7	43
Double Corona	6¾	48
No. 1	6½	42
Churchills	6⅛	44
Governors	6⅛	48
Dreams	5¾	46
Cafe Royales	5¼	44
Coronas	5¼	43
Margaritas	5⅜	28
Rothschild	4½	50

Hoyo de Monterrey Excalibur (Honduras)

This extraordinarily popular and well-made cigar is sold in the United States as Hoyo de Monterrey Excalibur but simply as Excalibur in Europe (so as not to conflict with the Cuban Hoyo trademark). It is a rich medium-to-full-

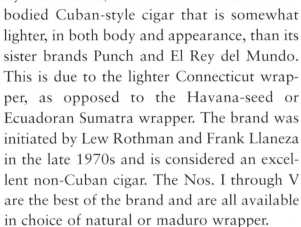

bodied Cuban-style cigar that is somewhat lighter, in both body and appearance, than its sister brands Punch and El Rey del Mundo. This is due to the lighter Connecticut wrapper, as opposed to the Havana-seed or Ecuadoran Sumatra wrapper. The brand was initiated by Lew Rothman and Frank Llaneza in the late 1970s and is considered an excellent non-Cuban cigar. The Nos. I through V are the best of the brand and are all available in choice of natural or maduro wrapper.

Model	Length	Ring Gauge
No. I	7¼	54
Banquet (tube)	6¾	48
No. II	6¾	47
No. III	6⅛	50
No. V	6⅛	44
No. IV	5⅝	45

JR Cigar Special Coronas (Honduras)

This sister brand to both the Puros Indios and Cuba Aliados is made in Danlí, Honduras, by Rolando Reyes

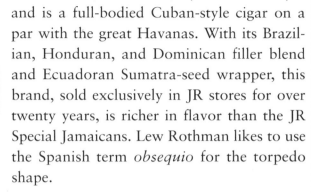

and is a full-bodied Cuban-style cigar on a par with the great Havanas. With its Brazilian, Honduran, and Dominican filler blend and Ecuadoran Sumatra-seed wrapper, this brand, sold exclusively in JR stores for over twenty years, is richer in flavor than the JR Special Jamaicans. Lew Rothman likes to use the Spanish term *obsequio* for the torpedo shape.

Model	Length	Ring Gauge
Victoria (torpedo)	7½	66
Pyramides	7½	60
No. 754	7¼	54
No. 2	6½	45
No. 54	6	54
No. 4	5½	45

JR CIGAR SPECIAL JAMAICANS (DOMINICAN REPUBLIC)

Originated by Lew Rothman in 1976, this brand was made in Jamaica until Hurricane Andrew (1992) damaged factories and forced a move to the Dominican Republic. There it is now made by the Quesada family of MATASA in Santiago. The quality is essentially the same as that of the cigars made in Jamaica, with a Connecticut wrapper, a Mexican binder, and a filler blend of Dominican *piloto cubano* and *olor* tobaccos. The predominance of *olor* makes it a mild to medium smoke, slightly heavier than a Dominican Romeo y Julieta or Casa Blanca, similar to the Avo and true to its Jamaican name and origin.

Model	Length	Ring Gauge
Rey del Rey	9	60
Mayfair	7	60
Pyramid	7	52
Noble (pyramid)	7	50
Churchill	7	50
A	6½	44
Fancy Tale (pointed foot)	6½	43
D	6	50
Bonita (torpedo)	6	50
B	6	44
C	5½	44

JR CIGAR ULTIMATES (HONDURAS)

The Ultimate series is made in Cofridia, Honduras, by HATSA (Honduran American Tobacco, S.A.), with a filler and binder of local blend and an oily Nicaraguan colorado wrapper. It is a rich medium-to-full-bodied smoke of superior quality, among the best cigars made in Honduras, and comparable to the great Havana brands. All sizes are available in a choice of four wrappers: EMS, natural, maduro, and maduro-maduro, with some adding a fifth choice of claro.

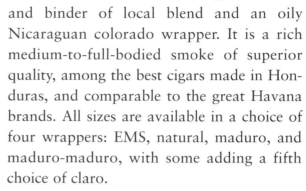

Model	Length	Ring Gauge
Presidente	8½	52
Super Cetro	8¼	43
No. 1 (natural wrapper)	7¼	54
Cetro	7	42
Slims (EMS)	6⅞	36
Double Corona	6¾	48
No. 5	6¼	44
Toro	6	50
Corona	5⅝	45
Petit Corona	4⅝	43
Rothschild	4½	50

JOSE BENITO (DOMINICAN REPUBLIC)

A pleasantly mild fifteen-year-old brand with a Connecticut wrapper, a Mexican binder, and a blend of Caribbean-based fillers, Jose Benitos are similar to Casa Blancas. They are made by MATASA at their Santiago factory in relatively small quantities, about 100,000 per year. The Magnum, with its 64 ring gauge (1 full inch), is one of the largest cigars available at retail.

Model	Length	Ring Gauge
Magnum	9	64
Presidente	7¾	50
Churchill	7	50
Corona	6¾	43
Panetela	6¾	38
Palma	6	43
Petite	5½	38
Rothschild	4½	50

JOSE MARTI (DOMINICAN REPUBLIC)

Of the two brands bearing the name of this Cuban revolutionary hero, this relatively new one is the milder. Its Connecticut wrapper, Mexican binder, and blend of Dominican *piloto cubano* and *olor* filler make it a medium-strength cigar. It is packaged in the old Cuban fashion—square-pressed into the box—meaning the first cigar can be very difficult to pry out, so be careful. They are high-quality, moderately priced, and made by Ramón Carbonell, whose father is also a cigar maker of repute.

Model	Length	Ring Gauge
Marti	7½	50
Palma	7	42
Maceo	6⅞	45
Creme	6	35
Robusto	5½	50
Corona	5½	42

Jose Marti (Nicaragua)

An even newer brand than its Dominican-made namesake, this heavy-bodied Cuban-style cigar uses an Ecuadoran Sumatra wrapper, a Havana-seed binder, and a blend of Havana-seed Nicaraguan and Dominican filler. It is made to high standards by Cuban expatriate Juan Bermejo at NATSA (Nicaraguan American Tobacco, S.A.). Possibly the best cigar produced in Nicaragua today, it comes in nine fairly large sizes, including the Masaya, which is named after a local volcano.

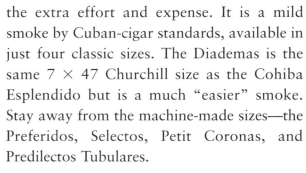

Model	Length	Ring Gauge
Rey del Rey	8½	52
Valentino	7	48
La Trinidad (pyramid)	7	48
Masaya	6¾	54
Robusto Extra	6½	52
Lonsdale	6½	44
Remedios	5½	44
Robusto	4½	52
Petit Lancero	4½	38

La Flor de Cano (Cuba)

Founded by the brothers José and Tomás Cano in 1884, this superior Havana brand is hard to find but well worth the extra effort and expense. It is a mild smoke by Cuban-cigar standards, available in just four classic sizes. The Diademas is the same 7 × 47 Churchill size as the Cohiba Esplendido but is a much "easier" smoke. Stay away from the machine-made sizes—the Preferidos, Selectos, Petit Coronas, and Predilectos Tubulares.

Model	Length	Ring Gauge
Diademas	7	47
Corona	5	42
Gran Corona	5⅝	46
Short Churchill	4⅞	50

LA GLORIA CUBANA (CUBA)

Another one of the most famous old Havana brands that made a comeback in the past twenty years, La Gloria Cubanas are now manufactured at the Partagas factory (revolutionary name: Francisco Perez German; look for those initials stamped on the box). The band features a Cuban señorita wearing a red feather boa on a yellow background. Although somewhat lighter than its sister brand, it is still a rich medium-to-full-bodied smoke, with a strong aroma and spicy flavor.

Model	Length	Ring Gauge
Tainos	7	47
Cetros	6½	42
Sabrosos	6⅛	42
Tapados	5⁵⁄₁₆	42
Minutos	4½	40

Medaille D'Or Series
(varnished 8-9-8 boxes)

Model	Length	Ring Gauge
Medaille D'Or 1	7⁵⁄₁₆	36
Medaille D'Or 3	6⅞	28
Medaille D'Or 2	6¹¹⁄₁₆	43
Medaille D'Or 4	6	32

LA GLORIA CUBANA (UNITED STATES)

This is an excellent medium-to-full-bodied Cuban-style brand with five models, made in the United States by Ernesto Carillo of Miami. It features Dominican, Nicaraguan, and Ecuadoran binders and fillers, with darkish Ecuadoran wrappers. Carillo is widely praised for his honesty and integrity and his top-standard craftsmanship, in the tradition of his Cuban ancestors. The robusto size, known as a Wavell, is highly recommended.

Model	Length	Ring Gauge
Soberano	8	52
Charlemagne	7¼	54
Churchill	7	50
Torpedo	6½	52
Wavell	5	50

LICENCIADOS (DOMINICAN REPUBLIC)

Introduced in 1990, Licenciados received a 93 rating in a *Cigar Aficionado* taste test, which effectively launched the brand. Like Cubitas and Jose Benitos, Licenciados are made by MATASA in Santiago, using a Dominican filler blend and light Connecticut shade wrappers for the standard series and Connecticut broadleaf for the Supreme series, which is maduro only. The Wavell model, a robusto, a size rapidly gaining in popularity, is available in either natural or maduro wrapper. The Licenciados is an excellent mild-to-medium-bodied smoke. There is a choice of maduro wrappers with the standard series.

Model	Length	Ring Gauge
Soberano	8½	52
Presidente	8	50
Panetela	7	38
Excelente	6¾	43
Toro	6	50
No. 4	5¾	43
Wavell	5	50

Supreme Series

Model	Length	Ring Gauge
500	8	50
300	6¾	43
400	6	50
200	5¾	43

MACANUDO (DOMINICAN REPUBLIC AND JAMAICA)

This world-famous brand, considered the best-selling premium cigar anywhere, was originated in a Cuban-owned factory in Jamaica in 1868.

In the 1960s General Cigar took over the operation, and the Macanudo became a best seller in the United States during the 1970s. Since 1983 the brand has been manufactured both in the Dominican Republic and in Jamaica under the expert eye of Benjamín Menéndez. It features superb workmanship, with Jamaican, Mexican, and Dominican filler, Mexican San Andrés binder, and Connecticut shade wrapper, available in a variety of colors. Many of the larger sizes come in a choice of wrapper: Cafe (Connecticut shade); Jade (double claro); and Maduro (deep brown, from Mexico). The Macanudo Vintage, which is made in Jamaica with a Dominican filler, is considered one of the finest cigars ever made, a really clean and beautiful cigar.

Model	Length	Ring Gauge
Prince Phillip	7½	49
Portofino	7	34
Baron de Rothschild	6½	42
Claybourne	6	31
Hampton Court	5¾	43
Crystal	5½	50
Hyde Park	5½	49
Duke of Devon	5½	42
Petit Corona	5	38
Caviar	4	36

Vintage Series

Model	Length	Ring Gauge
No. 1	7½	49
No. 7	7½	38
No. 2	6⁹⁄₁₆	43
No. 3	5⁹⁄₁₆	43
No. 8	5½	50
No. 5	5½	49
No. 4	5	45

MONTECRISTO (CUBA)

Named after the hero of Alexander Dumas's *The Count of Monte Cristo,* this classic twentieth-century Havana brand has, in the opinion of many experts and aficionados, staged a postrevolutionary comeback, to become once again the best of all Havanas.

The Montecristo is still produced in the H. Upmann factory where it was first introduced in 1935 by the Menéndez and García families, although the makers themselves have been exiled. (See Montecruz, page 200.) Alonzo Menéndez (the leaf man) and Pepe García (production) bought H. Upmann from the British firm Frankau. Montecristo was originally an Upmann model that became a separate brand of five cigars. John Hunter, a rival to Frankau, which handled Upmann exclusively, helped develop the Montecristo's famous yellow label with crossed swords. (The two firms subsequently merged and, as Hunters & Frankau, are now the importer of Habanos products into the U.K.)

When the Menéndez and García operation moved to the Canary Islands, José Manuel González (the legendary "Masinguila," considered by some the greatest cigar maker ever) stayed in Cuba to help guarantee the brand's continuing quality. In the early 1970s the brand expanded its offerings to include such classics as the A; the Nos. 1, 2, and 3; the Especial; the Especial No. 2; and the Joyita. A particular favorite is the No. 2, a pyramid or belicoso, $6\frac{1}{8} \times 52$. "Monties" have a slightly oily colorado claro wrapper, a superb aroma, medium to full flavor, and a tangy taste.

Model	Length	Ring Gauge
A	$9\frac{1}{4}$	47
Especial	$7\frac{1}{2}$	38
No. 1	$6\frac{1}{2}$	42
No. 2	$6\frac{1}{8}$	52
Especial No. 2	6	38
Tubos	6	42
No. 3	$5\frac{1}{2}$	42
Petit Tubos	5	42
No. 4	5	42
Joyitas	$4\frac{1}{2}$	26
No. 5	4	40

MONTECRISTO (DOMINICAN REPUBLIC)

This Connecticut-wrapped handmade bearing the world's foremost brand name is a relatively new offering of the Consolidated Cigar Company's La Romana operation. It's an excellent cigar, approaching the high standard set by the Macanudo, with mild to medium body, a little fuller than a Don Diego, but not quite as full as the Dominican H. Upmann, both products of the same factory. The torpedo-shaped No. 2 is a dead ringer for its famous Cuban counterpart. Consumers should be aware that there are many counterfeit Montecristos out there, both of the Cuban and the Dominican variety. Buy only from a reputable tobacconist who can guarantee authenticity.

Model	Length	Ring Gauge
Churchill	7	48
Tubos	$6\frac{5}{8}$	42
Double Corona	$6\frac{1}{2}$	50
No. 1	$6\frac{1}{2}$	44
No. 2 (torpedo)	6	50
Corona Grande	$5\frac{3}{4}$	46
No. 3	$5\frac{1}{2}$	44
Robusto	$4\frac{3}{4}$	50

Montecruz (Dominican Republic)

Founded by the García and Menéndez families in 1964 after their departure from Cuba, the Montecruz brand was first made in the Canary Islands, but it has been produced at La Romana in the Dominican Republic since the mid-1970s. Like its sister cigar, the Dominican Upmann, this is superior-quality merchandise, with an Indonesian shade wrapper, a Santo Domingo binder, and a Dominican and Brazilian filler blend. It offers a mild-to-medium-strength smoke, with an oily colorado wrapper, and comes in a wide variety of sizes, some in tubes. A version made for Dunhill has a lighter Connecticut wrapper. Montecruz has an elegantly simple brown and white band very similar to its Cuban cousin, the Montecristo.

Model	Length	Ring Gauge
Individuales	8	50
F	7¼	47
No. 200	7¼	46
No. 205	7	42
No. 255	7	36
D	6¾	38
A	6½	43
Colossus	6½	50
No. 210	6½	42
No. 250	6½	38
No. 201	6¼	46
C	5⅝	43
No. 220	5½	42
No. 282	5	28
Cedar-aged	5	42

Montesino (Dominican Republic)

Montesinos are made at the Fuente factory in Moca, Dominican Republic, from Dominican and Brazilian filler, a Nicaraguan binder, and a Havana-seed wrapper, which is medium to dark brown in color. They are classified as mild to medium bodied, a somewhat lighter smoke than the Fuente signature brand. They were originally a lower-priced version of the Arturo Fuente cigar, but when the finest Cameroon wrapper went into short supply in the early 1990s, the Montesino switched to a Connecticut wrapper, which changed its taste and resulted in an increased demand for the product. All sizes are available in a choice of natural or maduro wrapper.

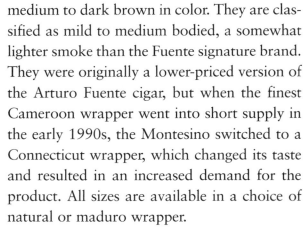

Model	Length	Ring Gauge
Napoleon Grande	7	46
No. 1	6⅞	43
No. 3	6¾	36
Gran Corona	6¾	48
No. 2	6¼	44
Diplomatico	5½	42

NAT SHERMAN (DOMINICAN REPUBLIC)

The elegant Nat Sherman shops in Manhattan have been among America's great cigar landmarks for over fifty years. The current one is at the corner of Fifth and Forty-second, with polished wood decor and an extensively stocked walk-in humidor. Joel Sherman runs the company now and in the early 1990s introduced four superior lines of Dominican-made cigars, each with its own special blend of tobaccos. The Exchange Selection, which is named after New York's telephone exchanges from the 1930s and 1940s and made from a blend of Latin American fillers, carries a light Connecticut shade wrapper, and has a mild flavor. The Gotham Selection, with a somewhat darker Connecticut wrapper and a blend of Dominican *olor* and *piloto cubano* fillers, delivers a well-balanced, spicy, mellow flavor. The Landmark Selection, with a Cameroon wrapper, a Dominican filler blend, and a Mexican binder, is slightly stronger in flavor with a taste of chocolate. And finally the City Desk Selection, with its darker Mexican maduro wrapper and a Dominican and Mexican filler blend, is a mild-to-medium-bodied smoke. The bands each feature the Nat Sherman store clock logo with a different background color: gold for Gotham, black for Landmark, dark green for Exchange, and red for City Desk. The cigars come in a good assortment of mostly larger ring gauges.

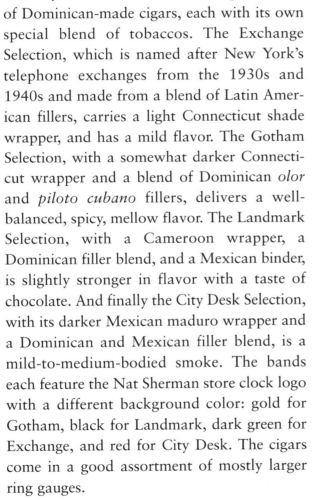

Model	Length	Ring Gauge
Gotham Selection		
500	7	50
1400	6¼	44
711	6	50
65	6	36
City Desk Selection		
Tribune	7½	50
Dispatch	6½	46
Telegraph	6	50
Gazette	6	42
Landmark Selection		
Dakota	7½	49
Algonquin	6¾	43
Metropole	6	34
Hampshire	5½	42
Vanderbilt	5	47
Exchange Selection		
Oxford 5	7	49
Butterfield 8	6½	42
Trafalgar 4	6	47
Murray 7	6	38
Academy 2	5	31

Partagas (Cuba)

This is the famous full-flavored brand with the distinctive red and white bands founded by Don Jaime Partagas in 1845. The factory, which still stands at Calle de la Industria No. 520 in Havana and is now officially named Francisco Perez German, is an interesting stop on any tour of the Cuban capital. Partagas and other fine cigars have been made there for over 150 years, except when it was closed for restoration from 1987 to 1990. The other house brands made in this factory are Ramon Allones and Bolivar. Montecristos, Cohiba Siglos, Robustos, and Esplendidos are also made there under license from those brands.

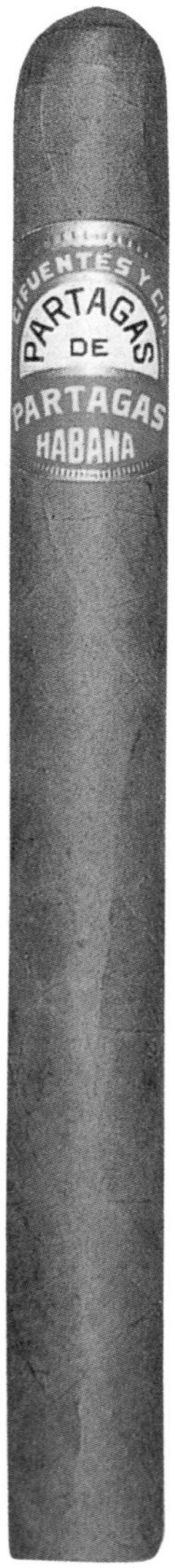

The Cuban ring says "Partagas Habana," while the Dominican says "Partagas 1845." Ernesto López and Jorge Concepción Luna, directors of the factory, consider the Dalia the flagship of the Partagas brand. The flavor is categorized as "full, rich and earthy" and receives the rare classification of "very full-bodied" from the world's foremost experts on Havanas.

Model	Length	Ring Gauge
Lusitanias	7⅝	49
Churchill De Luxe	7	47
Palmes Grandes	7	33
Partagas de Partagas No. 1	6¹¹⁄₁₆	43
Seleccion Privada No. 1	6¹¹⁄₁₆	43
Dalia (8-9-8)	6⅝	43
Lonsdale	6½	42
Corona Grande (8-9-8)	6	42
Culebras (twisted)	5¹¹⁄₁₆	39
Corona	5½	42
Charlotte	5½	35
Petit Corona	5	42
Series D No. 4	4⅞	50
Tres Petit Corona	4½	40
Shorts	4⁵⁄₁₆	42

Partagas (Dominican Republic)

The Partagas brand name has always represented some of the finest cigars ever made, with Ramón Cifuentes and Benjamín Menéndez the *conocedores*. The Cifuenteses ran the Partagas Havana factory for over a hundred years before the revolution; afterward Ramón Cifuentes brought his expertise to the Dominican Republic. Benjamín Menéndez, who created the Montecristo in Cuba, joined Partagas there, uniting two former competitors and colleagues.

The Partagas, with its Cameroon wrapper, Mexican binder, and blend of Caribbean-basin fillers, is an exceptionally well made cigar and definitely one of the top ten brands in the world. Owned by General Cigar, made in Santiago, it is the second-largest-selling brand of premium cigars after Macanudo.

The Limited Reserve, a fine vintage line, comes out in just two sizes; it's the same Jamaican-Dominican-Mexican blend as the regular Partagas line but with a special selection of superb Cameroon wrappers. Partagas is a medium-strength cigar, heavier than most of the other Dominicans, very smooth, and slightly sweet. The wrappers are colorado (EMS), but the Limited Reserve and Maduro models are available in maduro.

Model	Length	Ring Gauge
No. 10	7½	49
8-9-8	6⅞	44
No. 1	6¾	43
Maduro	6¼	47
No. 6	6	34
Limited Reserve		
Royale	6¾	43
Regale	6⅛	47

PENAMIL (SPAIN)

Penamil founder José Lorenzo, a native of the Canary Islands, learned the art of cigar making in Cuba in the 1920s. He married Mercedes Penamil, went into partnership with his father-in-law, Don Manuel Penamil, to found the brand, and eventually returned to establish its manufacture in the Canaries. José was jailed during the Spanish Civil War because he was a Cuban mason, but by 1940 he had revived the brand. When he died in 1973, his son Hiram took over the business, which continues under the name of Cigarcanaria. Penamils made for the U.S. market, with a blend of Brazilian and Dominican filler, a Mexican binder, and a Connecticut shade wrapper, were recently replaced by the Casa Buena brand. Penamils for the rest of the world are made from a fine blend of Cuban tobaccos, making them a modern-day European version of Clear Havana.

Model	Length	Ring Gauge
No. 30	7⅔	45
No. 57	7½	50
No. 25	7½	45
No. 18	7⅛	44
No. 16	7⅛	38
No. 17	6⅔	41
No. 50	6	50
No. 6	5⅞	41
No. 5	5⅓	41

PLEIADES (DOMINICAN REPUBLIC)

This mellifluously named brand, owned by the French national tobacco company, SEITA, was originally made in the Dominican Republic and shipped to a factory in Strasbourg for aging, quality control, and packaging. Now, due to the huge demand for premium cigars, those bound for the United States, where more than half a million units are sold annually, are shipped directly.

Pleiades come in cedar boxes with a rechargeable humidifier, which can be used for storing subsequent purchases. But be careful—it absorbs humidity at any level. If the boxes are stored in a tobacconist's humidifier at 70 percent, the cigars can be overmoisturized and develop mold. Although SEITA has switched suppliers in the past, the one constant has been MATASA, which also makes such fine brands as Casa Blanca, Licenciado, and Jose Benito. Pleiades are very high quality mild cigars, with Connecticut wrappers, Mexican binders, and a blend of Caribbean-basin fillers. Three new sizes—the Sirius, Orion, and Pluton (a robusto)—were launched in summer 1996.

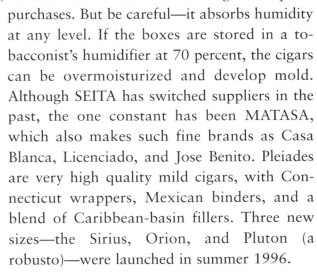

Model	Length	Ring Gauge
Aldebran	8½	50
Saturn	8	46
Neptune	7½	42
Sirius	6⅞	46
Uranus	6⅞	34
Orion	5¾	42
Antares	5½	40
Pluton	5	50
Perseus	5	34
Mars	5	28

POR LARRANAGA (CUBA)

The oldest brand of Havana cigar still in production (1834) was mentioned by Rudyard Kipling in his famous poem "The Betrothed," which ends with the line "And a woman is only a woman, but a good cigar is a Smoke." A less-celebrated line in the poem is "There's peace in Larranaga."

These are hard to find, mid to full flavored, and recommended by connoisseurs of traditional Havana flavor. The wrappers are oily, dark reddish-brown, with a nicely contrasting gold embossed ring. They are appropriate for an after-dinner smoke, rich and full of aroma, with a sweet strong flavor, although slightly less strong than the Partagas. There are machine-made versions in some of the handmade sizes, which are not considered premium cigars by most connoisseurs.

Model	Length	Ring Gauge
Lonsdale	6½	42
Corona	5½	42
Petit Corona	5	42
Small Corona	4½	40

POR LARRANAGA (DOMINICAN REPUBLIC)

A superior-quality mild to medium smoke, the Dominican Por Larranagas are made at the Consolidated La Romana facility with Connecticut shade wrappers, a Brazilian and Dominican filler blend, and a Dominican binder. To distinguish the Cuban and Dominican versions, the former have "Habana" printed on the ring, whereas the latter say "La Romana."

Model	Length	Ring Gauge
Fabuloso	7	50
Cetro	6⅞	42
Delicado	6½	36
Nacionale	5½	42
Robusto	5	50

MARCA INDEPENDIENTE DE TABACOS

POR LARRAÑAGA

ESTABLECIDA EN LA HABANA EN 1834

PRIMO DEL REY (DOMINICAN REPUBLIC)

This is an extremely well made brand from Consolidated with Dominican filler, along with a percentage of Brazilian Mata Fina, and a choice of wrappers: candela (double claro), claro (natural), and colorado (medium brown). The standard line has a Montecristo-type ring, while the Club Selection has a white ring with red and gold highlights and a coat of arms. The brand, which originated with the Morro Cigar Company in Florida in 1965, comes in a large variety of sizes and is a good bargain. It offers a heavier smoke than a Macanudo or Casa Blanca but still falls within the mild-to-medium-bodied range expected of a superior Dominican cigar.

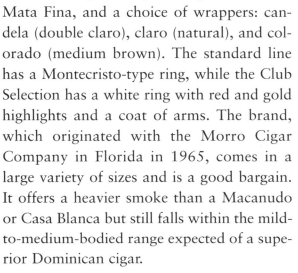

Model	Length	Ring Gauge
Aguilas	8	52
Soberanos	7½	50
Presidentes	6¹³⁄₁₆	44
Seleccion No. 1	6¹³⁄₁₆	42
Seleccion No. 3	6¹³⁄₁₆	36
Chavon	6½	41
Churchill	6¼	48
Seleccion No. 2	6¼	42
Reales	6⅛	36
Almirantes	6	50
Panetela Extras	5¹⁵⁄₁₆	34
Seleccion No. 4	5½	42
No. 100	4½	50

Club Selection

Model	Length	Ring Gauge
Barons	8½	52
Regals	7	50
Aristocrats	6¾	48
Nobles	6¼	44

PUNCH (CUBA)

One of the oldest Havana brands still in production, the Punch cigar was launched in 1840 by Don Manuel López. It shared its name with the famous British humor magazine of the time, and its label still features a colorful likeness of Mr. Punch of Punch and Judy fame smoking his cigar, with his faithful dog sitting at his feet, surrounded by cigar-production scenes. Their flavor is mild to medium bodied for a Havana and slightly sweet, with a spicy aroma and excellent bouquet. Certain sizes tend to be known by different names in different countries, so be sure to consult an expert about selection. Punches are made at the La Corona factory, now officially known as Fernando Roig. Look for the "FR" stamp on the box; also, be careful of machine-made versions of many of the brand's models, including the Exquisitos and Reales.

Model	Length	Ring Gauge
Diademas Extra	9¼	47
Double Coronas	7⅝	49
Churchill	7	47
Corona	5⅝	42
Punch Punch	5½	46
Royal Coronations	5½	42
Petit Corona	5	42
Coronations	5	42
Margarita	4¾	26
Coronets	4½	40
Punchinello	4½	34
Tres Petit Coronas	4¼	42
Petit Punch	4	40

PUNCH (HONDURAS)

Produced under the expert supervision of Frank Llaneza at Villazon, these, like their Cuban cousins, are superior-quality cigars with a mild-to-medium-bodied flavor. There are three series: Standard, Deluxe, and Grand Cru. The latter two series are available in maduro wrappers but maintain their delicate flavor due to careful aging of the tobacco.

Model	Length	Ring Gauge
Presidente	8½	52
Chateau L	7¼	52
Casa Grande	7	46
Largo Elegante	7	36
Monarcas (Tubes)	6¾	48
Double Corona	6¾	48
Lonsdale	6½	42
Chateau Corona	6¼	44
Punch	6⅛	43
Chateau M	5¾	45
No. 75	5½	43
Rothschild	4½	50

Grand Cru Series

Model	Length	Ring Gauge
Prince Consort	8½	52
Diademas	7¼	52
Britannia	6¼	50
Superior	5⅝	46
Robusto	5¼	50

PUROS INDIOS (HONDURAS)

This is the flagship brand of Rolando Reyes's Puros Indios Cigars, in Honduras, which also makes Cuba Aliados and JR's Special Coronas. Reyes is known for his ability to make the difficult larger sizes to the highest standards, and he certainly demonstrates it in this line, which features ring gauges up to 66 and lengths up to 18 inches! These renowned, rich-tasting cigars are full-bodied Cuban-style Hondurans with Ecuadoran Sumatra-seed wrapper, Cuban-seed Honduran binder, and a Dominican and Brazilian filler blend.

Model	Length	Ring Gauge
Chief	18	66
Gran Victoria	10	60
Piramide No. 1	7½	60
Victoria	7¼	60
Churchill Especial	7¼	53
President	7¼	47
No. 1 Especial	7	48
Palmas Real	7	38
No. 2 Especial	6½	46
Nacionales	6½	43
Piramide No. 2	6½	46
Toro Especial	6	50
No. 4 Especial	5½	44
Rothschild	5	50
Petit Perla	5	38

QUINTERO (CUBA)

The Quinteros—Agustín and his four brothers—were originally from Cienfuegos, near the Remedios growing region, where they founded their factory in the 1920s. They moved it to Havana in 1940. Quinteros are made from a light-flavored blend of Vuelta Abajo tobacco, quite mild on the scale of Havanas. The Churchill size is actually a classic Lonsdale or Cervantes, to use the Cuban factory name. Make sure you see the *"Totalmente a mano"* label on the box, since some of the models have machine-made versions.

Model	Length	Ring Gauge
Churchill	6½	42
Corona	5½	42
Media Corona	5½	40

RAFAEL GONZALEZ (CUBA)

These cigars offer a light-flavored, rich, sophisticated taste, also quite mild for Havanas. They are similar to the Montecristo in appearance; the rings and boxes reflect this similarity. But they are much lighter in taste and are made in the Romeo y Julieta factory (now Briones Montoto). The brand was introduced in 1928 by George Samuel and Frank Warwick for the British market; the Lonsdale shape was originated on special order from the Earl of Lonsdale, whose portrait used to be on the box. There are interesting instructions printed on the box:

"These cigars have been manufactured from a secret blend of pure Vuelta Abajo tobaccos selected by the Marquez Rafael Gonzalez, Grandee of Spain. For more than 20 years this brand has existed. In order that the Connoisseur may fully appreciate the perfect fragrance they should be smoked either within one month of the date of shipment from Havana or should be carefully matured for about one year."

This advice has a basis in fact, since the best Havanas will undergo a fermenting process and exude some natural oils once a year in the late summer, at least for the first few years after they're made, and shouldn't be disturbed at that time.

Model	Length	Ring Gauge
Slenderella	7	28
Lonsdale	6½	42
Corona Extra	5⅝	46
Petit Corona	5	42
Petit Lonsdale	5	42
Panetela Extra	5	37
Panetela	4⅝	34
Tres Petit Lonsdale	4½	40
Cigarrito	4½	26
Demi Tasse	4	30

RAMON ALLONES (CUBA)

One of the oldest Havana brands, the founding year (1837) is printed on its band. Allones, who was originally from Galicia, Spain, introduced color labeling, putting the Spanish royal coat of arms on his box, and also 8-9-8 packaging so that the cigars would not be squared, which had been the norm with Havanas. Allones cigars have been manufactured in the Partagas factory since the Cifuentes family took over the business in 1920. Like its sister brands, the Bolivar and the Partagas, it's a very full-flavored cigar of superior quality, made with a high percentage of *ligero* leaf, with good aging potential. The wrappers are dark, and the aroma is superb. It's definitely not a cigar for beginners or anyone who prefers a lighter smoke.

Model	Length	Ring Gauge
Gigantes	7½	49
8-9-8	6¹¹/₁₆	43
Corona	5⅝	42
Petit Corona	5	42
Panetela	5	35
Specially Selected	4¹³/₁₆	50
Ramonitas	4¹³/₁₆	26
Small Club Coronas	4⁵/₁₆	42

RAMON ALLONES (DOMINICAN REPUBLIC)

Another product of the revered Cifuentes family and General Cigar, which also makes the Partagas and Macanudo brands, Allones features a blend of Jamaican, Mexican, and Dominican filler, a Mexican binder, and a Connecticut shade wrapper. The cigar's overall impression is very much like the Macanudo, with superb construction and appearance, the major difference being that the Allones uses a darker strain of Connecticut shade wrapper. Culbro, the parent company of General Cigar, owns most of the fine Connecticut shade wrapper–growing area and thus is able to select the pick of the crop for its top-of-the-line brands like the Allones, which is classified as a mild-to-medium-bodied smoke.

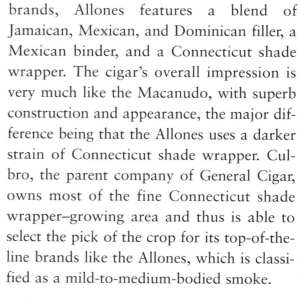

Model	Length	Ring Gauge
Redondos	7	49
A	7	45
Trumps	6¾	43
Crystals	6½	43
B	6½	42
D	5	42

Romeo y Julieta (Cuba)

This brand was originally introduced by Alvarez y Garcia in 1875. In 1903 the colorful "Pepin" Fernandez Rodriguez, who had recently resigned as manager of the Cabanas factory, bought the company and made it one of the biggest success stories in the history of cigars. Rodriguez was one of the great cigar personalities of all time. Making a large selection of personalized cigar bands for important personages, he is credited with the introduction of the Churchill, which is now sold in tubes and has a distinctive red and gold band and a superb aroma. He also had a successful racehorse that he named Julieta after his brand.

In general, the Romeo y Julietas are rich, medium-flavored cigars, among the very best available anywhere. However, avoid the tubed Nos. 1, 2, and 3 that don't have the "De Luxe" label; they are machine made.

Model	Length	Ring Gauge
Fabulosos	9¼	47
Churchill (tube)	7	47
Prince of Wales	7	47
Shakespeare	6⅞	28
Cedros De Luxe No. 1	6½	42
Corona Grande	6	42
Belicosos (shaped)	5½	52
Exhibicion No. 3	5½	43
Cedros De Luxe No. 2	5½	42
Corona	5½	42
Exhibicion No. 4	5	48
Cedros De Luxe No. 3	5	42
Petit Corona	5	42
Tres Petit Corona	4½	40
Petit Prince	4	40
Petit Julietas	4	30

Romeo y Julieta Vintage (Dominican Republic)

The regular Dominican and Honduran lines of R & J's are not widely available. Fortunately, the Vintage series, which was introduced in 1993 and is identified by a gold outline to the standard red and white band, is readily available in today's market and well worth the price. They are very fine cigars that feature elegant packaging and offer a mild-to-medium-bodied smoke. With their Connecticut shade wrappers, Mexican binders, and a blend of Caribbean-basin fillers, they are similar to another superior-quality Dominican-made brand, the Pleiades.

Model	Length	Ring Gauge
Vintage Series		
V	7½	50
VI (torpedo)	7	60
IV	7	48
II	6	46
I	6	43
III	4½	50

ROYAL JAMAICA

Hurricane Andrew, which devastated many areas of Jamaica in 1992, forced this brand's manufacturing to move to the Dominican Republic, where they are now made in a wide range of sizes in the mild-smoking standard line, which has Cameroon EMS wrappers. At the top of the line are two impressively large cigars: the 10½-inch-long Ten Downing Street, and the 9 × 64 Goliath, a full inch in diameter to deliver a large volume of very smooth smoke. The Churchills, Corona Grandes, Coronas, and Buccaneers are available in a choice of Brazilian maduro wrapper, which offers a more full-bodied smoke.

Model	Length	Ring Gauge
Ten Downing Street	10½	51
Goliath	9	64
Churchill	8	51
Giant Corona	7½	49
Double Corona	7	45
Doubloon	7	30
Navarro	6¾	34
Corona Grande	6½	42
Tube No. 1	6½	42
Park Lane	6	47
Director 1	6	45
Royal Corona	6	40
New York Plaza	6	40
Corona	5½	40
Buccaneer	5½	30
Petit Corona	5	40
Churchill Minor	4½	49
Pirate	4½	30

SAINT LUIS REY (CUBA)

This Havana brand was originally created by British importers Michael de Keyser and Nathan Silverstone in the 1940s. The cigars are superbly blended and manufactured, among the best of their kind, and relatively inexpensive, but they are also rare due to the small number produced. They are favorites of a number of Hollywood personalities, including Frank Sinatra and James Coburn. Made at the Romeo y Julieta factory, they are a full-bodied smoke with dark, smooth, oily wrappers and outstanding taste and aroma. (Make sure not to confuse these with the San Luis Rey cigars, which are made in Cuba for the German market and have a black label instead of the red and gold "Saint Luis Rey, Habana" trimmings.)

Model	Length	Ring Gauge
Churchill	7	47
Lonsdale	6½	42
Serie A	5⅝	46
Corona	5⅝	42
Regios	5	48
Petit Corona	5	42

Sancho Panza (Cuba)

Some connoisseurs would maintain that these cigars, quite popular in Spain but not as well known in Britain and elsewhere, are too light and shouldn't be considered among the greatest Havanas. Others prize them for that very reason. In any event, they are very well constructed, with a subtle, delicate flavor recommended for beginners or daytime smoking. The Belicoso has a torpedo shape and is probably the mildest Havana cigar in this size and shape.

Model	Length	Ring Gauge
Sanchos	9¼	47
Corona Gigante	7	47
Molino	6½	42
Panetela Largo	6½	28
Corona	5⅝	42
Belicosos	5½	52
Non Plus	5¹⁄₁₆	42
Bachilleres	4⅝	40

Santa Clara 1830 (Mexico)

Made in the famous San Andrés valley area, this brand was introduced in 1830 and is considered one of the top Mexican cigars. It is a mild-to-medium-bodied smoke with all-Mexican tobacco, including Sumatra-seed wrappers and local San Andrés filler. There is a choice of wrappers: Sumatra-seed colorado and Mexican maduro, the darkest of the maduro wrappers. A leaf that is world-famous for its ability to "take the heat," it is grown in the hot sun to a dark, thick, full-flavored maturity. (All cigars from Mexico are *puros* because until very recently cigar makers there were not allowed to import non-Mexican tobaccos.) Just four of the world's finest cigar brands offer a choice of this Mexican maduro wrapper in some of their sizes: Santa Clara, Te-Amo, Casa Blanca, and Macanudo.

The Santa Clara is a well-made cigar, with a typical Mexican "dry" taste. This is strictly a matter of preference and difficult to classify in terms of mild, medium, or strong body in comparison to Dominican or Cuban cigars. At some point, just about every non-Cuban cigar maker has made a "Macanudo-style" cigar; not the Mexicans. Some connoisseurs love the Mexican taste, others don't.

Model	Length	Ring Gauge
No. I	7½	52
No. III	6⅝	43
No. II	6½	48
No. VI	6	51
No. V	6	44
No. VIII	6	32
No. VII	5½	25
No. IV	5	44

SANTA DAMIANA (DOMINICAN REPUBLIC)

Made by Consolidated Cigar at their state-of-the-art factory in La Romana, this brand is named after a famous old Cuban *vega* and was introduced in 1993. It uses a Connecticut wrapper, a Dominican binder, and a blend of Dominican *olor* and *piloto cubano* filler tobacco for a medium-bodied smoke. It is a well-constructed, superior cigar, worth the price. The Seleccion line (Nos. 100, 300, and so forth), sold in the United States, has a somewhat lighter filler blend, whereas the European line, which uses traditional names, is more full-bodied. Hunters & Frankau, the great British importer of Havana cigars, markets the brand in the U.K., which is an impressive stamp of approval for any cigar.

Model	Length	Ring Gauge
Seleccion No. 800	7	50
Seleccion No. 100	6¾	48
Seleccion No. 700	6½	42
Seleccion No. 300	5½	46
Corona	5½	42
Seleccion No. 500	5	50
Petit Corona	5	42
Tubulares No. 400	5	42

Santa Damiana

SANTA DAMIANA

LA ROMANA

25 Fine Quality Cigars

TE-AMO (MEXICO)

Te-Amo, meaning "I love you" in Spanish, was introduced to the U.S. market in the late 1960s. It was the pioneer Mexican premium cigar on the international market and very quickly became a best seller. Not all experts give it the highest rating, mostly because the "dry" taste is not to everyone's liking. Nevertheless, Te-Amo is an important market force. It is available in a tremendous range of shapes and sizes, from 4 × 30 up to 8½ × 52, and a choice of light brown or maduro wrappers. The filler components are essentially the same as those of the other great Mexican brand, Santa Clara.

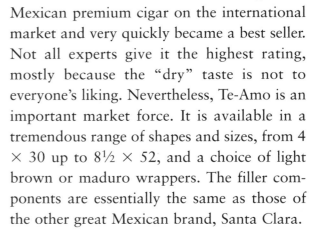

Model	Length	Ring Gauge
No. 6—C.E.O.	8½	52
No. 14—Churchill	7½	50
No. 28—Maximo	7	54
No. 17—Presidente	7	50
No. 1—Relaxation	6⅝	44
No. 3— Torero	6⁹⁄₁₆	35
No. 19—Toro	6	50
No. 29—Satisfaction	6	46
No. 2—Meditation	6	42
No. 4	5	42
No. 18—Torito	4¾	50

CORONITA · NATURAL

TE-AMO

SAN ANDRES VALLEY TOBACCO
100% HANDMADE CIGARS
IMPORTED · LONG FILLER
25 CIGARS

TEMPLE HALL (JAMAICA)

This venerable Jamaican brand was founded in 1876 by Cuban-exile cigar makers on the beautiful estate of the same name, the great house of which is pictured on the brand's gold label. Temple Hall is a product of General Cigar, which revived the brand in the early 1990s, and is similar to but somewhat more full-bodied than its sister cigar, the Macanudo. There are seven sizes, all with superb Connecticut shade wrappers, a Jamaican-Dominican-Mexican filler blend, and a Mexican San Andrés binder. The 450 robusto size is also available in the famous Mexican maduro wrapper leaf, known for its ability to "take the heat."

Model	Length	Ring Gauge
700	7	49
685	6⁷⁄₈	34
675	6³⁄₄	45
625	6¼	42
550	5½	50
500	5	31
450	4½	49

TOSCANO (ITALY)

Toscano, "the Tuscan" (plural Toscani), is Italy's famous brand, which has an irregular shape that makes for a stylish, rustic appearance. Wider in the middle and tapering at both squared ends, it is essentially a European cheroot. It offers a strong, dry taste that is recommended for those who like powerful tobacco flavor. The maximum ring gauge is approximately 35 at its widest point near the middle of the cigar, which is where the green, red, and white tricolor bands are placed, and tapers to about 26 at either end. Toscani are made from Kentucky tobacco, with a minimum aging period of six months. The Antico is aged the longest; it is also slightly larger in diameter. The Extravecchio is aged slightly less than the Antico. All three have a length of 15.5 centimeters, which is just over six inches. Another option, the Garibaldi, is the same size but is made from a milder tobacco. The Toscanelli ("little Toscani") are half length.

Model	Length	Ring Gauge
Antico Toscano	6¹⁄₁₆	35–38
Toscano Garibaldi	6¹⁄₁₆	34–35
Toscano Extravecchio	6¹⁄₁₆	34–35
Toscano	6¹⁄₁₆	34–35
Toscanello	3	34–35

VILLAR Y VILLAR (NICARAGUA)

The Villar y Villar brand name disappeared, along with others like Jose Piedra and Cabanas y Carbajal, when Castro abolished the nearly one thousand old Cuban marks in the early 1960s. It was thought to be gone forever, but fortunately Cuban expatriate Juan Bermejo of NATSA revived it. It is a heavy-bodied Cuban-style cigar similar to the Honduran El Rey del Mundo, with an Ecuadoran Sumatra-seed wrapper, a Nicaraguan binder, and a blend of Dominican, Nicaraguan, and Honduran filler tobaccos. It comes in a good selection of large ring gauges (50–54), which are increasingly popular, but it offers very little in the way of small cigars.

Model	Length	Ring Gauge
Bermejos	8½	52
Valentino	7	48
Laguito	6½	52
Special Corona	6½	44
Figaro	5½	44
Robusto	4½	52
Half Corona	4½	38

ZINO (HONDURAS)

This brand was created by Zino Davidoff himself in the mid-1980s, when his Davidoff cigars were still being made in Cuba. They are mild-to-medium-bodied Honduran-made cigars of superior quality that come in three series: the large-ring-gauged Connoisseur, introduced to coincide with the opening of the Davidoff store on Madison Avenue in New York City in 1987; the Mouton-Cadet series, which Zino promoted on a tour of America with Baronne Phillipine de Rothschild in the mid-1980s and which has a wine-colored band and reddish-brown wrappers; the regular series, with appropriate names such as Elegance and Tradition as well as the Latin pun Veritas (as in *In Zino Veritas*), which is an impressive 7 inches long with a ring gauge of 50. The Elegance size is also available in an aluminum tube under the name of Zino Tubo No. 1.

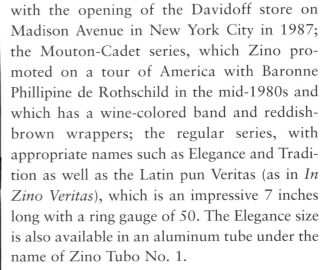

Model	Length	Ring Gauge
Veritas	7	50
Elegance	6¾	34
Junior	6½	30
Tradition	6¼	44
Diamond	5½	40
Princesse	4½	20
Connoisseur Series		
100	7¾	50
200	7½	46
300	5¾	46
Mouton-Cadet Series		
No. 1	6½	44
No. 2	6	35
No. 3	5¾	36

GLOSSARY

AMS (American Market Selection): another way of referring to double claro wrappers, which were traditionally the most popular on the U.S. market, although this is no longer the case; see also EMS (English Market Selection) or colorado, and SMS (Spanish Market Selection) or maduro

anilladora: the *fábrica* worker, traditionally a woman, who puts the rings on the cigars and packs them in their boxes

band: the small signature label wrapped around the cigar near its head; also known as the "ring"

belicoso: a thick cigar with a tapered head, generally with a ring gauge of 52 or more

binder: the leaf that is wrapped around the filler to hold the cigar together before it is enclosed in the wrapper

blender: the cigar maker responsible for the blend of tobaccos that goes to the rollers for assembling the cigars; the blending process is a closely guarded secret

bloom: when cigars ferment in the box they exude small amounts of oils that can dry to a white powder, which can be brushed off; it is not to be confused with blue mold, which causes a stain on the wrapper and can ruin the cigar

boîte nature: plain cedar-box packaging without vistas or other trimmings

booking: folding the filler leaves in half like a book before they are bunched and enclosed in the binder

bulk: a large pile or stack of tobacco leaves ready for fermentation

bunch: the filler and the binder, when they are ready for the wrapper

bundle: another form of packaging, where cigars are sold in sets of twenty-five to fifty, usually tied together with a ribbon

burro: a large stack or pile of tobacco leaves for fermentation

candela: another term for claro claro or double claro; see also AMS (American Market Selection)

cap: the piece of wrapper that covers the head of the cigar

capa: wrapper; literally, "cape" or "cloak"

capote: binder

casa de tabaco: curing barn on a tobacco plantation *(vega)*; usually wooden with a thatched roof

casing: another name for the *moja,* or spraying of the leaves to remoisturize them after drying or curing

catador: professional smoker or taster in a *fábrica* who tests a random selection of each roller's output

chaveta: a small semicircular sharp-edged instrument used by rollers for cutting the wrapper leaf and rolling the cigar; their only tool

Churchill: one of the classic cigar sizes, 7 inches by 47 ring gauge, named after the great British statesman

claro: one of the seven classifications of wrapper according to color and maturity; pale green to light brown

Clear Havana: beginning in the late nineteenth century, a cigar made in the Key West or Tampa area, from Cuban tobacco

cohiba: Cuban native (Taino) Indian word for cigar; applied in the late 1960s to Castro's personal diplomatic brand, which went on sale to the public after about a decade

colorado: one of the seven wrapper classifications according to color and maturity of the leaf; medium brown to brownish red; also referred to as EMS (English Market Selection)

colorado claro: the medium-brown-shaded wrapper; also referred to as "natural"

colorado maduro: the dark-brown-shaded wrapper; somewhat lighter and more aromatic than maduro

corojo: the Cuban wrapper plant, shade-grown and named for the famous old plantation where it was developed, El Corojo Vega; it has six categories of leaf, from top to bottom: *corona, centro gordo, centro fino, centro ligero, uno y medio,* and *libre del pie;* sometimes the top leaves are divided into *corona* and *semi corona,* making seven categories

corona: the classic midsize cigar, 5½ x 42; also, the leaves highest on the Cuban wrapper *(corojo)* plant

criollo: the Cuban filler plant

Cuban embargo: a U.S. law signed in October 1961 by President John F. Kennedy, prohibiting trade with Cuba in retaliation for Cuban nationalization of American businesses

Cubatabaco: formerly the name of the Cuban state tobacco company; as of late 1994, it became known as Habanos, S.A.

cuje: the pole used for hanging the bunches of tobacco leaves near the eaves of the curing barn

culebra: the most exotic of all shaped cigars, it is actually three panatelas braided together; literally, "snake"

despililladora: a stripper; the female worker in the *fábrica* who strips the stems off the leaves

diademas: a shaped cigar, essentially a large torpedo, at least 8 inches long, with a ring gauge of 40 near the head and 52 to 54 at or near the foot, tapering at each end

double claro: the lightest-shade wrapper; same as claro claro or *candela*

double corona: a classic larger cigar shape with dimensions of 7½ to 8 inches by 49 to 52 ring gauge

8-9-8: a form of packaging in which there are three rows of cigars in the box; eight in the bottom row, nine in the middle, and eight in the top; created so the cigars would not be pressed in and become square in shape

EMS (English Market Selection): the range of brown-colored wrappers that have been traditionally most popular in the U.K.

escogedora: a female cigar-factory worker who sorts leaves by color; the sorting process is known as the **escogida**

fábrica: a cigar factory

fermentation: the process by which harvested, cured tobacco leaves are placed in large piles; sap and ammonia seep out, starch in the leaves turns to sugar, and they acquire finesse and character; due to fermentation, tobacco for premium cigars contains less acidity, tar, and nicotine than cigarette tobacco

figurado: Spanish for "shaped"; any cigar that is not the standard cylindrical shape with parallel sides and rounded head—for example, torpedos, pyramids or *piramides,* perfectos, and culebras

fileteador: the cigar-factory worker who puts the trimmings on the boxes; after the *filete,* the ribbon of paper that seals the joints and edges of the cigar box

filler: the tobacco that makes up the interior of the cigar

flag cap: a wrapper leaf that is expertly twisted to form the cap of the cigar, rather than attaching a separate piece of wrapper; found only on certain superpremium cigars, such as the Cohiba Corona Especial

foot: the end of the cigar you light

galera: the cavernous room in a *fábrica* where the rollers sit at rows of tables and manufacture the cigars

gavilla: a roller's allotment of tobacco, usually enough for twenty-five to fifty cigars

gum: vegetable gum used as adhesive to attach the cap and/or the band to the cigar

Habanos, S.A.: the Cuban government company that manufactures and exports Havana cigars

habilitaciónes: collective term for the trimmings on a cigar box; there are ten types, including the *vista,* the *sello de garantia* (official government seal), and the *vitola*

hand: a bunch of (generally) five tobacco leaves sewn together and ready for the curing barn and/or fermentation

head: the end of the cigar you smoke

humidor: any sealed room or box used to keep cigars in good condition at 65–70 degrees Fahrenheit and approximately 70 percent or more relative humidity

hygrometer: a device that measures relative humidity; every humidor should have one

lector: a reader in a cigar *fábrica* who entertains the workers by reading from newspapers, magazines, or literary works; a practice that started around 1850

ligero: the strongest of the three types of tobacco leaves used for filler; comes from highest up on the plant, is oilier, and burns more slowly; literally, "light"; see also *seco* and *volado*

long filler: tobacco leaves running the full length of a cigar rather than chopped up, as in a machine-made cigar or cigarette

Lonsdale: a classic size—6¼ to 6½ inches long, with a ring gauge of 42 to 44—named after the Earl of Lonsdale

maduro: the dark, rich brown-colored wrapper; has less aroma and more flavor than the colorado maduro; sometimes called Spanish Market Selection (SMS); literally, "ripe"

media rueda: literally, "half wheel"; a bundle of fifty cigars; to reach one's *media rueda,* or half wheel, in Cuba means to turn fifty

mulling: a synonym for the aging or fermentation of tobacco

nicotiana: original name given to the tobacco plant in 1570; after the French ambassador to Portugal, Jean Nicot, who popularized it in his native country

olor: one of two major types of tobacco grown in the Dominican Republic; the native one, milder than the *piloto cubano*

oscuro: the darkest-colored, sun-grown wrapper; very dark brown, with strong flavor; less common in today's market than maduro, colorado, or natural wrappers; sometimes referred to as "maduro maduro"

panatela: a classic shape, longer and thinner, 5 to 7½ inches by 33 to 38; had its popular heyday in the late 1960s and 1970s; alternate spelling: "panetela"

papelito: an early cigarette, beginning in the mid-eighteenth century; made from cigar-factory scrap tobacco rolled in paper; literally, "little paper"

perfecto: a shaped cigar that is fatter in the middle, closed at its head, and tapered or closed at its foot, with a length of 4½ to 5 inches by 38; popular in the nineteenth and early twentieth centuries

petit corona: the classic smaller cigar, about 4½ inches long by 40 to 42 ring gauge

piloto cubano: Cuban-seed Dominican-grown tobacco

priming: synonym for harvesting the leaves from a tobacco plant

puro: popular Spanish name for a cigar; literally, "pure"; also, a cigar made from all-local tobacco

pyramid: a shaped cigar that flares from a narrow ring gauge at the head to a wide gauge at the foot (in Spanish, *piramide*)

ring: the small label that is wrapped around the cigar and is its signature; also known as the "band"

ring gauge: the diameter of a cigar, measured in sixty-fourths of an inch; for example, a ring gauge of 48 is $^{48}/_{64}$ inch or $^2/_3$ of an inch

robusto: a short, stocky size that has become increasingly popular in the 1990s; traditionally 5 to 5½ inches long with a ring gauge of about 50

roller: a cigar-factory worker who manufactures the cigars; *torcedor* in Spanish

seco: one of three types of tobacco leaves for filler; comes from the middle of the plant; has mild to medium flavor and aroma and a steady burn; literally, "dry"; see also *ligero* and *volado*

Siboney: legendary native Cuban martyr who, before being burned at the stake by the Spaniards, said, "If this is what Christianity is all about, I don't want anything to do with it"; when Castro nationalized all the old brands, the single state brand that replaced them was called Siboney

SMS (Spanish Market Selection): a maduro wrapper, traditionally the most popular in the Spanish market

stogie: the American nickname for a cheap cigar that was made in Conestoga, Pennsylvania, the center of native-leaf production in the early nineteenth century; one popular myth has it that it was so named because drivers of Conestoga wagons crossing the plains smoked them

stripper: a cigar-factory worker, traditionally female, who strips the leaves from the stem; *despililladora* in Spanish

tercio: a bale of fermented tobacco wrapped in palm bark ready for aging and/or shipment to the factory

torcedor: a cigar roller; literally, "twister"

torpedo: a shaped cigar that is wide in the middle and narrow at each end

vega: a tobacco plantation or farm

veguero: a tobacco planter or farmer

vista: a decorative label glued to the inside of a cigar box

vitola: the band or ring of a cigar

vitolphile: a person who makes a career or hobby of collecting cigar bands and/or other cigar-box trimmings

volado: one of the three basic types of tobacco leaves used for filler; comes from farthest down on the plant, is the mildest in taste, and burns fastest; the other two are *seco* and *ligero*

THE SHORT LIST

The finest cigars in the world can be purchased at:

JR Tobacco of America

Davidoffs Worldwide

Dunhills Worldwide

De La Concha, New York City

Havana Club, London

James J. Fox (St. James's), Ltd./Robert Lewis, London

La Casa del Habano, Paris

Mike's Cigars, Miami Beach, Florida

Sautter of Mayfair, London

Partagas, Havana

Casa del Tabaco, Miramar, Havana

Palacio de Tabaco, Capitolo, Havana

Gus's Smoke Shop, Los Angeles

Recommended reading:

BOOKS

Simon Chase and Anwer Bati, *The Cigar Companion*
(Philadelphia: Running Press, 1995)

Bernard le Roy and Maurice Szafran,
The Illustrated History of Cigars
(London: Harold Starke Publishers, 1993);
translated from the original *La Grande Histoire du Cigare*
(Paris: Flammarion, 1989)

Antonio Nunez Jimenez, *El Viaje del Habano*
(Havana: Cubatabaco, 1980)

Labels and cigar bands can be found through:

Dr. Orlando Arteaga

La Vitola

Galeria del Arte Litografico

Amargura 103

Habana 1 Cuba

INDEX